Alexander Hamilton

Dramas and Poems

Alexander Hamilton

Dramas and Poems

ISBN/EAN: 9783337337490

Printed in Europe, USA, Canada, Australia, Japan

Cover: Foto ©Thomas Meinert / pixelio.de

More available books at **www.hansebooks.com**

DRAMAS AND POEMS.

BY

ALEXANDER HAMILTON,
OF "HEUVEL."

U. S. VOLUNTEERS AND G. A. R. 182.

NEW YORK:
DICK & FITZGERALD,
18 ANN STREET.

COPYRIGHT, 1887, BY
ALEXANDER HAMILTON.

All Rights Reserved.

EDWARD O. JENKINS' SONS,
PRINTERS AND STEREOTYPERS,
20 *North William Street, New York.*

DEDICATED

BY PERMISSION TO

REV. JOHN A. TODD, D.D.,

MY FIRM FRIEND, THROUGH WHOSE FOSTERING AID I AM ENABLED
TO OFFER THIS WORK TO A GENEROUS PUBLIC.

"CANONICUS," "THE LAST OF THE NARRAGANSETTS,"

IS PRESENTED IN POETIC PROSE, AS BEING MORE IN CONSONANCE
WITH THE INDIAN STYLE THAN BLANK VERSE.

*"A'Becket" and "Cromwell" were so favorably received by the Press and
commended at the time in behalf of the Sanitary Commission, by
President Lincoln, Secretaries Seward, Chase, Stanton,
and Wells, Rev. Dr. Bellows, and the Poets Fitz
Green Halleck, Bryant, Morris, Willis, and
Lewis Gaylord Clark, that a reprint
may not be unacceptable.*

THE POEMS, PUBLISHED IN THE PRESS OF THE DAY, ARE NOW FIRST COLLECTED.

MY ILLUSTRIOUS GRANDSIRE HAVING MADE HIS NAME HIS OWN, FOR
ALL TIME—I ADOPT THAT OF HER, WHOSE PRAISE WAS EVER
THE FIRST SOUGHT AND THE DEAREST, "MY MOTHER,"

ALEXANDER HAMILTON,
OF "HEUVEL."

TARRYTOWN-ON-HUDSON,
June 1, 1887.

CONTENTS.

DRAMAS.

	PAGE
CROMWELL	1
THOMAS A'BECKET	1
CANONICUS	7

POEMS.

TO DEAR MOTHER	57
ON MOTHER'S DEATH	57
THE SHEPHERD	58
LINCOLN'S ACT OF FREEDOM	59
HAMILTON	60
NAPOLEON AND HAMILTON	62
SONNET—"CONTENTMENT"	62
SONNET—TO GRIEF	63
TO MY AUNT, SUSAN A. GIBBES	64
THE BUCKWHEAT FLOWER	64
TO MARY L——	65
TO MISS ——, A FAIR PIANIST	68
TO ——	68
TO MISS J. L.	69
THE BROOK	69
ON THE CONSECRATION OF "ST. ANN'S" CHURCH, MORRISIANA	71
THE HUDSON RIVER	71
SONNET—FAITH	72
SONNET—TO THE OAK	73
TO ——	73
TO ELIZABETH, OCTOBER, 1842	74

(v)

	PAGE
TO ELIZABETH, APRIL, 1843	74
TO ELIZABETH	75
TRUE LOVE	75
TO A VERY DEAR FRIEND	76
TO ——	76
TO CARE OPPRESSING A DEAR FRIEND	77
TO E. S. N.	77
TO THE ATHEIST	78
THE OLD MAN TO HIS WIFE	78
TO E. S. N.	79
TO E. S. N.	79
TO A CLOUD	80
TO E.	81
"ST. PAUL'S"	82
TO MRS. GEORGE L. SCHUYLER	82
TO ——	83
TO AN EVER GAY FRIEND	84
TO E. S. N.	84
FAIR WOMAN'S SMILES	85
TO A BROOK	85
THE MINSTREL	86
WRITTEN IN A VOLUME	87
ON WEIR'S PAINTING, WEST POINT	88
ON THE PAINTING IN CHANCEL OF WEST POINT CHAPEL	88
TO ELIZABETH	89
TO ELIZABETH	89
TO COUSIN ELIZA SCHUYLER	90
TO ELIZABETH	91
TO ELIZABETH	91
TO E.	92
CHRISTMAS	93
SONNET	94
TO MY ELDEST SON	95
ANTIETAM	95
CHANCELLORSVILLE	97
GETTYSBURG	99
TO E.	101
A LEGEND OF THE RHINE	101
TO E. S. N.	103

	PAGE
TO A CLOUD	104
TO E. S. H.	104
TO ——	104
SONNET	105
TO EMMA	106
ZENOBIA	107
TO E.	108
THE TROUBLED SPIRIT'S SONG	109
TO ELIZABETH	110
ON LAURENS HAMILTON	111
ON MY BROTHER LAURENS	111
TO-NIGHT	112
TO E.	113
DISAPPOINTMENT	113
TO A STORM	114
THE WALNUT-TREE	114
DYING CHILD TO HER MOTHER	115
TO MRS. SUSAN A. GIBBES	116
TO ——	117
TO ——	117
TO ——	118
TO E.	118
TO ——	119
TO ——	120
"THE DEATH BLAST"	121
TO JULIA S.	122
ON OUR MARY	123
TO ——	123
ON LEAVING MY COUNTRY HOME FOR CITY LABOR	124
"THE FROLICSOME PARSON"	125
ZION MEETIN'-'OUSE	129
TO GENERAL GRANT	131
SARATOGA	132

CROMWELL.

OLIVER CROMWELL.

At length the world begins to understand what an honest, earnest, God-fearing man Oliver Cromwell was.

Royalist writers have dwelt much upon his low origin and the humble pursuits of his early life. He had no occasion to blush for his pedigree. His father, Robert Cromwell, having married Elizabeth Steward, purchased an establishment which had been used as a brewery.

A few years after this he died, leaving a young family to the care of their mother, who, by her skill and industry, not only provided funds to support her family in a respectable station, but even to supply her daughters with such fortunes as recommended them to suitable marriages.

This estimable lady, like Charles the First, was descended from Alexander, Lord High Steward of Scotland, and thus they were cousins in the eighth or ninth degree.

Born at Huntington, on the 25th day of April, 1599, and soon the only survivor of three sons, Oliver became a great favorite with his mother, who, though a woman of excellent sense, was of a too indulgent temper.

"The love of truth," says a writer of his day, "will not permit us to extol either the docility of his temper or the literary triumphs of his genius—while at school, he being described as 'playfull and obstinate.'"

Hinchinbrooke House, the seat of his uncle, Sir Oliver Cromwell, was generally one of the resting places of the royal family when on their journey from Scotland to the English capital.

In the year 1603, King James, accompanied by his young son Charles, then Duke of York, afterward King Charles the First, paid a visit to Sir Oliver Cromwell, by whom they were entertained in the most sumptuous manner.

Charles and young Oliver disagreed, and in a scuffle young Oliver drew blood from the royal nose. Sir Oliver reproved his nephew, when, it is related, King James rejoined—"Nay, nay, it will teach the boy to respect the rights of his subjects."

Milton, the immortal poet, who knew him well, does not ascribe to him high accomplishments in literature. Bishop Burnet says, "he had no foreign language, and but a little Latin."

He remained but about half the required term at the University, and was then sent to London to attend to the study of the law at Lincoln's Inn, "but making nothing of it," he soon returned home.

Sir Philip Warwick, no uncandid judge of his manhood, gives a far from flattering account of his earlier days, but says: "After a time he became converted, and declared himself ready to make restitution unto any man who would accuse him or whom he could accuse himself to have wronged. Soon thereafter he joined himself to men of his own temper who pretended unto transports and revelations."

Residing at Saint Ives, he attended the Established Church, and was intrusted with the civil business of the parish, but was not on good terms with the clergy.

Having completed his twenty-first year, he married Elizabeth, the daughter of Sir James Bouchier, of Essex, by whom he received a considerable addition to his fortune and regained the affection of his uncle, Sir Oliver, and his relations the Hampdens and Barringtons, whom he had alienated by his thoughtless or undutiful conduct.

The next seven years of his life we can learn but little of, except that he became very rigid in his manners and devoted much time to religious duties. His house was ever open to the Non-conformist ministers, whose consciences did not permit them to comply with the ritual of the Established Church. He preached in support of their principles and joined them frequently in public prayer.

This paved the way for his popularity at Huntington, and soon procured him the honor of representing that borough in the third Parliament of Charles the First. Milton says, "That being now arrived to a mature and ripe age, all which time he spent as a private person, noted for nothing so much as the culture of pure religion and an integrity of life, he was grown rich at home and had enlarged his hopes, relying upon God and a great soul in a quiet bosom for any, the most exalted times."

In his domestic life he was happy. His affection for his wife and family, being marked and tender, was by them heartily returned.

He was always active when matters of religion were brought before Parliament, and his course at an early day shows the bias which his mind had taken and the ground on which his opposition to Government was thenceforth to be maintained.

Sir Philip Warwick describes his appearance in Parliament in 1640, "as untidy in his dress, his stature of a good size, his countenance full and reddish, his voice sharp and untunable, but his eloquence full of fervor."

Discontent with Charles's administration of the Government soon leading to overt acts, we find Cromwell, at the age of 43, on the side of the people, at which period, in 1642, the play opens.

CROMWELL:

A TRAGEDY, IN FIVE ACTS.

PERSONS OF THE DRAMA.

OLIVER CROMWELL, Commoner, General, then Protector.
IRETON,
INGOLDSBY, } His sons-in-law.
FLEETWOOD,
DESBOROUGH, his brother-in-law.
PYM,
HAMPDEN, } His friends.
HOLLIS,
OLIVER and RICHARD, Cromwell's sons.
GENERAL LAMBERT, his friend.
GENTLEMEN of NORFOLK, SUFFOLK, HERTFORD, ESSEX.
WHITLOCKE, WHALLY, LENTHAL.
BRADSHAW, HARRISON, MARTIN, GRIMSHAWE, LUDLOW.
ASHE, ALLEN.
SIR HARRY VANE, COLONEL OAKEY, SIR ARTHUR HAZELRIGG.
MR. LOVE and MR. PEET, RICH, STAINES, WATSON.
MAJOR SALLOWAY, CAREW, LISLE.
LORD MAYOR OF LONDON.
AMBASSADORS from FRANCE and SPAIN.
COLONEL JEPHSON, ASHE, SIR CHARLES PACK.
ATTORNEY-GENERAL.
QUAKER FOX, a great merchant.
SPEAKER.
KING CHARLES.
REGINALD HASTINGS, } His friends.
and others,
LADY CROMWELL, wife of Cromwell.
LADY ELIZABETH CROMWELL, his daughter.
LADY ALICE LAMBERT, wife of General Lambert.
PATIENCE, an attendant.
TRADESMEN, CITIZENS, and SOLDIERS.

Scene—ENGLAND, mostly in LONDON—A. D. 1642–1658.

CROMWELL.

ACT I.

SCENE FIRST.
A street in London.

CITIZENS *enter from opposite sides.*

FIRST CITIZEN.

Which way, my friend?

SECOND CITIZEN.

Unto the Commons.

THIRD CITIZEN.

What for?

SECOND CITIZEN.

To seek redress.

FIRST CITIZEN.

To seek redress for what? The last taxes drained our purses, robbed us and ours of our homes—why needs our King more moneys?—we have no wars.

SECOND CITIZEN.

The Pope, who rules this wife that rules
Our King, exacts new tributes.

THIRD CITIZEN.

Down with the Pope! if needs must be,
The Queen!

FIRST CITIZEN.
And the King too!

THIRD CITIZEN.
Nay, nay, we love the King! he's Stuart blood!
Let's to the Commons! [*Exeunt.*

SCENE SECOND.

The House of Commons.

PYM, *rising.*
Fellow-Commoners of England! her bulwark
And her boast, with love and loyalty to King Charles
I rise—if sad my visage, sorrow is at my heart—
To state that he would violate all his bonds
Demanding further supplies of us.

[HOLLIS.
And I deny that we should grant
Them to him. At the very outset of his reign,
More a Papist than a Puritan at heart,
Charging that we, his people, sparingly doled out our
  supplies,
He, in defiance of all law, his first Parliament dissolved.
A second he convoked, but finding that
Still more intractable, its speedy dissolution
Was its fate; and he, without the show
Of legal right, fresh taxes raised, and the chiefs
Of the opposition into the cells of felons threw.
Is this the meed of patriots?

HAMPDEN.

My friends, we may not yield to these demands;
The Star-Chamber we have swept away,
The High Commission, and the Council of York.
Thomas Wentworth, late Earl of Strafford, has expiated

His great crimes by axe and block;
Laud is immured in yonder Tower;
The Lord Keeper finds refuge in a foreign land;
And King Charles has bound himself never
To adjourn, dissolve, or prorogue this Parliament,
Which here doth meet, without its own consent,
To serve its God, its country, and its King!

   REGINALD HASTINGS (*Royalist*).

Ay, its wronged King!—robbed of age-founded
Hereditary rights! He loves his country.

      PYM.

Indeed! then now what mean these discontents
In Ireland? The Rebellion of the Roman Catholics
In Ulster has been planned nearer home.
Our Queen one of that faith, our King of no faith
At all, though Protestant avowed.

   REGINALD HASTINGS (*Royalist*).

If Church and King no reverence command,
In gentle courtesy leave our fair Queen at peace.
Heed ye well, that when the Church shall fall, then falls
 the State.

CROMWELL *enters and takes his seat on L. H., nearest footlights.*

    CROMWELL, *aside*.

Two fierce and eager factions it would seem,
And nearly matched. Be the King wise and true,
All will be well with him and his tried friends,
While we, perforce, must seek our homes in other climes.
But he will fail, the people's rights must triumph,
And henceforth two great parties in this realm

Shall ever contend for the mastery.

PYM.

I move that a remonstrance be presented
To the King, enumerating all the faults
Of his administration, expressing the distrust
With which his policy is still regarded
By the people, and their inability
To endure fresh taxes—but let it be expressed
In love and true allegiance.

HAMPDEN.

I second this.

CROMWELL, *aside*.

My thoughts! my sentiments! tho' gemmed in eloquence.
The current of events I'll note, and use them
As befits me.

SPEAKER.

The motion ye have heard.
All in its favor rise—

[*All rise except Royalists.*

'Tis carried—by eleven votes majority.

HOLLIS.

His Majesty promises well; but yestere'en
Falkland, Hyde, and Colepepper were invited
To become the confidential advisers
Of the Crown.

PYM.

We'll see how he will keep his promises.
But lo! whom have we here?

Enter the Attorney-General and the Sergeant-at-Arms.

SPEAKER.

What would the Attorney-General of the realm,
Of England's Commoners?

SCENE II.]   CROMWELL.

ATTORNEY-GENERAL.

Our Liege commands that I do impeach
Before the House of Lords—Lord Kimbolton,
Pym, Hollis, Hampden, Hazelrig, and Strode,
Commoners of England, for high treason.

Great commotion.]   Sir! sir!   [*From several voices.*

CROMWELL, *rising and advancing.*

Do I hear aright! The King would impeach
These gentlemen?

ATTORNEY-GENERAL.

You do—the Sergeant-at-Arms,
In the King's name, demands of the House
The persons of these six gentlemen.

CROMWELL.

By your leave, we will consult
On this. You may retire.   [*Exit Attorney-General.*
My friends, this is too true.
* Here are private lines, just borne to me,
Which counsel that you instantly consult
Your safety. The King himself approaches
With an armed band.

Great outcry.]   The King! the King!
[*From several voices.*

HAMPDEN.

We'll but retire till the whirlwind's past,
And then prepare for storms—where is the treason now?

CROMWELL.

'Twere well—retire.   [*Exeunt six members.*
Aside.] Oh, Thou! to whom, in humble, heart-felt fealty

---

* From the Countess of Carlisle, sister to Northumberland.—*Hume.*

1*

I knelt in early youth; unto whose helping hand
I've trusting clung in manhood's stormy hours,
Nerve me with lion's strength, that singly I may brave
My coun'try's foe, and save her from this tyranny.
    Turning to Commoners.]
Be not dismayed, my friends. He's but a man,
Like one of us. Now must we prove unto the wide world
For every age—that steadfast, true, God-serving hearts
Are never left to fall. Hark! they do come.

King CHARLES *enters with armed attendants.*

CHARLES.

Where are those whom I would impeach?

CROMWELL, *advancing.*

In safety, Sire.

CHARLES.

How so?

CROMWELL.

God keeps them, Sir.

CHARLES, *aside.*

*We battled in our youth, and he o'ermastered me,
Must we now war in our age till he o'erpowers me?

CROMWELL, *advancing.*

My Liege and royal kinsman, is this nobly done?
The forest's monarch, royalty's best type,
Singly pursues his prey, never in troops.

CHARLES.

Cromwell, I am—

---

* King James paid a visit to Sir Oliver Cromwell at Hinchinbrooke House, in September, 1604, taking with him his son Charles, when he and the future Protector disagreed, and Oliver so little regarded the dignity of his uncle's royal visitant, that he made the royal blood flow in copious streams from the Prince's nose.—" *Cromwell and his Times.*"

CROMWELL.

    My King, whose surest safeguard
Is his people's love, and that he best secures—

CHARLES.

        Cromwell, you are our kinsman;
Else—

CROMWELL (bowing), *aside.*

        The Sheriff's deputy would fulfil
His office.
      My Liege, I'm, as you know,
But a plain country gentleman, not used
To courtly phrases, nor the arts that cloak
The thoughts of courtiers. I would counsel
You in love, and beg you'd learn of nature,
And behold how the majestic monarch
Of the mount maintains his proud estate,
Spreading afar his roots in genial soil.
He on his own strength relies for vigor
To sustain his outstretched arms.
                    He never seeks
From arid rocks sustenance to imbibe,
Else would his branches die, his foliage fall!
The source of all your strength, your people's purse,
Is well-nigh drained—although their cup of loyalty
Still to the very brim is full. Deem me not rude,
But banish this hired troop—'tis a rough setting,
And out of keeping with your royal heart,
Whose richest casket is your people's love.

CHARLES.

I thank you, Cromwell, for this truthfulness,
Though verily it grates; for I have feasted
On flattery so long, that frankness

Is a new dish and out of course. I would
That you were with me, not against me.

CROMWELL.

So am I, and would ever be, reigned you yourself,
Not food for parasites, who'd sap your strength,
Your very life, for self-advancement.

CHARLES.

I would those gentlemen would wait on us.
Counsel this, in love to us, and come with them;
We should together prop up the Stuart House,
Sprung from the self-same source—
      I would consult with you.

CROMWELL.

Our consultation were a futile act,
Old counsellors still about you.

CHARLES.

      But come, though
I'll not yield in this.
    [*Exit* CHARLES *and attendants.*

CROMWELL.

There goes a noble heart, but so bewitched,
And so long trained in course of fell deceit,
That even I dare not trust him, he is
So hackneyed in these Romish ways.——
I'll see my friends and serve them if I can,
Save them I'm sure to do—
     For this have I resolved !
Here has Charles wrecked all hopes, all chances
Of success. Commoners of England! now assert

Your rights.   Compliance to his will ceases
To be a virtue.
                    Each to his home
In London; our fortress that, well garrisoned
With tried and loving hearts ; urge them with prayer
True succor to entreat ; and legions from the Lord
Will join our ranks.   Proclaim aloud throughout the land
Unto the wide, wide world,
" That where the Spirit of the Lord is, there is Liberty."
We are but as one man in this, I believe—
Is it not so?
                    ALL *exclaim, retiring,*
                              But one! but one!

                    CROMWELL, *going out.*
                              Let's on!
Where are the friends thou hadst,
My King, but one short hour ago?
This thy last act has made each man thy foe!   [*Exit.*

SCENE III.

Street in London.

PYM, HAMPDEN, *and* HOLLIS, *stand on one side ; deputations from various trades pass, exclaiming,* " Privileges of Parliament! Privileges of Parliament!"

                    PYM.
         It all works well.   The Mercers these!
And here another comes!

                    HAMPDEN.
              The Porters these!—a God-fearing, honest
Class!   Another yet!

HOLLIS

The Apprentices! bold and reckless dare-devils
Are these, but honest as the sun.

HAMPDEN.

Stand ye apart—the King! [*They retire one side.*
The Beggars come
The other way—we'll note their salutation
As they meet him.

King CHARLES *enters with attendants, and they pass on. Deputation of Beggars pass, exclaiming,* "Privileges of Parliament!" *and one calls, as they pass out,* To your tents, O Israel!*

HAMPDEN.

Wormwood to you, my King!
My pity for you drowns your wrongs to me.
This is Cromwell's house. We must with him consult;
Long have I known him; he is of all
"The man for the times," in spite
Of his rough exterior. If he lives, he'll be
The foremost man of every age. [*Exeunt.*

SCENE FOURTH.

Interior of Cromwell's House.

CROMWELL, *alone, strides across the stage.*
This fire at my heart o'erheats my brain!
Would I could play the woman, and in tears
Weep out my rage—no! no! they would but scald

---

* The words employed by the mutinous Israelites when they abandoned Rehoboam, their rash and ill-counselled sovereign.—*Hume.—Clarendon.*

My furrowed cheeks, and sear with life-long scars.

* * * * *

To think that men so gentle and so pure,
So elevate in nature, that they look
On earthly pride and pomp, as shines the sun
Upon this tinselled scene, mere work of men's weak hands,
Should be thus hunted down like wolves,
While, lamb-like, spite of all their wrongs,
They are bleating out their love for him,
And urging gentle treatment of their tyrant King.

LADY CROMWELL *enters.*

My Lord, my loving Lord! what moves you thus?

CROMWELL.

My dearest wife, thy love ever was the brook
Whereat I slaked my thirst and cooled
My fevered brow. By nature I was never gentle:
Rough and uncouth in form, unhammered iron
Both my heart and hand—I am o'erwrought to-day;
But now thou comest, I shall grow calm and cool,
For you can mould me as you will, dear love.

LADY CROMWELL.

But what is this, my Lord?

CROMWELL.

Hast thou not heard, how, mid the hot debate
Upon his new demands,—Pym, Hampden,
Hollis, and our friends, urging a mild remonstrance
To his will and wishes,—first there comes
A message from the King, that they should be impeached,
And then a secret letter sent to me,
Informing that in person he would seek them,
Of which I instantly advised.

Scarce had the Attorney left the Commons, when the
    King,
Forgetful of all promises, all pledges,
Forgetful of his honor as a man,
Forgetful of the sacred office of a king,
And all its great attendants, rushed in
With a rude band of hired menials,
And did demand the persons of these gentlemen!

          LADY CROMWELL.

You did not yield them up?

          CROMWELL.

                        No, but I told him
That God kept them, as He ever does the just;
That He would preserve them.

          LADY CROMWELL.

      Spake you thus unto the King, my Lord?

          CROMWELL.

I did; in what is he more than mortal like us?

          LADY CROMWELL.

His power!

          CROMWELL.

         He has no power now. He had
Until this hour; till now the Commons inclined
To him, despite of all their wrongs.
But this last act awoke the slumbering fires
At their hearts; the ebullitions of their rage
Burst forth as the long smothered volcano's flames,
And swallowed all things up. The streets of London
Are with hot lava filled; none but spirits kindred
To them may safely sojourn there.

       Enter PYM, HAMPDEN, *and* HOLLIS.

Gentlemen, you're welcome, very welcome! Here

For a time you're safe! [*Shouts heard.*]
What means this outcry
And this violence?

PYM.

Our wrongs have taken voice:
All London is aroused.

HAMPDEN.

And we must seek
How best to quell this turbulence.

CROMWELL.

True, true!
It were not well that it should spend itself;
We yet may need some little fire to light
Us on our way. Hampden, we have too tamely borne
Our wrongs, more like weak children, 'neath the brutal
    rule
Of some tyrant guardian, than the people's friends,
Intrusted with the care of their dearest rights.
Strike not these shouts with leaden weight upon your
    hearts,
Upbraiding as they fall?

HOLLIS.

They do; and we must act
For them, if Charles dissolves not our Parliament.

CROMWELL, *much excited.*

Dissolve this Parliament! He shall tear
This form limb from limb.
Till that the weak pulsation of this heart
Shall be sole sign that ever it was mortal,
Ere he shall dare do that! We have been too tame!
    *   *   *   *   *   *
I have advised that Parliament seize the town of Hull,

Where there is now a magazine of arms;
That Goring, at Portsmouth, be required
To obey no commands but theirs;
And instant arming of the Londoners
Take place. That Essex be made General
Of Parliament—but here is Ireton!

　　IRETON *enters.*] What news, my son?

IRETON.

The people all enraged, the King has gone
To York, whither the nobility, in crowds,
Do follow him.

CROMWELL.

　　　　　　　　　Nobility!
The tinselled nobles follow him. He
Is their only hope. I would he had them all;
Their touch but taints;
The true nobility are ours! What more?

IRETON.

Essex is made General of the Parliamentary forces,
And news is just received that Charles has raised
His standard at Nottingham.

CROMWELL.

'Tis well! England is born again!
After a slumber of six hundred years,*
The Anglo-Saxon shall awake to life!
Where was thy guardian angel, treacherous King,†
When thou compelledst that small band
Of peaceful spirits who had embarked
For the new world to disembark, and, toiling, here,
Drag out a mean existence, when plenty,
Peace, virtue, Religion, there were free,
As God first made them unto all mankind?
Since thou wouldst have me great, thou must not murmur

---

　　* A'Becket's murder.　　　　　　† 1634.

That thou madest me so. Though I may never tread
New England's virgin soil—bear through her wondrous
    wilds
The banner of the Lord—teach the Red Man
That his Great Spirit is ours—that we are but one—
I'll sow such seeds that ages yet unborn,
Throughout the world, shall bless the day
Cromwell from peaceful intents was torn,
And forced to be a Man.
                        But much there is to do;
King Charles's army will be in bright plumage decked;
Rupert is a master-spirit in the charge,—
He has trained troops, while we have, at best,
A rabble crew, will never stand the onset
Of the foe!
            Gentlemen, do you each to your
Several homes. Hollis, in London, enroll
The stoutest artisans of our faith.
Pym, there are many kindred spirits will follow
You where fiercest is the fight; drill them
Into strict obedience, for a steady front
Is what we most shall need. Hampden, my friend,
At your own home there are at least a thousand
True and steadfast hearts; hasten you thither,
And prepare them all, and let each and every man
Account himself the Lord's. Ireton will to his friends,
And raise a troop of horse; while I'll to Ely,
And arouse all mine.   *   *   *
                        Pardon me, gentlemen,
In counselling thus the choicest spirits
Of the land,—myself an humble citizen,
Though servitor of God,—I do presume too much.

            HAMPDEN.
We came not, Cromwell, for honeyed words,

But counsel, and you counsel give,—such counsel
As we sought. The whirlwind bows all trees
Of weaker growth; old England's oak still holds
His head erect, an emblem for us all.
Be thou that oak!

CROMWELL.

Then since you've sought from me, let us,
Each and all, distrustful of his single strength,
Seek from our God His guidance and support;
And with a pledge, that, as we shall strive
But for our England's honor and supremacy,
So when her *people's rights* are well secured,
We'll lay aside our arms.

[*Exeunt* PYM, HAMPDEN, *and* HOLLIS.
Enter, on opposite side, his daughter ELIZABETH, *son*
OLIVER, *and* LADY LAMBERT.

My own fair daughter and my gallant son;
And thou! most lovely Lady Lambert, dost thou brave
This scene, venturing through London's waves tempestuous,
To see how fiercely they are chafing here?

[*Striking his breast.*

My children dear, ever does kind Heaven send
Its comforts with its cares.

LADY LAMBERT.

My husband absent,
It were but fitting that his glory's partner
Should learn what griefs assail our cause,
That she might timely forewarn him in words
Of gentlest love, not let them rudely burst
Upon his ear, too oft assailed already;
Emboldened by these thoughts, your most fair daughter,
Venus-like, ushered me to the light of day,
Thou England's Sun!

CROMWELL.

    Grace in your speech, no less
Than in your form!—henceforth shall Cromwell
E'er in heaviest hours welcome you,
Dearest lady, amidst these his best counsellors
(As such, my wife and children ever proudly owned).
My son, it seems the will and pleasure
Of the Lord that I, who his servitor
So long have been, should take an active,
It may be, foremost part with my long well-tried friends
In England's cause.

OLIVER.

Father, the King!

CROMWELL.

    Reigns, son, but for himself.
He doth forget the trust God hath reposed in him,
Thus choosing him His Vicegerent. Go you with Ireton,
Your brother now—a father in my absence he will be
To you. Ireton! my eldest son,—the hope and love
Of manhood's earliest hours, the pride of present years,
And promise of my age,—I do intrust to you;
Make him a soldier, but a soldier in the Lord;
A warrior like yourself, I ask no more;
Now take him with you, and enroll your horse.

IRETON.

Father, it shall be so.

OLIVER.

    Come, Ireton, I am eager
For the fight; I'll not disgrace my lineage
Or my name.

CROMWELL.

    Well said, my son, may Heaven be with you.

IRETON.

Hark! "Cromwell" fills the air as well as gilds the walls;
All London's streets proclaim the people's will,
And call to arms.   [*Exeunt* IRETON *and young* OLIVER.

CROMWELL.

Not theirs, but God's!
His high behest I must, I will obey.   [*Exit* CROMWELL.

LADY ELIZABETH.

O dearest Lady! what a rived heart is mine;
My duty weighed against my love.   I may not pray
For either cause.

LADY LAMBERT.

Cheer thee, dear girl!   Your father
Is no foe unto the King, but unto his dishonor.

LADY ELIZABETH.

Think you that he will hearken to our love?

LADY LAMBERT.

You are as nobly born as this Young Charles,
But custom sanctions not an honorable love
Between the prince and subject.

LADY ELIZABETH.

Sweet friend,
That is the worm that gnaws! No other
Ever could be mine,—none other would Charles have;
He loves me purely, worships me as though
I were a saint from Heaven.

LADY LAMBERT.

I pray thee, think no more of it,
Insatiate—it is man's way—but satisfied—beware!
He is by birth a King!   They deem all creatures
Made but for their pleasure and their will—ay,

Even earth's fairest, such as thou, sweet girl.
Beware! beware! [*Exeunt.*

SCENE FIFTH.

A Large Tent.—An Encampment.—Night—Table, Books, and Taper.

CROMWELL.

Is this a dream, or dread reality?
Have those strange thoughts I dwelt on in my youth
Thus taken form and shape? or have I on visions
So long feasted that my mind, o'erwrought, wanders
Mid quicksands will my hopes ingulf?
'Tis night; no sound, save the trusty sentinel's tread,
Who keeps his watch, humming some holy strain,
And praying God to guard his earthly hopes
As he shall guard His cause.
       It is no dream.
A nation's wrongs have forced a nation's heart
To burst the cerements of kingly love,
And make a bold assertion of their rights;
Rights born of Heaven, conferred by God;
Not to be lightly or unvalued worn.
 Kneeling.] His hand I see in this—to whom I kneel
In humble supplication for His aid,
His counsel, and His care. A distant tread—
A challenge—they have passed;
It is those valued friends I summoned here.
I summoned here!—Why would they make me first?
Essex and Fairfax are of nobler rank,
Though not more *nobly born.* For am not I
A kinsman of the King?—might have been
King myself! might have been king myself?
I see no weird women on this heath;

There are no spirits in the air, I know,
To whisper this to me! It is no whisper,
Though it sounds as though 'twere thunder-born,
And drowns my every thought but this:
That I might have been king! And so I might,
As well as he who now doth wear the diadem:
From Alexander, Lord High Steward of Scotland,*
Both are sprung—Charles traces back through a long
    line of kings,
His ancestor being the elder son; while I
Am scion of that noble house, descended
Through my sainted mother, eleventh in succession
From that Lord's third son, while Charles is but the
    twelfth
From his eldest born.
There glares the curse of primogeniture!
The times have changed, and so must human courses.
I will be king—king in the service of the King of kings,
And reign pre-eminent o'er the hearts of men.
[*Enter several gentlemen escorted by the sentinel.*]
My friends.

GENTLEMAN.

    Cromwell, your messenger urged
All haste, or we had not intruded on the night
With the day's business.

CROMWELL.

    You're very welcome,
And I thank you heartily. So long unused
To every public charge,—my little knowledge
Being but from books,—this glittering harness
But uneasily fits, and, like an untutored steed,
I must be trained to it. But now I learn
That Lord Capel advances upon Cambridge

* Noble.

With both horse and foot; that many
Of the old nobility are hastening up in arms.
   Aside.] I'll sound these gentlemen!—
"We must consider seriously, my friends, how acceptable
"A service to the King ours would be,
"To keep five whole counties in his obedience."

GENTLEMAN.

Is there then hope of him?

CROMWELL.

There is always hope with life. Bad counsellors
Are his curse. We must be a sheet-anchor
To the State; fast holding amid the gales
That fiercely assail her now; but see
What honors, what rewards, the storm o'erpast,
We then may justly claim for such true loyalty.
"What troops are there in Essex now, who have
"The honor and happiness of the King at heart?"

GENTLEMAN OF ESSEX.

Three thousand; two of stalwart hearts on foot,
One thousand the best mounted in the land.

CROMWELL.

I know your stables are most choicely filled;
Your riders are?

GENTLEMAN OF SUSSEX.

A God-fearing, prayerful, preachful set—

CROMWELL.

In our cause chief elements of success.
And yours of Suffolk?

GENTLEMAN OF SUFFOLK.

Two thousand—all well-armed, brave artisans.

CROMWELL.

A brawny race—I've met with them. And yours
Of Hertford?

GENTLEMAN OF HERTFORD.

Three thousand and three hundred
When all told—with most delicious voices
And great prayers.

CROMWELL, *smiling*.

Less music shall we need, then.
'Tis very well—for 'tis expensive, and all we save
We gain. And how of Norfolk?

GENTLEMAN OF NORFOLK.

Jockeys in Norfolk,—
Every man's a horse. Some fifteen hundred
Chanting cherubs, with good steeds,
And fifteen hundred well mounted as at their birth.

CROMWELL.

You're pleasant, sir!

GENTLEMAN OF NORFOLK.

It is but pleasure that I've entered on—
A game of chance—'tis true, a boisterous game.
The winner—who can tell?

CROMWELL, *aside*.

'Tis a shrewd fellow—what does he mean?
  Ironically.]   Gentlemen, you deserve
Much love and many honors from your King.
Meet me here with your best speed, six days
From this, with all the forces you can raise.
Bring all your saints from Hertford, and Norfolk's
Chanting cherubs!   [*Exeunt Gentlemen.*

A saintly crew—I'll use them.

Sentinel enters and hands papers.]
What now? from London! from Hampden, too?
Reads.] "Spare nor goad nor spur, but speed to London;
Now the Commons sit in consultation
Upon proposals made by the Lords in favor
Of a peace. Haste, or our cause is lost——"
Lost! Lost! no, no! thou noble spirit, tried friend,
And truest gentleman that England boasts.
No cause is lost, with Hampden on its side.
God watches with the virtuous—they ne'er fail;
Though they may fall, 'tis but as sets the sun to-day
To rise the brighter on to-morrow's morn.
True virtue never fails——
     My horse—my fleetest horse!
My Ironsides, an' you will——
 GENERAL LAMBERT *enters.*] Remain you in command,
My trusty friend, for I must post to London.
Read this—it is for thee alone; observe
The strictest discipline—religious exercises
Thrice a day; with purest sentiments inspire
The men; let them have no time for idle thoughts
Or ribald jests.
And this, the "Soldier's Bible,"* give to each,
Where, from the Holy Scriptures,—THE CHARTERS
OF THE LIBERTIES OF MANKIND,—selections
Most appropriate may be found;
Thus may each daily say or sing
The praises of his God.
     The morn now breaks,
And I must speed away on matters of great moment

---

* Cromwell had appropriate quotations made from the Holy Scriptures, printed upon a sheet folded into sixteen pages, a copy of which was given to every soldier under his command.

To our cause—   [*Distant Reveillé heard.*
" What is to do? I know not what I would have,
Though I know what I would not have."

GENERAL LAMBERT.

You have not rested now for some three nights;
Nature will be outworn—

CROMWELL.

        Good friend, my country calls;
I may not rest for many a night—
  Aside.] It may be never more.
Farewell! God speed you all.

LAMBERT *walks back towards the tent.* CROMWELL *exits.*
Curtain falls slowly.

END OF ACT I.

ACT II.

SCENE FIRST.

Room in Cromwell's House.

Lady Cromwell, Lady Alice Lambert, *and* Lady Elizabeth Cromwell, *enter.*

LADY CROMWELL.

Hark, how the shouts of a maddened populace
Come like the surges of a raging sea,
Lashed into fury by contending winds,
Proclaiming some new-born wrongs heaped
On their already overloaded backs! My King,
My King, why goad them unto frenzy?

LADY LAMBERT.

     The roar hath passed,
And now falls on the ear as murmur
Of a distant sea, subsiding into peace.

LADY ELIZABETH.

Yes, lady mother, now notes of joy and voices
Of glad welcome fill the air, as though
Some mighty conqueror approached, laden
With new-born honors.

LADY CROMWELL.

   'Tis Pym they name, and Hampden,
Cromwell's friends. Why do they rank him first?
Would we were safe upon New England's shore!
I dread this sudden greatness. My King! my King!
Oh, thou art ill-advised; thy gentle, true,

And trusting nature is abused. Why cast
You from you all would be your friends,
And leap into this den? Sweet Lady Alice,
Where is now your lord? Lambert has potent voice
With this rude crowd. He should be here
When Cromwell is away.

LADY LAMBERT.

It is thy Lord Cromwell's order he observes,
That keeps him from the hearts that love him best.
The Parliament sent him hence to raise
Fresh troops, and he returns not till they summon him.
But here are worthy gentlemen—
     Hampden, England's pearl,
And Pym, the gorgeous ruby of the times.

   HAMPDEN *and* PYM *enter, saying*,
     At your service, ladies.

LADY CROMWELL.

You're very welcome, gentlemen, for our woman fears
Have magnified the noise in London's streets
Into things terrible, and our timid hearts
Beat quickly for those friends we know do brave
The storms. When hast thou heard from my honored
  Lord?—
'Tis strange that I must question you of him,—
I, who ne'er passed a day without his smiles,
From that proud hour when first I called him
Lord, till, leaving Nature's bright and lovely walks,
We sought a home mid London's dreary walls.

HAMPDEN.

You may expect him ere the sun hath set;
Most urgent matters call him here. [*Giving letters.*

Sweet Lady Lambert, from your honored Lord,
A trusty messenger these lines hath brought.

LADY ALICE.

My Lord! my honored Lord!—

HAMPDEN.

Most fair Elizabeth, thy smiles I woo
To win me to forgetfulness. Would that I had
A son, and he might win your love, that I might call
You daughter—thou brightest jewel in our Cromwell's
  home.

LADY ELIZABETH.

Kind Sir, I am not worthy of such praise,
Far, far more honored than my poor deserts,
By your o'er-estimate—

[CROMWELL *enters.*
Rushes to CROMWELL.] My father, my dear father!

CROMWELL *salutes each.*

My child, my dearest child, my honored wife,
Fair Lady Alice,—and my friends—
  [*Giving a hand to* HAMPDEN *and* PYM.
      My friends, ye are true friends
Indeed,—thus, mid the many calls our country
Makes, to offer solace to these o'ertasked hearts.
Hampden, how idle are the glories of the world;
How vain, illusory, the gifts which shine
Most gorgeous to our view! How rich in blessings
Is that peaceful country life, where we had dwelt
So long. How valued was the privilege granted us
Of studying in great Nature's book,
Written by God's own hand. I am already
Sickening of this scene of turmoil and of strife,
And envy even the untutored savage

Who may roam at will, and worship the Great Spirit
Unrestrained, in Nature's wondrous temples—
His, his is freedom—there the soul may soar
Where'er its Godlike nature bears it,
And such adoration render as the spirit
Feels, of essence like itself.
                            'Tis not the material form
That alone untrammelled makes us freemen;
But the immaterial sense that teaches us
That we are heavenly born—that this life's
But a pilgrimage.

LADY CROMWELL.
                            My dearest Lord, you think
Too deeply; you magnify our cares!
God gives us charges, but He gives us, too,
Ability to fulfil them; he praises best,
And the best service renders, who loveth best
Whatever is imposed by Him.   There is
Some occult blessing e'er in store, whatever our trials.

CROMWELL.
True, my sweet comforter—my saint-like wife—
Seeing letter in LADY ALICE'S *hand, who starts.*]
    Fair Lady Alice!   From your lord, I ween—
                            How fares my friend?

LADY ALICE.
Well as his friends could wish.

CROMWELL.
Shouts heard.]   Hampden, what mean these cheers?

HAMPDEN, *going to window.*
Cheers for our friends—our true and steadfast friends.
Unto the Lords' proposal for a peace,

The Commons had well-nigh yielded;
For two long nights, an angry, hot debate
Gave us but a slight majority.

CROMWELL.

What! are we, then, so weak in friends,
Or were they overawed?

PYM.

      Uncertain of their strength;
And hearing Charles gathered fresh forces
Every hour, many did quiver, while
Some men quailed!

CROMWELL.

Brave hearts! Why, they should tougher grow,
Like steel, the more they are hammered on.
This gives *me* new strength! What said the Londoners
To this?

HAMPDEN.

  They called them cowards, truants
To the trust the people had reposed in them.
Now, the foremost of our citizens do parade
The streets with drums, and fifes, and martial music;
While banners flaunt the air; and call
Upon the populace to enroll in the defence of London.

CROMWELL.

This, that daunts them, gives me new strength,
Nerves me for mightier trials. I'll seek
Their leaders, and inflame their hearts
With the pure fires of Liberty!
      This is no time
For woman's fears! Quivered and quailed,
You said, when that their country's welfare

Was at stake—   [*Turning to his daughter.*
    Why, I would offer up this,
My dearest child, on Liberty's altar,
For a sacrifice, and deem it cheaply bought,
Though my heart writhed in agony at the deed!
Come, we'll unto our friends.
Exeunt Ladies on one side.]
    [CROMWELL, PYM, *and* HAMPDEN *exeunt on the other.*

SCENE SECOND.

Streets of London, at nightfall.—Popular Commotion.

FIRST CITIZEN.

Down with these fickle Commoners, and give us men!

SECOND CITIZEN.

Give us those spirits dare assert our rights!

THIRD CITIZEN.

Men sprung from Nature; not the tinselled forms
That glisten, to dim at the mere touch of breath.

FOURTH CITIZEN.

Give us our Pym!

FIFTH CITIZEN.

    Our Hampden!

SIXTH CITIZEN.

        Our Hollis!   But here they come.
    Enter PYM, HAMPDEN, *and* HOLLIS.

HOLLIS.

Thanks, my friends, thanks; this gives me hope;
For I had feared Peace had most truly rusted out

Not only our arms, but hearts; that our English valor,
So famed, was gone.
But twenty miles apart, for ten days the foes sought each
    other.
The battle of Edgehill was fought; and he who was
The conqueror, after a good night's repose,
First left the field! Essex retiring to Warwick
With his carpet knights;
The King, with his show troops, too glad to escape
A second fight, fell back on his old post
At Banbury, leaving five thousand Englishmen
On the field. This Rupert is a hot-headed
And bold partisan—unequalled
In the sudden and fierce onslaught;—
But there's, as yet, no general in the field.

HAMPDEN.

But there is in the LAND. The man is born
That shall be styled—
      "THE BEST THING EVER ENGLAND DID."
Nurtured in peaceful arts, of stalwart form,
Sustained in all his trials by his faith in God;
Looking on life, as written in His book,
A scene of obligations must be filled
By each in his due course; not seeking
How he may evade, to him, God's seeming stern,
But justice-born commands.

CITIZENS.

Cheers for Hampden, Hollis, Pym—
Cromwell enters.]   And Cromwell, too.
Cheers for the people's friends.

HAMPDEN.

Thanks, thanks, my gentle friends.

CROMWELL.

Thanks, thanks, ye noble hearts, no longer
Would be slaves. 'Tis true, in loyalty you love
Your King; but he's no King who violates
All rights, all obligations, and forgets his royalty.
For royalty is born of God, and to be honored,
Must be worn as wears the Lord his attributes.
Has not he raised his banner against you
At Northampton? Has not Edgehill been fought,
And Marston Moor? The reeking wounds of thousands
    call from earth
For vengeance on their heads so ill advise,
While hosts of departed spirits knock
At Heaven's gate, witnesses from this dread scene;
I would not stir you up to rage by asking
Of those dearest friends you've lost; I would not wake
The sleeping lion at your hearts by asking
For your butchered young!
                          But, in Religion's name,
I'd ask if 'tis ordained, expressed,
Or even implied, that one man's wicked will
Shall trample on a nation's rights? I find
No record of it in the Word of God,—
The true authority for all man's acts.
Some are there, who would have you yield tamely,
Submissively; I tell you, no! You have a sacred trust,
Untarnished to transmit to ages yet unborn.
But let your work be in the spirit of the Lord!
Consider deeply, how high the trust that God
Has given in endowing reason—likening
To himself mere worms of earth. See how the world
Has grown in temporal, since spiritual gifts
To it were known! The seed is sown, the culture

By Heaven taught, the harvest's all your own.
Your King has forced you into arms;
For years you've tamely borne all your wrongs
Granting supplies—for what? that while you're poor
He and his pampered menials might be rich.
There is no halo hanging about his name;
Has England's glory ever been his aim?
Is there one single act, in all his long and peaceful reign,
Adorns the page of history? No!
But his wilful violations of your rights
Outnumber the sea-shore's sands!
I would not urge you, friends, against your King;
There's a divinity doth guard that name.
But since this Charles has raised his standard
Against his people and their Heaven-born rights,
He has become no more than their common foe.
When he is mindful of his proud estate,
Transmitted to him through a line of kings,
Banishes from his side the assassins of England's honor,
He will be in his people's hearts enthroned,
And there more proudly gemmed than e'er was
Egypt's queen; religions hosts his never-sleeping guard,
So long as virtue shines his diadem.
In the mean time, prepare we for the worst;
Forewarned, hereafter we must be found forearmed.
I must to the field and face this "people's foe." [*Exeunt.*

SCENE THIRD.

Room in Cromwell's House—Morning.

Lady Cromwell, Lady Lambert, *and* Lady Elizabeth *at a table, sewing.* Patience, *an attendant.*

LADY CROMWELL.

Good Patience, thou hast brought no news to-day.
Go hearken what the gossips say below.
                                    [*Exit* Patience.
Dear Lady Alice and my fair daughter,
The one the bride of Lambert—you our Cromwell's pride,
There is sad news to-day! Charles and his friends
Are carrying all before them in the west.
At Stratton they have overcome our Stamford;
At Lawnsdown, too, with dreadful loss of life,
The Royalists gained the victory; and Bristol,
Second city in the land, in riches and in greatness,
Has been taken.

LADY ALICE.

My Lord—

LADY CROMWELL.

Is safe with Essex—[*to Elizabeth*] where your father is.

LADY ELIZABETH, *aside.*

My father! mine's a divided interest.
Which father do I mean—my source and spring of life,
Or him, my source of hope, love, happiness,—
The father of my Charles? Oh, dreadful day
That ever I was born to know such misery!

LADY CROMWELL.

Who comes?
[PYM *and* HAMPDEN *enter.*]

PYM.

Your friends and servitors.

LADY CROMWELL.

What news?

PYM.

None but ill news.
A king is warring against his people;
His people, serpent-like, against themselves.
Our Edmund Waller—the courtly gentleman,
The poet, scholar, and the soul, 'twas thought,
Of honor—has been detected in a foul conspiracy.
He and his brother Tompkins and friend Chaloner
Are hung! There was no course but this.

HAMPDEN.

The battle of Newbury has been fought
And the pure Falkland's fallen, with "peace"
Upon his lips. Both armies worsted—London's militia,
As Anglo-Saxons ever do, equalling the veteran's valor—
Have retired to winter quarters, and we may soon
Expect our friends. Essex is no great general.

LADY ALICE.

Then Cromwell will be home—your Lord and my Lord—
Lambert will be home!

LADY ELIZABETH, *aside.*

And my Charles, where?

PYM.

Your Cromwell is the soul of our arms.
He found a rabble crew, and formed
A bulwark for our liberties.
      In Newbury's fight
Our troops were felled by Rupert's fierce onslaught
As hurricane fells forest-trees, till Cromwell
With his netted foot, his mettled cavalry,
A rocky front opposed, as breasts the firm-based mount,
Now frowning in the clouds, now in the sunshine gleaming,
The waves that lash its iron sides—mere mockery.
Fairfax and CROMWELL are our sole hope,
His name alone a legion.
      Yet more than this,
He's not found only in the fiercest fight,
But in the Council stands pre-eminent;
Let but a friend of Cromwell's propose a step,
And all the way shines bright, where was but gloom.
Were he like us, seeing no Charles, all would be well.
His kinsman of England, with his regal rights,
Falls like a shadow on his noble heart
And palls his arm—though all his *love* is England's.

HAMPDEN.

We have one hope, and that is, that this Charles
May yet be guilty of deceit towards him,
And sever all their bonds. My friend—
 IRETON *enters.*]

IRETON.

Is my friend Cromwell here?—my father,
For I have won that name winning his daughter's love.

 CROMWELL *enters.*]

PYM.

My country's hope!

IRETON.

My father!

LADY CROMWELL.

My honored lord!

LADY ELIZABETH.

My father!

LADY ALICE.

And my—friend!

CROMWELL.

Love and esteem to each and all—
My honorable wife!
To LADY ALICE.] My lovely lady! my children!
To PYM.] Mine and England's truest friend,
You've seen the cloud that lowers in our skies
Coming as comes the snow, a leaden pall,
Sent from the Ice-King's Court, as though in league
Against us. You'll see it all dispelled
As morning mist before the Day-King's messenger.
Ray after ray now rises, and each one glistens
Brighter than the last; rolling its folds away.
I would preserve my King, while quelling
Our foes; I would that he might wear his royalty—
An emanation from the Deity;
If he will not, he is no King. He summons now
One portion of the land to war upon the other.
Scotland is all in arms, and in his cause
Would wreak her vengeance upon England
For her imagined wrongs—wrongs which have made
Her great. One of the brightest jewels

In earth's diadem, "*Great* Britain" speaks
Her fame unto the wide, wide world.

IRETON.

You, her general, speak of others' wrongs;
Sees thy noble nature not thy own?

CROMWELL.

What means my son? thy brow is clouded.

IRETON.

Thine ear apart—these women and their tongues!—

CROMWELL.

Indeed—it must be weighty.
 Cromwell *and* Ireton *apart.*] [*Exeunt others.*

IRETON.

Since you took Hilsdon House and kept Oxford
In alarm, even the foe do pit you against
Prince Rupert; the King, hearing this, himself
Exclaimed:
 "I would some one would do me
The good service to bring Cromwell to me,
Alive or dead."

CROMWELL.

    He flatters me!
But I'll not favor him with my presence yet.
The time will come when we'll stand front to front.

IRETON.

But more, he has dispatched letters to the Queen
Touching your life.

CROMWELL.

   My life! 'tis in God's hands!

IRETON.

Concealed in a saddle—they will be sent
To a certain tavern on the coast near this,
And thence to France.

CROMWELL.

We will dispatch some trusty friends
To seize them—yet stay, we'll be those friends
Ourselves. Come, you are ever ready
For the scene of danger. We'll seize this saddle
Ourselves. It may not prove an easy one
To Charles. We'll borrow some troopers' cloaks
And morions. Come, away! *[Exeunt.*

SCENE FOURTH.

A Camp.—Parliamentary Officers advance.—General's tent in front.

FIRST OFFICER.

So a deputation has been sent to Scotland
To negotiate a treaty.
     Our lamb-like Parliament
Are sick of war, ere they have heard its sound.
Our troops too, all unpaid, as well as we—
Where is our General Cromwell? He is the man
For times like these! Essex and Fairfax
Are too tamely given.

SECOND OFFICER.

   Too true, alas!—for now the battle
Of Naseby is fought, and Colonel Monk has joined
Our cause—but here comes Ireton, and Cromwell too.
 IRETON *and* CROMWELL *enter.*]

CROMWELL, *with a letter*.

Weak and perfidious tyrant! Here has he sealed
His own destruction.
                    Forsooth he is courted
Alike by both factions, but rather thinks
To close with the Presbyterians.
                        His French Madam,
Her whom they ycleped our Queen, reproaches
Him with making too large concessions
To those villains;—and here he writes:
"But, dear heart, rest thou assured
That I shall in due time know what to do
With these rogues, who, instead of a silken leash,
Shall be fitted with a hempen cord."
Look to it, Charles, thy head is not so firm
On thy shoulders as it was an hour since.

IRETON.

It may be he thus speaks to please his dame.

CROMWELL.

And so would hang us some fair day,
By way of gallantry to his spouse!
There is no longer a King in England!
Her monarchy died within the hour,
Though it be aged sixteen hundred years.
Harrison, return at once to camp! Arouse
Our troops! rekindle the stifled flames
Into a blaze!—restore the confidence
Of the army in its leaders; assure them
We have abandoned all intention
In favor of this King.
                    Ireton, what said

The Parliament to the conditions I would propose
Unto the King?

IRETON.
They did address them to him,
And he returned an obstinate refusal.

CROMWELL.
What then? Speak quickly!

IRETON.
The vote of non-addresses was passed.

CROMWELL.
Then is Charles in fact, though not in words,
Dethroned!
We will keep down by military awe
The majority in Parliament.

IRETON.
But blow after blow on all sides falls upon us!
The Scots invade! The fleets in the Thames
Have hoisted the royal colors; risings
In Norfolk, Suffolk, Essex, Kent, and Wales;
Divisions among ourselves—Fairfax,
Governed either by his wife or by his rigid
Presbyterian principles, refused to lead
Against the Scots. May it not be suspected
That these movements are contemplated
With secret complacency by a majority
Of the Lords and Commons?

CROMWELL.
What of that?
He is not the only general in the land—
We'll find another. The Master Genius
Of the times shall rise, and against all

Alone suffice;—who greater, purer, than our Hampden?
Hasten you unto Fairfax; govern him;
See that he suppress the insurrection
In the South. In Wales I will subdue the revolt;
And while they think me there, I will to Scotland.
I'll drive them to their hills—these Highland Chiefs.
Haste ye to the South! keep up the drooping spirits
Of our troops.

IRETON.

It shall be done. Fare you well.
Giving letter.] But ha! I did forget—I found this letter
In my tent—it is addressed unto the troops.

CROMWELL.

Ha! Ha-a-a-a! What devil's work is this? Ho, there!
Soldier enters.]
Are my brave fellows prepared for the review?
We soon shall meet the foe.
       The victory must be ours.

SOLDIER.

They but await their General.

CROMWELL.

       I will attend.
[*Exeunt* CROMWELL *and others through his tent.*

SCENE FIFTH.

Scene changes to troops drawn up in line prepared for the Review—Let this be done by drawing aside the General's Tent.

CROMWELL *advances with Officers—a letter in his hand—and says:*

Ha! My brave soldiers in the Lord—
What! Discontent? What! Fears? Whose lines

Are these would stir you to revolt?
                                To revolt
Against whom? Against yourselves—for 'tis yourselves
Who would fall, if you fail. Has not
" The Almighty set his Canon against
Self-slaughter?" 'Tis this it bids you do—
A suicidal act—No! no! it cannot be—
The bare thought of such a dreadful deed
Strikes terror in your hearts, and tears, I see—
Tears of contrition, the only tears
The Independent soldier ever sheds,—
Steal mournfully down your cheeks.
                            I can no more—
You never will, I know, desert your Lord!
Desert your wives—your babes—your homes!
Desert your General and this holy cause!

TROOPS.

Never! never! never!
Rear high our standard—lead us to the fight!

CROMWELL, *unfurling a flag.*

The victory is won!—" The Lord of Hosts is with us!
The God of Jacob is our refuge."—On, Ironsides, on!

TABLEAU.

Curtain Falls.

ACT III.

SCENE FIRST.

Streets of London—Whitehall.

A crowd of Citizens.

FIRST CITIZEN.

The King! the King!

SECOND CITIZEN.

What king?

THIRD CITIZEN.

Why our King, King Charles,
Escorted now from Hurst to Windsor
By our Colonel Harrison.

FOURTH CITIZEN.

What, have we earthed the fox at last,
Despite of all his cunning? "He who publicly recognized*
The houses at Westminster as a legal Parliament,
And at the same time made a private minute
In Council declaring the recognition null.

FIFTH CITIZEN.

Ay, and publicly disclaimed all thought
Of calling in foreign aid against his people;
At the same time privately soliciting it
From France, Denmark, and Lorraine.

SIXTH CITIZEN.

He denied that he employed Papists, at the same time
Privately sent to his generals, directions to employ

* Macaulay

Every Papist that would serve; publicly
Took the Sacrament at Oxford, as a pledge
That he never would even connive at Popery;
Privately assured his Popish wife that he intended
To tolerate it in England, and authorized
Lord Glamorgan to promise that it should
Be established in Ireland—and then attempted
To clear himself at his agent's expense,
Who received, in the royal handwriting,
Reprimands, intended to be read by others,
And eulogies, to be seen but by himself.
Why, even his most devoted friends complain
Among themselves, with bitter grief and shame,
Of his crooked politics. His defeats, they say,
Give them less pain than his intrigues."

SEVENTH CITIZEN.

A prisoner, he will seek to cajole
And undermine our Cromwell—who now returns
Triumphant from the North.

SIXTH CITIZEN.

     Let the poor king
Pass privately to Windsor—admiring crowds
Will yet attend his way.

SEVENTH CITIZEN.

    Ay, ay, his way to heaven or—

SEVERAL CITIZENS.

All hail to Cromwell!—Cromwell comes—Cromwell,
Our hope, our trust.

  [CROMWELL *enters, with Soldiers and great state.*]
      Thanks—thanks,
My friends and fellow-soldiers in the Lord;

The fight is fought, the victory is ours.
Praise and thanks to Him, the God of battles,
Who smiled upon our arms; not unto me—
His humble instrument. Give thanks, give thanks!

TROOPS AND CITIZENS.

Amen! Amen! Amen!

IRETON.

Onward, brave troops.
[*Soldiers and Citizens exeunt.*
To CROMWELL.]—General, the King has gone to Windsor.

CROMWELL.

Is sent, you mean—[*Aside.*]—and THENCE!!
To IRETON.]—Bid Whitelock, Widdington, Lenthal, and
 Dean
Unto a private conference.

IRETON.

Where?

CROMWELL.

Where? Where but here, at Whitehall?
[*Exit* IRETON.
Charles at Windsor! Cromwell at Whitehall!
Charles king in title, but in power how fallen!
And I, Oliver Cromwell, master of this realm.
It is a vain and idle thing in me
To strive to keep my thoughts among the herd,
When all will have me great. It has been whispered
That the King must die; some men of blood,
Warriors austere, who've ruled the nation
Now for many months, meditate a fearful vengeance
On the captive King.* Where was engendered

* History of Indepency. Part II.

This most horrid thought? Where could it be
But in his most unrighteous acts, who, wrong
On wrong upon his people heaping, has reared
A power crushes beneath its might all reverence
And all love. I will not harp on this,
Nor ever will consent to shed that royal blood—
A deed inexpiable, and which will move
The grief and horror of the world. Some call
Me hypocrite; I am no fool. Charles the First
Dead—vengeance all wreaked—his faults all flown
With him, Charles the Second—next of the royal line—
Will rise in youth and innocence, and veiling
All his father's faults, that sainted blood will cry
Aloud to Heaven for vengeance on his judges.
I ne'er will sanction this, have I but power
To save him.* [*Exit* CROMWELL.

SCENE SECOND.

Scene changes to Room in Whitehall.—A Royal Bed.—WHITELOCK, WIDDINGTON, LENTHAL, and DEAN, writing at a table.

CROMWELL *enters.*

ALL.

General, you are welcome once more to London.

CROMWELL.

Thanks, my friends, thanks. Would that myself
Were the less kindly greeted, and my poor King
Had but his measure of his people's love.

WHITELOCK.

General, that thought was idly born, though born
In reverence; nothing will now suffice
But—

* Heath.

CROMWELL, *throwing himself upon the royal bed.*

Nay, name it not; there ever are expedients left,
Asked in sincerity in a virtuous cause,
Heaven-sent. I would devise some plan
For the return of the secluded members
To their duty in Parliament. An answer
Of the Lower House to the messages of the army,
Counselling gentleness, and a Proclamation
Drawn, to be issued by the Lords and Commons
For the settlement of the nation. I pray you
Have this speedily done. [*Exeunt.*

CROMWELL, *alone.*

What am I now to do if this should fail?
I would not that his royal head should fall;
And yet it may not reign. The people all are mine;
The soldiers too; but only mine while I am
Charles's foe. Thus far has Heaven smiled
Upon the Independents' cause—a cause
By their forbearance sacred made; but let
That royal blood be spilt, each drop that falls
Will cleanse out an offence.
My Ironsides name must e'er untarnished be;
In our rare camp, no drunkenness or gambling e'er is seen;
No rights of peaceful citizens disturbed,
And woman's honor is most sacred held.
Hampden and Pym are in their graves—
Alas for England, and for me!—Hampden fell [genets,
On Chalgrave field, and Pym now sleeps with the Planta-
While Buckingham, Strafford, Laud, lie in their bloody
    graves.

IRETON *enters.*

General, a missive— [*Handing a letter.*

CROMWELL.

Nay, a letter.

IRETON.

'Tis from the Queen.

CROMWELL.

The Queen! what Queen? This curse of queens
Has brought his royal head unto the block!
Ireton, my son, I see it all.
It shows as black as yonder stormy cloud,
And laden with Heaven's wrathfulness.
They shall not kill my King. He yet shall live.
What would this Queen?

IRETON.

A pass to return to England.

CROMWELL.

Nay, nay, that would be fatal. Her Popish name
Would whet the axe. Her presence give the blow.

IRETON.

The States of Holland, too, have interposed.

CROMWELL.

Unwisely done; they have interposed ere now
As England's foes—this is too fresh in memories
Of the people and the troops.

IRETON.

Colonel John Cromwell,
Commissioned by the Prince of Wales,
Would wait on you.

CROMWELL.

Go tell him I may not see him.
Tell him I know his errand. He knows

I would have saved my King—would he have saved
Himself—will save him if I may.   [*Ireton exits.*
I see it all; there is but one man left in England,
The world asserts it; that man is—who?
One Oliver Cromwell, late a plain country gentleman.
What trick would Fortune play me? Fortune!
The heathen's boast. In this enlightened age,
The Scriptures teach, man has no fortune
But a destiny; clothed with due powers,
Guided by an almighty hand, so long
As Virtue's plain ways and walks, by Conscience
Sentinelled, are trod, no foes can come,
And his great charge fulfilled; God's appointed end
Is reached.   If in his trust he fails, he falls
Forever; if he is true, he lives till the doom
Of time.   There is a leaden weight about my heart;
A pall enshrouds my thoughts.
May Heaven give me strength in this dread hour.

BRADSHAW *enters.*

General, there is no treating with this Charles.
He will be King, or nothing.

HARRISON AND GRIMSHAWE *enter.*]

HARRISON.
                    That shall he be
Before to-morrow's sun.

CROMWELL, *rising and advancing.*
                    Nay, nay, my masters!
Such unseemly haste betokens malice, not justice.
Since 'tis your will his royal head must bow
To dust, remember he has been our King.
Let this our deed, at which the world shall stand

Amazed, at least the semblance of justice wear.
Deposed, dethroned, tried in the face of all the world,
For wrongs against his people and his realm,
He as a KING should die,—a warning
For all after times.
            Remember, He whose servitors
We are, was by the accursed unbelievers
Dragged unto His ignominious and most bitter death;
Remember how Nature yawned; how the sun
Shrunk from earth, in horror at the sight;
And the whole world convulsed. Remember, too,
How, God Himself, He rose; how His blessed name
Drowns every sound where'er 'tis heard, when
Every head in reverence bows, and every knee is bent;
How they, in theirs, are wretched wanderers through the
        wide, wide world,—
No land, no home, not even one resting-place!
I counsel, that you ponder well on this,
Lest that, too late, you learn your fatal error.

HARRISON.

General, are you against us? The troops—

CROMWELL.

                            Are MINE!

BRADSHAW.

General, sign here our sentence—

CROMWELL.

Our sentence!—nay, nay!—not mine, not mine!
Oh! I would stay your suicidal hands;
You know not what you do!   [*Exit* CROMWELL.

BRADSHAW.

Our General not with us? Have we raised
A power we may not curb?

HARRISON.

I'll hasten, and stir up
The troops; if they demand it, he will yield.
His heart is with us, 'tis his hand that fails.

GRIMSHAWE.

It never failed till now. He would not have
Us act so unadvisedly. 'Tis for ourselves,
Not Charles, he counsels this. Let but the people
And the troops require, and he will sign the sentence.

BRADSHAW.

Then each unto his several friends; insist
Upon our sentence being passed, and executed
Without delay. [*Exeunt.*

SCENE THIRD.

Cromwell's Room.

CROMWELL, *alone.*

Is it come to this? that I, who ever sought
But paths of peace and righteous ways, must steep
My soul in blood, or lose my life? There's nothing left
But this. My life! and what is life, that I should weigh it
Against eternal death—deepest damnation—
For this murder foul—for murder sure it is!
Who comes?—[IRETON *enters.*]—Ireton, my son, what
    means this haste?

IRETON.

The troops are murmuring that you stay their will;
The populace cry out, that they will have his blood.

CROMWELL.

So have they cried before from the oldest time,

Yet rent the air (their act scarce o'er) with wailings.
Ireton, my son—Charles the First dead, Charles the
    Second
Lives, most potent of the twain. Charles the First
Living (imprisoned, an' you will), there is no Charles the
    Second,
And the Commons are rulers of the realm!

IRETON.

The Commons now are rulers of this realm—
Cromwell their General—soon their KING.
                    [CROMWELL *starts at this.*
For we, your troops, are masters of the land.

CROMWELL, *looking earnestly, fixedly, and sternly at* *IRE-
    TON, *goes up to him.*

There have been spectres, witches, weird women,
In the olden times, so teach the nursery dames;
Which of all these art thou?—wouldst drag my soul
To ruin, offering thus the diadem
For a blood-stained hand? Canst thou be Ireton?—
My son? Father to those darling babes
Caressing, fondling, call me grandsire?
My daughter's husband?—art a man? Put out
Thine hand,—'tis flesh and blood! Let me but gaze
Upon that face,—those locks;—they live, as I have seen
Them in the battle fierce, bristling with fury.
Those eyes,—so cold, so china-like,—are thine.
There are no smiles.
    [*Half aside.*] I never saw a smile upon his face.
This hand—this cold and clammy hand— * * *
How didst thou win my daughter's love? Nay, nay,
Hast thou not entwined thyself about my heart?
Thy serpent beauties sure are basalisks! * * *

    * Ireton, "the man of blood."—*Clarendon.*

*The vision, Ireton, said not I should be King,
But "*greatest* man of England."

IRETON.

How such, but King?—
See, here is Grimshawe.

GRIMSHAWE, *entering*.

General, the people
All, with one accord, demand his death.

CROMWELL.

Grimshawe, the troops are there to preserve
The law, which knows no populace
And no partisans.

HARRISON, *entering*.

General, the troops are with the tradesmen siding,
And all demand his death.
Here is the warrant, wanting but your signature.

CROMWELL.

Is it come to this?—leave it, pray leave it!
Leave me all, awhile.

[*Exeunt all, save* IRETON, *who goes to one side.*
RICHARD CROMWELL, *enters.*]

Ha! what wouldst thou, son? Com'st *thou* to urge
This bloody act? Why am I thus encircled by fierce
hearts?

RICHARD CROMWELL.

Father, you are o'erwrought—you mistake my purpose.

CROMWELL.

Nay, nay! you, like the rest, would rather be great
Than good. I tell you, Virtue's is the only crown
That's worth the wearing.

* Clarendon.

RICHARD.

So have I learned,
From the first lesson that I conned with you
Till this dark hour of melancholy tasks.
Father, upon my knee I do beseech you, sign not that!
I'd rather toil from sun to sun in the far
Western wilds,—the turf my couch, the sky my canopy,—
Than have this dear hand stained by an unworthy act,
Much less give warrant for our monarch's death.

CROMWELL, *embracing him.*

Richard, my son—thou art my son—indeed
Thou art; I never prized you at one-half
Your worth. [*Seeing* IRETON.] Ireton, he reads a lesson
Unto you, and them—those bloody men.

IRETON.

He knows not the world. He is too young—
The age of lovers, when, with mincing steps,
They track fair maids, with silvery tongues;
This their high ambition.
     Here comes your fairest daughter.

CROMWELL.

Go ye, and learn the people's and the soldiers' wills;
I would be alone with her.
     [IRETON *and* RICHARD *exeunt.*
It may be she would unfold the delicate leaves
Of her young heart unto her father's love,
As doth the tender flower to the ever-cheering sun.
 ELIZABETH *enters.*] My dearest child!

LADY ELIZABETH.

Father, your looks are sad, your eye is heavy,

And on your brow the clouds of care, not anger!
  Half aside.] I augur well from this.

CROMWELL.
    Why so! what wouldst thou ask?

LADY ELIZABETH.
A life!

CROMWELL.
   A life! Whose is it that I hold the tenure of?
Sure I am grown great, when life is in my gift—
But I ne'er sought this power.

LADY ELIZABETH.
           My King's.

CROMWELL.
Alas! it is not mine to give or keep.
All that I may do I have done; I am no longer
Master of myself, but slave to thousands.
Hark to the rabble's cry!—a cry for blood;
Hark to the murmurs of my troops!
Most melancholy sounds that ever fall
Upon a leader's ear.

LADY ELIZABETH.
          Better hear this
Than Conscience's upbraiding voice should break
The silence of the midnight air, bearing
The shrieks of mothers, daughters, children grown,
Ay, infants, too, ever to your restless couch.

CROMWELL.
Stay! stay! No more—no more!

LADY ELIZABETH.
           One thing, and I have done:
You ever said, you loved me best of all.

I have loved you as never other loved ;
And I would make you partner in my young heart's hopes,
Which you may turn to joy or bitterness
Which shall it be ? It is your daughter,
Father, asks you this. One word, and life and love,
Or misery till death !

CROMWELL.

Nay, nay ! how so ? Speak, speak !

LADY ELIZABETH.

I love our Liege's son, and he loves me ;
His father saved—and thou canst do it—
Your daughter his son's bride—my father lives
In honor and in glory ; the glory
Of a great, a virtuous deed !
Spurn this base rule ;
'Tis but a mob's, who'll turn against you,
Gratified or no.

CROMWELL.

But Charles has sought my life—would seek it again—
And with my life my country's liberties.
Great Brutus slew his best friend for Rome ;
Should Cromwell do less for England, thou noble girl ?

LADY ELIZABETH.

Ay, father, this is true ; but, Cæsar slain,
Was not the curse of blood upon their heads,
And early, ignominious deaths their lot ?
'Twere best to ponder on it. Oh, now I see
You're moved ! Give me that hideous paper,
Whose words gleam out like peace-pursuing fiends.

CROMWELL.

Nay, touch it not ! If Charles and England

Both can live, he shall; if one must die,
His was the smallest evil of the two.
The times, my child, are changed—

        England is new-born.
The spirit of the far Western clime new nature
Has infused into us all. We must move on,
Untrammelled by old customs, which do bind
The hands, as Popery binds the soul.
The Priest has fallen! The Spirit of the Lord
Is in the land; and where He is, there is Liberty.
Daughter, I would that I might grant thy prayer;
This Charles is e'en a noble boy; if I may save
His father, child, I will. First England—then ourselves.
But hark! what notes are these?—a funeral dirge—
What other of the heroes of the age has fallen?

 IRETON *enters.*]

To ELIZABETH]—Daughter, pray retire.

          [ELIZABETH *exits.*
Speak, Ireton, speak! what means your grief?

IRETON.

Cromwell, my father! you are a soldier,
And a Christian, too. Rally around you
All your strength, for you have need of it.
The bolt has fallen on your house.

CROMWELL.

My house? my house? My son! my son!
Where is my Oliver?

HARRISON, GRIMSHAWE, *and others enter, escorting a bier.*
What noble form is this? My child's! [*Falls on it.*
Almighty God, have mercy on me now.
My boy! my boy! speak, speak!—no voice to answer
Mine, that ne'er was heard in vain.

Hushed is the sweetest music I e'er heard;
Fallen the noblest form I e'er beheld.

HARRISON.

General—

CROMWELL.

Can ye not spare me but a little while,
My masters? Surely, the State's service
Gives me time to weep my first-born,
And most fondly loved. How happened this,
And where?

HARRISON.

Hastening to London with a small force,
Sir John Elliott, with a troop of the late King's Horse,
Assailed him. A Cromwell living, he a Cromwell
Died—most bravely fighting to the last.
Upon the news being brought, I hastened
With full force, and found my boy—
For he was mine, as yours—all England's—
For all loved him—honored him.

His murderer
Is ours—is to die ere set of sun. His purpose
Was to hold your Oliver a hostage for the King.
The King suggested this; so say these lines.

[*Showing* CROMWELL *the papers.*

CROMWELL.

In Charles's hand! Give me the warrant;
Blood will have blood. He who slew the son
Can have no mercy at the father's hand.

[*Signs the Warrant; then kneels by the bier.*

My son! my son!

TABLEAU.

Curtain Falls.

END OF ACT III.

ACT IV.

SCENE FIRST.

The House of Commons.—The Statue of CHARLES thrown down, and on its pedestal written, "The Tyrant, the last of the Kings, is gone."—In session.

BRADSHAW AND GRIMSHAWE *advance.*

BRADSHAW.

So amazement sits upon the land, and discontent
Broods everywhere.

GRIMSHAWE.

'Twas thus that Cromwell,
Who now is away in Ireland in our service,
Told us it would be, and charged upon us
Moderation.

BRADSHAW.

He signed the warrant for King Charles's death.

GRIMSHAWE.

Who had not done the same, like circumstanced?
Open and secret threats—letters anonymous—his son
thus sacrificed.

BRADSHAW.

He who foresaw the storm, should best know
How to still it.
      A resolution has passed the Commons,
That as the Lords seceded during the trial
Of their King, so henceforth we shall make
No more addresses to them, nor receive
Aught from them; that, as the existence
Of the Upper House is not only useless,

But dangerous, it ought forthwith to be abolished.
I also move the extinction of monarchical
Government in England, and declare it
High treason to proclaim, or any otherwise
Acknowledge Charles Stuart, commonly called
Prince of Wales.
    Let all in favor now in silence rise.
They all rise, uncovered.]

BRADSHAW.

The Lord doth smile upon our acts.
Amen.

ALL.

  Amen.

BRADSHAW.

Hereto, then, I affix our great seal, whereon
Is inscribe !—" On the first year of freedom,
By God's blessing restored, 1648."
Let now a Council of State be formed,
To consist of forty-one members, of whom
I do propose that Cromwell, Fairfax, St. John,
And the younger Vane shall be; upon them
Shall devolve all the duties which formerly
Attached to the Crown and its ministers
In the two Houses.

GRIMSHAWE.

   I would add you, friend Bradshaw,
To the same, and now do put it to the vote.

SPEAKER.

All in its favor rise.   [*They rise.*
Our Government is formed, and we adjourn. [*Exeunt.*

SCENE SECOND.

Whitehall.

LADY CROMWELL, LADY ALICE LAMBERT, LADY ELIZABETH CROMWELL.

LADY ALICE.

Dear Lady Cromwell, hast thou no news from Ireland?
Some three months have already passed;
No tidings could be trusted from your Lord
And mine.

LADY CROMWELL.

No news direct, but rumors of success;
Success such as has ever crowned
Our Cromwell's arms. Come, my fair Elizabeth,
Thy song, thy voice, should be attuned to joyful measures,
Thou peerless child of greatness.

LADY ELIZABETH.

Nay, of griefs!
There is no balm in gold or grandeur
To the wounded heart; mother, I have not sung
For months, except his dirge.

LADY CROMWELL.

Fie, fie! why must thou be
A puling girl, and weep for thy boy lover,
Forgetful of the greatness that surrounds thee?

LADY ELIZABETH.

Mother, thou hast crossed o'er the stream
Upon whose bosom Love's bark floats, and left
Its flowery banks for the thick chaparral,
Where the acactus, with its gorgeous hues,
Hides the sharp stings await the venturous foot.

This gorgeous grandeur blinds your eye sedate;
Fear lest its dazzling glories lead to ruin.

LADY CROMWELL.

Thou bird of evil omen! yet most fair
Of my fair brood, why flew the barb from the sole quiver
Could most deeply wound, that pierced thy bosom—
A wound must rankle, never to be healed by him?
Nay! cheer thee, child; there are a hundred heroes
Woo thy hand; ay, titled, and with wide domain,
Thou shouldst be mother to a race of men;
I would be grandam to the sweetest crew
That ever revelled o'er a gay parterre.

LADY ELIZABETH.

You might have been grandam to a long line
Of kings!

LADY CROMWELL.

And will be yet.

LADY ELIZABETH.

The dream was to my father, and no more.
Attendant enters.]

PATIENCE.

Madam, some gentlemen await on you.

LADY CROMWELL.

My Lady! Girl—will you never learn? admit them;
Daughter, receive them graciously.
BRADSHAW, GRIMSHAWE, *and* MARTIN *enter.*]
Ah, worthy Master Bradshaw, and my friends,
Grimshawe and Martin; your smiles betoken news—
Good news; haste give it me!

LADY ALICE.

And me; for I am trembling with loving eagerness.

BRADSHAW.

Temperance, fair dame, is next to chastity
In maiden hearts.

LADY CROMWELL.

Pray ye, what says my Lord?

BRADSHAW.

That Ireland is ours—Drogheda, Wexford,
Duncannon, Waterford, Estionage, Carrick,
And Passage Fort are won. The first-mentioned
Four, with loss of life; the last, surrendered.
All of your friends are well; Lord Broghill
Did good service to our cause, and the wild Irish
Fell.

LADY ALICE.

It was Lord Cromwell's voice that won him over.

LADY ELIZABETH.

My father's voice was ever wisest.

BRADSHAW.

Sweet child
Thou sayest well, and soon may thank him for us all;
I'd have no sweeter spokesman than yourself,
To render him the homage of our hearts.

LADY CROMWELL.

Why soon? Surely the war is not yet over.

BRADSHAW.

His services are needed nearer home;
The Parliament have summoned him;
Our General Ireton is with him now,
And well may take command, though Cromwell has
Full liberty to appoint whom best it pleases him.
The Council waits, and we must take our leave.

LADY CROMWELL.

Farewell, gentlemen. My thanks to you.
[*Exeunt Gentlemen.*
Sweet Lizzy, see—I am mother of great men,
If not of kings: "Our General Ireton!"
I would that Richard loved an active life,
Not pondering o'er dull tomes—a carpet knight.
Alas! my Oliver! He was a hero from his birth.

A trumpet and people's cheers.

LADY ALICE.

Hark ye, the shouts! It is our General comes.

CROMWELL *enters, saluting each.*

My honored wife, my Lady, and my love—
How glorious shine your beauties at this hour;
A joyous greeting for your truant Lord.

LADY CROMWELL.

Who should have come with lute upon his arm.
Such sweet words on his lips. How fare you,
My dear Lord?

CROMWELL.

A little weary, though right well.
How does our honored Lambert's lovely wife?
He bade me bear you this. [*Kissing her.*
I need not ask;
A garden of sweetest flowers by moonlight seen
Scarce rivals you.

LADY ALICE.

Nay, pardon me, but rather
By the light of yon bright orb, just resting
Now upon the throne of day—a herald
Unto thee, our General and our Lord, it shows thy way.

CROMWELL.

Be but a harbinger of peace, and I shall thank
You, sweet one.
   Turning to Elizabeth.]—My fairest child,
Where is thy smile—thy kiss?

LADY ELIZABETH, *kissing him.*

There, my *great* father—pardon me!

CROMWELL.

                       What means
This coldness in you, who ever rushed
Into my arms—or stood on tiptoe, eager
To embrace, when stayed in your approach?
What! can it be that I am grown so proud
And great (if I am, I did not know it),
That even my best-loved daughter is awe-filled?
If so—away with honors, glories, fame, and power—
I'd rather rule by love than majesty.   [*Turns away.*

LADY CROMWELL.

Nay, she has grown timid, Sir, of late;
She sings no more—nor smiles.
   Aside to ELIZABETH.]   Thou foolish girl!

CROMWELL.

                       I see it all.
Farewell, domestic joys—the innocent joys
Of home!
My generalship I purchased
With my dear son's blood; my country's safety,
With my daughter's love!
Why, what a bawble is aggrandizement!
The serpent eye of Jealousy—the soft voice of Deceit—
The blandishments of men who favors seek—
Eye-service everywhere—but nothing from the heart!

I had it once—all that the heart could ask:
My son's, my daughter's. Charles stole his life;
His son, her love—I know not which the weightiest loss:
Hers, 'tis a lighter grief to miss him here, a warrior
In heaven—than see her like a delicate flower
Lose her bloom, and perish leaf by leaf—
My girl! My boy! my brave, my noble boy,
My Oliver—why should I weep? He serves
In heaven now, while I am serving Heaven
Upon earth.
    I must attend upon the Council.
Exeunt Ladies the other.]   [*Exit one side.*

SCENE THIRD.

Grand Council-Chamber, Westminster—Counsellors seated—A Trumpet.

BRADSHAW.

Hark to the trump! Our General comes;
He has proved himself a gallant officer—
The General of the age.

GRIMSHAWE.

    As he has proved
Best Counsellor in our cause—
    Welcome unto our General!

As CROMWELL *enters, with Officers and armed Attendants, the Counsellors rise.*

CROMWELL.

Thanks, my good masters—fellow-Counsellors!
Thanks for this welcome of my humble self,—
The honored instrument of Heaven's will,
To whom all honor, power, glory, is given.
 They all uncover their heads.]

BRADSHAW.

On earth as heaven.   Amen.

CROMWELL.

Our arms victorious—Ireton, my son,
I have left in Ireland, supreme.
In all my sieges, battles, storms, assaults,
I deemed that mercy best would be consulted
By speediest termination to our war,
And therefore pray ye think, if you would harshly judge
My course,
"How much the evils attend
Upon a few instances of severity
In the outset, are compensated
By the cutting off long years of obstinate resistance."
Finding the Irish such a wild and savage race,
I felt that I was forced to string myself
Even to acts of seeming cruelty and horror;
Their arms not turned upon their foes,
They turn upon each other—with scarce a cause of wrong.

GRIMSHAWE.

In Henry the Second's reign, Cambrenses
Wrote—"that the only way to civilize
The Irish was to exterminate them
And seize their estates."

CROMWELL.

   Nay, my good masters!
I would not have that Emerald Isle,
The great capital out of which our debts
Are paid, our services rewarded, our acts
Of bounty performed.   Win them to peace
And love, by gentlest arts; now that they, knowing,
Fear your power, teach them that 'tis not your intention

To extirpate the nation—for now in flight
They seek a refuge from their wrongs; at least
Some fifty thousand have already left the land.
I would that they were taught the peaceful arts,
Then plenty soon would follow in their train,
Poverty be a stranger to that land, most blessed
On earth, and virtue reign lord paramount.

BRADSHAW.

We will debate on this, and act as you may counsel.
But now we have received news from Scotland:
They have proclaimed young Charles their King,
And King of England, Ireland, and France.

CROMWELL.

But have they made him such? Best as it is—
Better that now while our troops are flushed
With victory. Trouble not, my masters;
We will dispel their force as sun the mist.

BRADSHAW.

Thou dauntless man—now learn what for thy services
The House appoints. [CROMWELL *bows*.
The Palace of St. James thy residence,
With such attendants as beseemeth thee
And them; large grants of land
                    To their victorious General,
Most full approval of your every step,
And, with entire confidence in your ability
And faithfulness, they, on behalf of all England,
Give their thanks.

CROMWELL.

Nay, my good friends, Whitehall is well enough.

BRADSHAW.

For you, 'tis true, who love the tented field.

CROMWELL.

Nay, would I were out of the trade of war,
And here in council with you at Westminster.

BRADSHAW.

Till then thy wife and children are our most valued
  guests;
While you are caring for the State away,
Here must we guard them cheerily.
                               We have sent
To learn Lord Fairfax's will as to the conduct
Of the war in Scotland, and he declines
Assuming the command—'tis thought, at instance
Chiefly of his Presbyterian wife; but says
That should the Scots England invade, he would be ready
To lay down his life.

CROMWELL, *aside.*

             How all things tend to my advancement;
I could devise naught better.
Aloud.] "Notwithstanding his unwillingness, I pray
Ye may continue him General of your army,
For I would rather serve under him, than command
The greatest army in all England."

LUDLOW.

                               Fearing your views
Were such, we've sent a committee to advise
With him.   [CROMWELL *going.*
         I pray you do not withdraw yourself,
Nor yet, in compliment and humility,
Obstruct the public service by your refusal.
Stay yet awhile, and learn what Lord Fairfax
Further says; our committee come.

COMMITTEE *enter.*

               Still on his purpose bent,

Lord Fairfax's Secretary at the door awaits
To surrender his commission, if we
Think fit to receive it.

     CROMWELL.
    Did ye remind
Him that the Scots had invaded England
Since the recognition of the solemn League
And Covenant, and in direct contravention
Of its letter as well as spirit; that now
They meditate another inroad, under the banners
Of Charles Stuart, whom, without the Commonwealth's consent,
They have proclaimed Sovereign of the three kingdoms;
And therefore if there must be war, 'twere best
To choose the enemy's country for the scene,
Than permit a hostile army to penetrate
Into the heart of this nation, already wasted
By the ravages of our own civil dissensions?

     COMMITTEE.
We did, my Lord. He still refused.

     CROMWELL.
Then, my masters, if ye do receive surrender
Of his commission, which I would counsel
Ye temperately to consider, though *I* know not
What else to do, since he will die to all his former glory,
"And become the monument of his own name,"*
Which every day'll wear out, there should
For his past services recompense be made
 Aside.] (Their future General may require the like),
A liberal recompense.

     BRADSHAW.
So let it be; receive we the commission,

   * Cromwell's words.

And grant to him two thousand pounds a year.

LUDLOW.

Two thousand pounds!—scarce enough, my friend; for
  you or us
It would suffice.

CROMWELL.

Greatness, my masters, brings
Great charges in its train; make it five thousand pounds
  a year;
Now, I pray ye, excuse me.   [*Retires one side.*

BRADSHAW.

Our General counsels well; so let it be.
Admit his Secretary.
  Secretary enters.]   Young Sir, we do accept
Surrender of your Lord's commission;
Bear this to him, with our best thanks—
A settlement upon him for his past services
Of five thousand pounds a year: so would our General
  Cromwell.
This being disposed of, now I would propose
That our Lieutenant-General be Captain-General
Of all the land forces; that his commission
Be instantly drawn up; and that the Council of State
Hasten the preparations for the Northern expedition.

ALL.

Let it be so.

BRADSHAW.

The commission is prepared; I will affix
The seal. Captain-General, I salute you—now—my friend!
CROMWELL *bows to them, when they retire, and then advances with commission in his hand.*

CROMWELL.

Captain-General of all the land forces of England,

Then supreme ruler, under Heaven, of the realm!
Why am I raised to all this honor? I sought it not.
It must be that I am by high Providence
Selected for the accomplishment of great purposes;
"May it not be as instrument of the will divine,
As writ in Holy Scripture, which shadows forth
The triumphs and felicities of the Messiah's kingdom?"
  LUDLOW *enters.*] Ha! Ludlow, my friend!
  Aside.] I do not understand this man.

LUDLOW.
General.

CROMWELL.
Thou art cold—why so? Hast thou suspicion
Of my integrity, as servant of the public?
Dost thou suppose that I would be their master,
Seeing I am grown so great in power?
Believe me, I am but Heaven's instrument.

LUDLOW.
Enough, enough! I should not doubt you.

CROMWELL.
No, you should be the very last to do so.
Incumbent it may be on me many things to do,
Even extraordinary in the judgment of some men,
Who, now opposing, would bring ruin on themselves,
On me, as well as on the public cause.
But here I do declare that all I do
Shall be but for the people's good, for whose welfare
I am prepared to sacrifice my life.

LUDLOW.
We may not doubt you, General, in this.

CROMWELL.

You should not, with the past proofs you have;
All my desires are to settle the nation
In a free and equal commonwealth.
There are no other means to keep the old rulers out;
And, in all reverence and humility, I must say
I feel it is the Lord's design His people
To deliver from every burden.
HIS WILL AND WISE DECREES TO ME I READ
In " that the Lord at thy right hand shall strike
Through kings in the day of His wrath;
He shall fill the places with the dead bodies;
He shall wound the heads over many countries;
The people shall be willing in the day
Of *thy power*—thou art a priest forever."
There have I my commission. I will reform
The clergy and the law; the sons of Zeruiah
Are still too strong for us.
      Wilt thou not aid me
To fulfil God's will? I need the services
Of such as thou, godly and gallant gentlemen.

LUDLOW.

Most gladly, General, if in God's service.

CROMWELL.

It is; wilt thou accept the Lieutenant-Generalship
Of Ireland?

LUDLOW.

   I will—most sensible of the honor
You now do me.

CROMWELL.

   Then hasten preparation.

Ireton has returned, and I would you were there.
Farewell. [*Exit* LUDLOW.
    He may be troublesome. I would remove—
During my absence in the North, where, should reverse
Befall me—the more violent republicans,
Of whom he is one; they might take advantage,
And place the power of the State in other hands.
Oh, curse of greatness!—I do already feel
That I have more to dread from former friends
Than enemies avowed.
      The army I will make
Subservient to my ulterior plans;
I'll separate the interests of the soldiers
From those of their old commanders;
I will dismiss many of the " godly party,"
And give their places to men who make
Arms their trade.
While Fairfax stands an empty name, I'll mould the army
To my mind—" weed out the godly," they are
Bad fighting men, and fill their rooms with such
As make no question for conscience' sake;*
But I must do it gently, and unperceived
By the eyes of men. I need no " agitators;"
They are as two-edged swords—I must not cast
Them only to one side, but have them under foot,
And, if needs be, grind them into powder;
So shall I distribute all my fanatics far apart
In different regiments.
     We will have
No convocations now of saints.
 IRETON *enters*.] Ha, Ireton, what news?

IRETON.

Bad—as ever.
    * Cromwell's words.

CROMWELL.
Give it me.

IRETON.

Three of our bravest captains are arraigned
For a conspiracy against your life,
And now are before the Council of State, in the
Adjoining chamber.

CROMWELL.

My life! what would they with my life?
They value it at more than I do, if they'd steep
Their souls in perdition—their good names
In infamy.
       Who are they, and their cause for it?

IRETON.

Rich, Staines, and Watson—they have confessed
That in a dream they were advised to it,
In words of Scriptural cant.

CROMWELL.

       In the adjoining chamber,
Do you say? Not yet condemned? I'll make
An example of them for all time. Come with me.
       [*Exeunt.*

SCENE FOURTH.

Room adjoining Council-Chamber.

RICH, STAINES, *and* WATSON, *before the Council.*

CROMWELL *enters with* IRETON.

What meaneth this, my good masters—and ye,
My well-tried captains, conspiracy against my life!
Why would ye take it before the eyes of men?

Ye who might have had it tens of thousand times,
Unseen by all save the unseen eye of God?
My body-guard, ever in the closest fight;
Ye easily had mistook me for a foe;
My sentinels, at silent hour of night,
When all about me slept save ye yourselves—
Ay, and my very cup-bearer wert thou, my Rich,
When I was faint at Naseby—fie, fie, Sirs!
Shame on ye, pitiful, sneaking, and poor knaves
That ye are! see how ungrately ye had been to me—
How treacherous, cowardly to yourselves!
What would ye further with them, Sirs?

BRADSHAW.

A hempen cord!

CROMWELL.

      Your pardon, my good Bradshaw,
And my thanks, my friends, in that you deem
My life worth three—with your good leave, I have
A condign punishment for them.

BRADSHAW.

Pronounce it thou—against you their offence.

CROMWELL.

'Tis this: that ye be taken hence—what! do ye start
And tremble? ye poor weak fools! do ye fear
Death now? ye who ne'er knew fear before?
I have oft marked ye well, Sirs—I say, shall be taken
Hence—taken to my troops—all your bonds loosed—
Conscience awakened from this dreadful lethargy,
Ye shall your deed anticipated see
In all its naked horror—*upon the rack*—
Ye tremble—see what mean things a guilty conscience
Makes, e'en of the stoutest and the bravest hearts;—

Upon the *rack*, I say—ay, upon the *rack*
Of *conscience* ye shall lie—a living testimony
Of my judgment, and show unto the world
The vengeance Cromwell takes upon his private foes.
But woe to those whom he shall find the State's.
Go hence, and let me hear no more of this.
When that ye deem my country needs my life,
Come then and take it—'tis freely hers.
Release their bonds.

BRADSHAW.

Thou great and glorious soul,
The State would thou shouldst have a private guard.

CROMWELL.

I have it, friends; but in the private thoughts,
The secret heart of every Englishman.
With God upon my side, these canting fools
Will prove a better bulwark than ten thousand guards.
Now join in prayer and thanks to Heaven, my friends,
Then will I unto Scotland.

[*They kneel, and curtain falls.*

END OF ACT IV.

ACT V.

SCENE FIRST.

Council-Chamber.

BRADSHAW, GRIMSHAW, *and* MARTIN.

MARTIN.

What news to-day from Cromwell?

BRADSHAW.

Our foes dispersed at Derwent, Dunbar,
Indeed, where'er he met them; at Edinburgh,
He lies sick with a grievous fever;
Two skilful doctors to his aid I've sent,
And, by God's providence, I trust he may be saved.
The State can spare him not; though here he writes,
"Indeed, my Lord, your service needs not me—
I'm a poor creature, have been but a dry bone,
And am still an unprofitable servant
To my Master and to you." But, Heaven
Be praised! our Goddard writes, he mends;
And the same hour brings advice that the young Charles
In arms towards England comes.

GRIMSHAW.

And this from Cromwell;
Which doth intimate that all his forces
Withdrawn beyond the Forth, temptation thus
Is thrown in Charles's way, to confide himself
And cause to the English nation, whose loyalty
He would test.

He our General further entreats that we,

The Council of State, collect what force
We can without loss of time, and give Charles check
Until he shall o'ertake him. Lambert, with the cavalry,
Is sent to join brave Harrison at Newcastle,
To watch their motions, and straiten them on their way,
Though not to risk a battle.
    Enter an officer.]   Ha! what news?

OFFICER.

Major-General Massy and the Earl of Derby
Have been repulsed by Lilburn at Wigan,
And Charles has entered Worcester, where
He has solemnly been proclaimed by the Mayor,
Amid the loud acclamations of the gentlemen
Of the county.

BRADSHAW.

Charles at Worcester!—haste ye and rouse our friends;
Bid them use all speed to meet our Cromwell,
And aid him in his "crowning victory;"
For such shall this fight be. Haste ye, and urge on
Our supplies and men. Haste all!   [*Exeunt.*

SCENE SECOND.

Troop before Worcester.—Hour, Daybreak.

Troops enter and form in line of battle, crying, "Long live the Commonwealth of England!" "Long live CROMWELL!" *who enters with* IRETON *and* OFFICERS.

CROMWELL.

Thanks, thanks, my brave friends and fellow-soldiers.
What news, my Ireton?

IRETON.

The Bridge of Upton, held by General Massy,
Lambert has carried against fearful odds,
Leaving their General wounded on the field.

TROOPS.

Praise be to God!—long live our gallant Lambert!

IRETON.

Fleetwood has forced the passage of the Team.
A bridge of boats over the Severn at Bernhill
Thrown; at Powick, too, a fierce attack was begun,
And pike to pike they fought at set of sun.

CROMWELL.

Day dawns, my troops—nay, 'tis the sun himself;
            [*Sun breaks through clouds.*
Nature has veiled our brave intents;
So "let the Lord arise, and let His enemies
Be scattered."*

Martial Music; cannon at first near, then more distant. They charge upon the enemy; fresh troops come on the stage, and charge after charge.

On, my brave troops! on! on!
They break—their King doth turn—Ha! ha! brave boys!
I profess they run. The victory is ours;
The Commonwealth is safe. Let all our thoughts
Tend to His honor, who hath wrought
So great salvation, and let not wantonness
And pride follow this crowning mercy.

            OFFICER *enters and presents papers.*

OFFICER.

From the Council of State to their General Cromwell.
                        [*Retires.*

---

* Psalm lxviii.

CROMWELL.

The fight is fought; the victory is gained;
The Scots subdued; *their* Charles the Second fled;
What now remains to do?—Much, much—there is
A war within this *heart*, far fiercer raging
Than all outward foes. Down, fell ambition,
With your fiend-born crew, which feast upon its members
Ere 'twill die!
    Now, as I have in arms,
So must I seek in peaceful arts to raise
The power of England.
 Looking at the papers.] They do salute me here
As though I were their King, and would escort
Me in great state to London. My home, a palace—
And in each address greet my ears with loftier adulation
Than e'er was lavished on the scion
Of an hundred kings!
 IRETON *enters.*] Ha! Ireton—'twas bravely fought—
A word with you.
    The power of Parliament
Must be lowered!—its duration limited—
All political offences committed
Before Worcester's fight must be forgiven,
Except some certain cases.

IRETON.

This is well thought; 'twill make you friends.
It is decided Parliament be dissolved
Three years from this.   [*Exit.*

CROMWELL.

    Three years!—but see, here are

Enter WHITLOCK, WHALLY, DESBOROUGH.]

Our friends. Ha! Whitlock, Whally, Desborough—

What think ye, Gentlemen—
Were it best to perpetuate the Commonwealth
On fixed principles, or re-establish a mixed form
Of monarchical government?

WHALLY.

                      General, our friends,
The army, will not have a Monarchy.

WHITLOCK.

I would advise revival of the ancient Constitution—
King, Lords, and Commons—'tis better adapted
Than a Republic to the laws, the habits,
The feelings of Englishmen.

CROMWELL.

                Well spoken, learned friend,
But pray, whom would you recommend unto the throne?

WHITLOCK.

Charles Stuart or the Duke of York, provided
They submit to our conditions.

CROMWELL.

  Aside.]   Humph! [*Aloud.*] Methinks
They never will. 'Tis true, somewhat
Of a monarchical government would be most effectual,
If it could be established with safety
To the liberties of the people as Englishmen
And Christians.
                Methinks I have heard you do propose
Reduction of the army and of their pay.
By your leave, deem you this wise?—pray you,
Weigh it well, as also in all other retrenchments.
Rather let speedy and effectual means
Be taken for the propagation of the Gospel,

And all arrears due the army be paid forthwith.
Remember you their services and privations
In the course of a long war.

      See ye not, my friends,
That this paltry junto of statesmen who preside
At Westminster, the miserable remains
Of that illustrious body first met in 1640,
Actuated by no feelings but the love
Of power and emolument, intend
To keep the precious fruits of victory
To themselves, in their own hands, and condemn
The army to poverty and degrading insignificance?
'Twould be unjust, disgraceful, that men
Who never saw the tented field, nor suffered
In the long campaign, should enjoy
Those things for which the army have so often
Shed their blood. Let them now be in possession,
They never will resign; but, in defiance
Of the people and our soldiery, exclude
From all share in the government every man
Of truly patriotic principles.

     Whally, pray you draw up a petition
To this effect, and vindicate your rights.

WHALLY.

We will.

DESBOROUGH.

Ay, and hasten to present it.
   [*Exeunt* WHALLY *and* DESBOROUGH.

WHITLOCK.

General, may not this course be deemed,
To say the least, hasty and unconstitutional,
Thus to address the Parliament—in either hand
The sword or the Petition?

CROMWELL.

      You, Whitlock, are a lawyer,
Who by your code must work; men of the world
And soldiers, let their natures teach.
You are a very faithful, most efficient Lord Commissioner,
But, I fear much, look not into the root of the times.
You have met our officers, learned their views—
" What think you, if a man should take upon himself
To be a king; would it not cure all ills?"

WHITLOCK.

The remedy, I think, were worse than the disease.

CROMWELL.

Why think you so?

WHITLOCK.

     As to your own person,
The title of king would be of no advantage.
You have already the full kingly power.
It might awaken jealousies—besides,
The King of Scots yet lives; the people look
Upon him as their natural King.

CROMWELL.

The King of Scots—[*Aside.*]—why died he not at Worcester?

WHITLOCK.

I would propound your Excellency should send
To him, and have a private treaty with him;
Secure yourself and friends; make you and your posterity
Forever great—the name of Cromwell an example
For all time. He will accept any condition,—
Besides, there is a rumor in the land,
That there's a link binds Charles to Cromwell's House.
You have a daughter—pardon me—most fair;

This Charles is young, and once did consort with her—
[CROMWELL *starts*.
Wherefore not wed them?* Then your right to rule,
As his Prime Minister, no man could dispute.

CROMWELL.

He has already sought my daughter's hand;†
But have I the right to jeopard my dear child's peace,
My country's honor and prosperity,
By trusting one so profligate, so prodigal,
So lost to all fair fame as he?
        I cannot think of it.
I have refused her hand. Meantime, I would suggest
That the sovereign power be placed
In the hands of a Commission of forty persons,
Chosen from the Army, the Senate,
And the Council of State. What think you of this?
Some of our friends do counsel it.

WHITLOCK.

      I fear
'Twere dangerous to dissolve the House; besides,
Your Excellency, the formation of the proposed Commission
Is quite unconstitutional.

CROMWELL.

      Ever the lawyer, Whitlock.
I thank you for your friendship, and when you have
Leisure from the cares of state, which I know
Weigh heavily on you, will further counsel take.
Good day, my friend—my honest friend.
        [*Exit* WHITLOCK.
He wed my daughter! That may not be.
'Twas by my act his father died. This Whitlock

---

* Russell.   † Pictorial History of England.

Is very honest—the spokesman of the times.
None but a Stuart can, it seems, be king.
The vision said, I should be greatest man, but did not
    say *the King!*
We'll look to this.
  INGOLDSBY *enters.*] Ha! Ingoldsby, my friend!

INGOLDSBY.

Advised of what your and the army's feelings
Are, the Commons now are urging through the Bill
For their own dissolution, encumbered
With all the provisions to which the military are opposed.

CROMWELL.

Did none object to this? Had we no friends there?

INGOLDSBY.

Harrison most sweetly and most humbly
Conjured them to pause, while I came here
To counsel you to act. Your presence is much
Needed there.

CROMWELL.

    Thou hast well done,—*now is the time
To act.* We'll hasten unto Westminster.
Call Colonel Worsley and my Guard.   [*Exeunt.*

SCENE THIRD.

House of Commons in session—Westminster.

CROMWELL *enters with* INGOLDSBY, *and takes his seat on one of the outer benches, and beckons to* HARRISON.

CROMWELL.

Harrison, I judge the Parliament now ripe
For a dissolution.

To ST. JOHN.]   My friend, my friend, I have come
With a purpose of doing what grieves me
To my very soul, and what I have earnestly
With tears besought the Lord not to impose
On me; but there is a necessity, in order
To the glory of God and the good of the nation.

HARRISON.

Sir, the work is very great and dangerous.
I desire you seriously to consider before you
Engage in it.

CROMWELL.

You say well; we will consider on it.

SPEAKER.

The Bill for the dissolution of this House,
With due restrictions on the military power,
Having been well debated, I move the question
Now be taken.

CROMWELL (*to* HARRISON).

This is the time—now must I do it.
Addressing the House.] My friends, my friends, have we
fought and bled for this?
Left we our homes, our wives, our babes, to make
The sward at best our beds, if not our graves,
While you, self-seekers and profane, denying justice,
And oppressors all, lapped in luxuries,
Found uneasy rest even upon your downy pillows—
We fasting when you feasted—the elements
Fiercest beating on our unprotected heads,
While you sat sheltered by your blazing hearths,
Idolizing the lawyers, constant advocates of tyranny?
And for what did we this?   Returning
Victorious over every foe, to find reward

In glory, honor, ease, and plenty? Homes where
We might rest our wearied frames, and nurse
Our racked joints to health again?
                              Was this our return?
No, no; not so; no comfort for your tools;
Months of our pay in arrears; our crying babes,
Crying but for the crumbs fall hourly from your tables;
Our weeping wives, heart-riven by their sufferings;
While we, disabled in your cause that ye might feast,
Have not wherewith to break our fast. But, Sirs,
Your time has come. The Lord has disowned you;
He has chosen more worthy instruments
To perform His work.

SIR HARRY VANE.

                    Sir, Sir, I never have heard
Words so unparliamentary and offensive,
And uttered, too, by our own servant,
Whom we have so fondly cherished; whom,
By unprecedented bounty, we have raised
To the elevation on which he now stands.

CROMWELL.

Come, come, Sir; I'll put an end to your prating.
This must not, shall not be. Ye shall disgorge
A portion of those rights which ye so long
Have preyed on. Ye would be masters; fit masters
Ye shall be, but of yourselves alone.
Here die your tyrannies, ambitions, robberies,
And oppressions of the public.
                    Ho, there! without! [*Soldiers enter.*
BEHOLD YOUR MASTERS! *I*, their and God's instrument.
For shame on you, vile leeches that ye are!
Go, get you gone; give place to honester men;
To those who will more faithfully discharge

Their trust. You are no longer a Parliament!
I tell you, you are no longer a Parliament!
The Lord, the mighty Lord, has done with you;
He has chosen other instruments for His work.

SIR HARRY VANE.

I do protest against this proceeding.

CROMWELL, *laughing*.

Oh, Sir Harry Vane! Sir Harry Vane!
A vain protest—most vain. The Lord deliver me
From Sir Harry Vane—ha! ha! ha!
 Taking MARTIN *by the cloak.*] Thou art a lecherous
  knave—retire;
We must have modest men here!
 To another.] Thou art an adulterer—begone!
You taint the very air.
 To another.] Thou art a drunkard and a glutton—
Away! a very beast!
 To another.]   And thou an extortioner—
The rack were thy just doom. Millions hast thou
Kept on it. God gave even you a conscience.
Go—for now you'll find it—go to your solitude.
I have your ill-gotten, heart-wrung gains.
Ye are dishonest and corrupt livers all,
A shame and scandal to the profession
Of the Gospel.

SPEAKER LENTHAL.

  I do refuse to withdraw,
Unless I am compelled to leave this chair.

HARRISON *leads forth two of the military, at a sign from* CROMWELL, *to make a show of force, and, laying his hand on* LENTHAL, *assists him to descend. About eighty, among whom is* ALGERNON SIDNEY, *follow this example, and move towards the door.*

CROMWELL.

It is you who have forced me to do this.
I have sought the Lord night and day, that
He would rather slay me, than put me on
The doing of this work.

ALDERMAN ALLEN.

It is not yet too late
To undo what has just been done.

CROMWELL.

This from you, Sir?
You, who have defrauded the public to the amount
Of some hundred thousand pounds, as Treasurer
Of the army! Take him into custody,
Until he answers for this peculation.
Fixing his eyes on the mace.]
What shall we do with this fool's bawble?
Here—carry it away.
He snatches the Act of Dissolution from the hands of the Clerk.]
Lock fast the door, and bring the keys—
I will unto Whitehall.

[*He retires, and the door is locked.*

SCENE FOURTH.

Whitehall.—Council of State—Council of Officers waiting Cromwell's return.

CROMWELL *enters.*

My friends, my fellow-soldiers, I have been sorely tried;
I did not think to have done what I did;

But, perceiving the Spirit of God
So strong upon me, I would no longer
Consult flesh and blood, but let the Spirit act.
Behold the spoil—the mace, the keys of the lower House,
The Act of Dissolution—the Parliament is no more.

OFFICER.

How mean you, General? The Parliament no more?
This course can only lead to ruin and confusion.

CROMWELL.

Leave that to me. Have I ever yet failed?
I will do much more good to the country
Than ever could be expected from Parliament.
Aside.] Ireton, a word with you. [*They retire one side.*

COLONEL OAKEY.

Means so hypocritical, the end will sure be bad.
What could be passing in the General's mind,
When he praised the Parliament so highly
To the Council of Officers, and yet proceeded
Immediately afterwards to eject them
With so much scorn and contempt?

DESBOROUGH.

True, true; if ever the General drolled in his life,
He has drolled now. We must look to this.

CROMWELL.

Gentlemen, if you are here met as private persons,
You shall not be disturbed; but if as a Council
Of State, this is no place for you; and since
You cannot but know all that was done at the House
But this morning, so take notice that the Parliament
Is dissolved.

BRADSHAW.

Sir, we have heard what you did
At the House in the morning, and before many hours
All England will hear it; but, Sir, you are mistaken
To think that the Parliament is dissolved;
For no power under heaven can dissolve them
But themselves. Therefore take you notice
Of that.

SIR ARTHUR HAZELRIG.

Ay, indeed; this is true.

MR. LOVE AND MR. PEAT.

Ay, true; most true.

CROMWELL.

Ye too, Gentlemen! I thank ye, Sirs.
All England soon will hear it; and, hearing, know
That the Parliament would have sent their officers
And soldiers into private life, upon diminished pay,
And stripped of all influence those who had made
Them great, and England to be feared.
The Army and the Navy both, in their addresses
Unto me, declare that they will stand or fall,
Live or die, in support of these my measures.
The populace throughout the land will thank me
For it; ay, and chant hymns of triumph
O'er your fall; magnify the name of the Lord,
Who has broken the mighty, and cast
The proud down to the ground.

Aside.] Ireton, 'tis well
We have done what we have; these statesmen
Are fast becoming adepts in our policy.
Had but the Bill for dissolution passed,
Those neuters—those, I mean, of the Presbyterian interest,
Who had not consented in our measures—

IRETON, *interrupting him*.

The King's death and the Army's measures.

CROMWELL.

Ireton, no more of that; name it not,
Name it not! When memory calls it up,
My heart is blanched, and what I have to do
I do by halves—those hated hours shadow
All my days.

IRETON.

The wisdom of your acts
Refutes all charges, and should dispel such thoughts.

CROMWELL.

It may be so; but enough of this.
By interposing my authority just when I did,
The dispute I limited to a body
Of men who, for reasons various, had ceased
To be longer popular—call it as you may,
My good fortune or my great political wisdom.
My friends, let now a Council of State
Be appointed, to watch over the peace and safety
Of the Commonwealth, and superintend
The present management of public affairs,
In number thirteen—nine military and four civilians;
A Scriptural number, and vouchsafed to us
By Him whom here we seek to serve. Sir Harry Vane,
Pray you be one of us.

SIR HARRY VANE.

Thank you, General; though the reign
Of the saints is begun, I shall defer my share
Until I go to Heaven.

CROMWELL.

Or to ——, as it best pleases you;

All have a right to choose their company.
Beckoning them to one side.]
Good Major Salloway, and Carew, my friend,
Prithee, your care and counsel. I know not how
I can sustain this weight now falls upon me.
Thoughts of the awful consequences make me tremble.
Free me, I prithee, from the great temptation
Laid before me. Go ye, I pray, forthwith
Unto Chief-Justice St. John and Mr. Selden,
And together draw some instrument of government,
Which may take the power out of my hands.

SALLOWAY.

The way to free you from this temptation
Is for you not to look upon yourself
To be under it, but to rest persuaded
That the power of the nation is in the good people
Of England, as formerly it was.

CROMWELL.

      Thou speakest well;
My many cares at times obscure my thoughts.
I pray you, then, summon our chief officers
To meet me at Whitehall forthwith, where they may consider
What 'twere best to do.

SALLOWAY.
   We will.

CROMWELL.
     Do it forthwith.
'Tis well. Some private business calls me now—
Prithee, attend to this. [*Exeunt* CAREW *and* SALLOWAY.
    Ireton, read ye their thoughts?
We must be wary.

IRETON.

Ay, and bold; the power is yours.

CROMWELL.

And I will keep it. I will conclude the treaty
With the Portuguese Ambassador, suspend
The four Judges do offend, and make
Two new appointments; nominate new Commissioners
Of the Treasury and Admiralty; continue
The monthly assessments of one hundred and twenty
    thousand pounds
For an additional half year. For form's sake,
I will submit it to my Council of State;
It will sanction it in the eyes of England.
'Twere well, I think, too, for form's sake,
That we and our Council of State
Should nominate a Parliament
Of holy, pious men. Did our ministers
In the several counties send returns
Of persons faithful, fearing God,
And hating covetousness, who may be deemed
Qualified for this high and important trust?
I'll choose, say, an hundred and fifty to serve for certain
    places
In the three kingdoms.

IRETON, *showing a list*.

They did—are here—and I have chosen them.

CROMWELL, *laughing*.

'Tis well—a goodlie
If not Godlie company. There are an hundred and fifty,
    we,
That is, you, my Ireton, and I, know to be true
And faithful. You will observe

They did appear personally at Whitehall
On the *Fourth Day of July*, 1653—
This shall be hailed throughout the world
As Freedom's Birthday. Attend on them;
Go you, and send me instant word how they conduct.
[*Exit* IRETON.
Enter the Quaker Merchant Fox.]
Most worthy friend,
What wouldst thou have? A merchant prince,
Most honored of God's instruments—link
In the priceless chain of peaceful arts
That bind all climes together—source
Of England's glory—God's treasurer on earth—
Trustee immaculate of the wealth He gives,
In charity's sweet offices to dispense—
Mid heaviest charges e'er has Cromwell's ear.

FOX.

My ship from India—her cargo priceless—
Is by the Spaniards, in the Channel, taken.

CROMWELL.

Your ship! Truly thou say'st her cargo's priceless—
'Twas England's honor that she convoyed hither.
And in the Channel too!—at our very doors!
But what matters that? Were it in farthest seas,
Our flag should be immaculate. Their wealth
Has made these Spaniards arrogant.
'Twill prove the curse and ruin of their land—
Misused, abused, the trust forgotten.
Thou shalt be recompensed ten days from this;
Make out your charges; 'tis England's cause;
Our Blake shall straightway seek their argosies.
Monuments of your goodness fill the land,
Which the most loses in your loss.

FOX.

My duty—nothing more—no praise in that—
My habit and my home I have—'tis all I need-
The rest is for the State.
                    So do I humbly take my leave.

CROMWELL.

God's peace be with thee.   [*Exit Quaker* Fox.

An Officer enters and hands a note to CROMWELL, *saying,*
"From General IRETON, my Lord;" *then retires.*

CROMWELL *alone, takes the note and reads.*

The Parliament are met—my goodlie, Godly
Parliament—no, no, not mine, but Barebones'.
What a name! They would o'erturn all known forms
Of law and government, would I but let them.
I have failed indeed in this. They are worse
Than were the Danes or Normans. Those fellows,
Preaches, Feakes, and Powell, preach that Cromwell
Is the Man of Sin—the Old Dragon and the Beast
Foretold in the Revelation. I've had enough
Of this fooling. Ireton! Ireton, I say!—
There's terror in his looks and name—
  IRETON *enters.*] My son, go to the House,
Forthwith—bid the members repair to Whitehall,
And give back their authority into the hands
Of him from whom they had received it.
If these reformers, who are some thirty—
I know them all—ask for a warrant, call in
A company of soldiers; take my own guard,
If needs be; clear the House, and hither bring
The keys. It must be done—this the best way
To do it.

IRETON.
And shall be.
CROMWELL.
He likes this service.
What a stout heart that is! My Oliver's was even such,
But Richard's is a gewgaw for fair dames.
CAREW *enters*.
General, the Military Council have decided
That, finding Parliaments such unstable
And unwieldy things, that you be solemnly
Installed the Lord Protector of the Commonwealth
Of England, Scotland, and Ireland, and do await
Your presence in Westminster Hall. They beg
You'll pardon this lack of ceremony,
But the State requires it.
CROMWELL.
Thanks, my good friend;
I will attend, though I would rather not assume
Fresh cares.   [*Exit* CAREW.
IRETON *enters with Speaker, bringing keys.*
CROMWELL.
Ha! Gentlemen; welcome, Gentlemen;
  With a smile.]
My son, you did escort them in due form.
SPEAKER.
We would resign the power you conferred on us,
Unworthy instruments, unequal to the task,
And pray for your dismission.
CROMWELL.
Nay, my good friend,
Why so? How is this? You have scarcely entered

Upon our service; but if it needs must be,
Why, it must be. I have appealed to God
Before you already. I know it is a tender thing
To make appeals to God. Then fare ye well
[*Speaker exit one side;* CROMWELL *and* IRETON *the other.*

SCENE FIFTH.

Westminster Hall.

A Chair of State, with a rich carpet and cushions.—A Commissioner of the Great Seal at each hand.—The Judges on both sides.—The Lord Mayor and Aldermen on the right, and the members of the Council on the left.—Triumphal Music.—CROMWELL enters with a splendid retinue.

CROMWELL.

My loving, honorable, and much honored friends,
Why would ye summon me, an humble citizen,
To leave the calm and equal walks of privacy,
For the toilsome and uneasy race of greatness?
I thank ye for the honors ye would confer;
But pray ye to confer them on one worthier.

INGOLDSBY.

Cromwell's the name, the worthiest England
Ever bore, to wear the honors that her people give.

LISLE.

Here is the institute of Government,
Duly sealed, and here am I to administer
The oath gives unto England's sole and only use
Her worthiest son, as Protector of the Realm.

CROMWELL, *raising his hand.*

Since such is your and the people's gracious will,
Here do I swear, in all humility,

Her honor to preserve by land and sea,
From pole to pole.

The Lords Commissioners deliver up to CROMWELL *the Purse and Seals.*

LORDS COMMISSIONERS.

The purse and seals, your Highness;
Pointing to the Chair of State.] And that your seat.

LORD MAYOR OF LONDON.

This too, with London's love and loyalty, my sword.

CROMWELL.

Nay, Sir, as Cromwell's friend, keep this.
In greatest stress the Londoners e'er proved true;
So may I find them ever.
Advances.]
Protector of the Realm—in all things King, save name!
The wide world envies me—the air is rent
With praises of my deeds—each act a virtue,
And many great acts mine that never yet
I dreamed of. So runs the world; a few short years
Protector of the Realm, a few short minutes
May be your span of life. But for this mail,
[*Strikes his breast.*
Some secret foe had long ere this probed
My heart's mysteries, and unveiled to earth
What Heaven only knows; for all my deeds,
Ay, even my motives, yet shall be unfolded
To the world, though it may be not until
Long hereafter; but probed they will be.
Regicide one age, the next I shall be lauded
To the skies as Godlike, Freedom's Father!
Strange destiny is mine—an humble wanderer
In a savage clime, I thought to be,

When he, whose head paid forfeit for the act,
Compelled my sojourn here, and made me
More than King; for I've o'erleaped all wonted forms,
And out of the line direct, though of royal blood,
I reign entire master of the Realm—
Its meanest and its mightiest, officers to my will.

ATTENDANT, *advancing*.

Ambassador of France, my Lord.

CROMWELL.

Give him admittance.

AMBASSADOR.

France sends her greeting unto the Lord Protector,
And woos his friendship and his favor.

CROMWELL.

We thank His Majesty, and trust the love
Our people and ourselves now entertain
For him may be preserved. Say this is
From Cromwell unto Mazarin. Prithee,
Your presence at our feast to-day.
    Presenting him to Ladies.] Our Lady Cromwell,
And our friends, fair Sir.
    Officer hands a paper.] From Spain an Ambassador
Attends. France *and* Spain—France *or* Spain—
Now come the troubles of our greatness.
Portugal too doth wait; and from the Netherlands
There is an embassy; the United Provinces
Now sue for peace, on terms most favorable
To us—which we will grant, for our great Blake
Has swept the seas even of Von Tromp
And his masthead broom. The triumphs of our flag
Shed a glory on our rule unequalled

By the past—if Cromwell lives, never to be equalled
In the *great hereafter.*

I'll have no foreign wars, our foes subdued
Or peace insured; for there are troublous tongues
Enough at home. Though scarce established
As their Lord Protector, idle, venomous spirits
Do menace me—even the Preachers dare denounce me.
The system I in Ireland adopted, speedily worked
My ends; I'll try it here. Ireton, I have heard
That our late friend, Harrison, wags his tongue
Against us. He was a master spirit in our cause;
May prove such against us. The Tower
Were the safest place for him. There's likewise
A stubborn, wrongheaded schoolmaster called Vowell,
Who has been most treasonable in his course;
He is not of much note, and has few friends
To feel revenge—let him be hanged—
'Twill give their idle brains somewhat to muse
Upon; and that young fellow, Gerald,
I've seen the boy, a murderer by his looks—
Let him swing for it—be instant—
No paltering now. [*Exit* IRETON.
    Faith, I would rather have taken
A shepherd's staff than this Protectorship.
My Genius hates this show of greatness.
New England should have been my home;
No shadows would have crossed my pure intents.
There the untutored savage I might have moulded
In the true ways of life; in nature and association
They're prepared. Here, every tree
And stone, ay, every star tells men of Princes
And their pageantry. The history of all times
Teaches of despots and despotic rule.

Though for some short-lived season men may have tried
Self-government, 'twas e'er to fall under an iron hand,
That crushed them into obedience.
                            I have been swept along
By the swift current of fierce events, and find
Myself upon a throne—a throne of cares and fears—
My myrmidons, jealousy, hate, deceit,
And all the fellest passions of the human heart.
Men do not love me—why, they cannot say,
Save that I have o'ertopped them. [*Enter* INGOLDSBY.
                            Ha! Ingoldsby—
What news?

                    INGOLDSBY.

            Great discontent among
Our quondam friends.

                    CROMWELL.

              Why so? Have I not told them
I would not be lord over them; but one that is resolved
To be a fellow-servant, to the intent
Of this great affair?

                    INGOLDSBY.

True, true; but now the House debated, whether
They should consent to have the Government
Vested in a single person and a Parliament,
And carried it but by five voices.
    Enter IRETON.]

                    CROMWELL.

                          Indeed! what more?

                    IRETON.

One said, that as God had made him
Instrumental in cutting down tyranny
In one individual, so could he not endure

To see the liberties of the nation shackled
By another, whose right to the Government
Could not be measured otherwise than by the length
Of his sword, which alone had emboldened him
To command his commanders.

CROMWELL.

And yet they thrust it on me.
What more was said?

INGOLDSBY.

Another as the Prophet
Unto Ahab said—" Hast thou killed and also
Taken possession?"

CROMWELL.

Such words of me! I had not dreamed
They thought it. Killed, did they say? You know
I did not do it; it was ordained by them;
My signature wrung from a father's bleeding heart,
At sight of his eldest son a corpse transfixed.
If this is my reward
For years of toil—for fondest hopes crushed
At their consummation—for Heaven's own ways
(Mine were then most pure), all set aside,
And worldly courses taken—hereafter
I will be ruler of myself and of this realm—
Preserve my life, though at the cost of myriads.
I have made England great, greater than e'er before,
And I will rule. Ingoldsby, let them say on,
Ay, gibe like monkeys—I tell you, Sir,
The time will come when they will offer me
The crown. Go you, and order three regiments
To march into the city; seize the most noisy
Of these brawlers; place a guard at the door
Of the House, and lay this recognition

On a table in the lobby, for their signature.
I have foreseen all this, and now *will know*
My friends.   This binds them neither to propose
Or consent to alter the Government
As it is now settled in a single person
And Parliament.   I will have my spies
In every regiment, in almost every house,
And in the very bed-chamber of this Charles II.,
As they clepe him—at Cologne and at Paris.
I have done with peace and rest—there is
No rest for me but in the grave—the grave.

This kingdom I will divide into military governments,
To arrest, imprison, and bind over
All dangerous and suspected persons,
Without the power of appeal to any
But the Protector himself and his Council;
And all who have borne arms for the King,
Or were of the royal party, shall be
Decimated.   There will no longer be a cant
Of liberty.   They are not fit for it,
Who fatten on distrust, and, gorged,
Would fill the realm with it.   There now are
In the ports a hundred ships of various sizes;—
Penn and Venables shall hasten to the settlements
Of Spain and seize on them;
Thence to James River, and reduce to allegiance
Unto me, those colonies which dare adhere
To Charles, cleping themselves the " Old Dominion;"
I'll give them a new rule, whose seeds shall yet
O'ertop the world;—while Blake shall add
To his well-won honors, and seize Spain's treasure-ships.
France must be our friend, even though Spain
Is our foe; yet now proposes I should be seated

On the throne. Ireton, go you and give my order
That Penruddock and Groves be beheaded at Exeter;
Jones and his friends be hanged; the residue
Who were concerned in the rising at Salisbury,
Be sent to Barbadoes and sold as slaves!
Issue my declaration, prohibiting
All sequestered clergymen of the Church
Of England from preaching or using the Liturgy,
As ministers, either in public or private;
And command all Roman Catholic priests
To quit the kingdom under pain of death.
Forbid the publication in print of any news
Whatever, without permission from the Secretary of State.
There are three argosies in port, taken by Blake;
See that Friend Fox be recompensed—this done,
The residue retain for England's honor.
Thus Cromwell seeks redress.
Send instantly an embassy to the Duke of Savoy,
To intercede in behalf of the persecuted Vaudois.
Our brother of France unites in this—we will it so.
Then let him haste to Rome, with our command
That all persecutions of God's elect shall cease,
Or Cromwell's cannon's roar shall echo
Through St. Angelo. [*Exeunt.*

Enter COLONEL JEPHSON, ASHE, *and* SIR CHARLES PACK.

COLONEL JEPHSON.

My friends, what may we do to stay
These plots against our General and ourselves,
Which rise on every hand at every hour?

ASHE.

Make him our King!—beseech him that he will be pleased
To take upon himself the Government

According to the ancient Constitution—
Then will their hopes and plots be at an end.

SIR CHARLES PACK.

This was my thought; and here have I prepared
An humble address and remonstrance
Of the knights, citizens, and burgesses now assembled
In the Parliament of the Commonwealth,
Praying he will accept this power.
The title I have left blank—shall we present it?

JEPHSON.

Ay, and fill the blank with KING. We'll find him
In the Tapestrie Chamber. Come, we'll present it
On the instant.   [*Exeunt.*

SCENE SIXTH.

Whitehall.

Enter CROMWELL, LAMBERT, FLEETWOOD, *and* DESBOROUGH.

CROMWELL.

Oh, what a troublous thing is greatness!
I once knew peace—sweet peace of mind—but it is fled
Forever. There is no safety now for me
From dastard cut-throats, save an armed guard,
And all the attendants make kings slaves.
Free in my nature, I would have been free,
Free as the wild deer roves New England's woods.
He stayed me in my course of usefulness,
And made me what I am now, what I am yet
To be. Fleetwood my son, my brother Desborough,
And my friend Lambert—*they* would have me king,
These lawyers and civilians—what think ye

Of this name?   The power I have is greater
Than any king's for ages past.

DESBOROUGH.

Nay, Cromwell, entertain it not;
There is more matter than you perceive in this;
Those who would put this on you, sure, are no enemies
To Charles Stuart.

FLEETWOOD.

Methinks it would draw ruin on yourself
And friends.   General, eschew this act.

CROMWELL.

Oh, ye are a couple of precise, scrupulous fellows.
Lambert, what say you?

LAMBERT.

           As do these friends, your kinsmen,—
Touch not the diadem.

CROMWELL.

Well, well, I would do naught without consent
Of the army.   Hasten to the House, and put them off
From doing any thing further in this matter.
But lo, whom have we here?

Enter SPEAKER *and others.*

SPEAKER.

My Lord, herewith do I present to you
The humble petition and advice of the Parliament,
Setting forth the advantages of regal government,
And the nation's confidence in a new Sovereign—
Yourself their choice.

CROMWELL.

My gentle friends, I thank you, but must decline.

SPEAKER, *presenting the diadem.*

Here is the diadem.

CROMWELL.

What! would ye tempt me
With this golden bawble, which at the best
Is but a feather in a man's cap? I should not be
An honest man, did I not tell you that I
Cannot accept of the government, nor undertake
The trouble and charge of it. I, who have tried it
More than any one—indeed, I cannot undertake
The government with the title of King.
This receive, I pray you, as my answer
To this great and weighty business.*

SPEAKER.

This must we to the Parliament relate,
Who'll much regret refusal to their will.

CROMWELL.

Give them my thanks;—as Lord Protector
I will rule the realm as God directs me.
'Tis a weighty trust; I pray ye lighten it
As best ye may, by your collected wisdom,
Unto which I'll bow, so long as England's welfare
Is your aim. My thanks to one and all;
My friends, at even I will meet ye. [*Exeunt.*
The diadem of England mine! Her fleets,
Her fortresses, her coffers, armies, all are mine!
All save her people's love—that which I most
Had prized—and yet they'd have me take
The name of King—that bane of greatness.
I sought it not, and ne'er will own it. I have made
England great, Scotland and Ireland too,
And won a name which shall be mine alone

* Cromwell's words.

For every age throughout the world. I made
My people free—redressed their wrongs, and placed
The power in their own hands—but ah, alas!
I found them ill prepared for self-government;
They are so trammelled by old ties and customs.
Whitehall and Westminster, St. James, the Tower,
All speak of regal rule; old laws and usages
Are seared upon their hearts; they cannot walk
In the new paths I've marked; paths must be laid out
In a new land, where there is naught but freedom
To be seen. There in New England I might have fixed
The People's Rule—a rule that shall o'ermaster
Every other form, and last till the last trump
Shall sound, *if men but unto themselves be true.*
Ah! that dread tertian ague seizes now!
Why comes this sickness on me at this hour?
Thou bleeding form, thou canst not say I plucked
Thy diadem to perch it on my brow. Years
Now have numbered their troublous minutes o'er,
And yet thou visitest me, thou murdered King.
I will descend unto your charnel-house,
And gaze upon your slumbers—peaceful slumbers.
Shall such be mine? [*Takes a light.*
    IRETON *enters.*] Ha! Ireton! what now?
Thy brow doth lower portentous as the thunder-cloud.

IRETON.

An old and faithful soldier of your guard
Craves instantly the Lord Protector's ear.

CROMWELL.

Give him admittance. He should have said
His General's. I hate these titles from my long-tried
    friends.

Soldier enters.] Ha! what wouldst thou, my brave fellow?

SOLDIER.

Full credence to my tale, and instant action,
To cut short a deed too dreadful to be thought on.

CROMWELL.

What deed? Speak! speak!—how every tale unmans me!

SOLDIER.

One Dr. Hewett, Sir Henry Slugsby, and he
Who was brave Colonel Sexby, with him
Who is called Snydercombe, gave me this purse
And these bright jewels, in order to procure
Admittance to the chapel at Whitehall.

CROMWELL.

They are my friends. You did accept and gave it them.
Was it well done? I saved your life at peril
Of mine own at Drogheda, striking aside
The pike was at your throat—and you'd risk mine
For a paltry bribe!

SOLDIER.

Ay, those wild Irish—

CROMWELL.

Nay, nay, not so;—they are a gallant and a misused race.
See their condition now under just laws;
Their land is teeming with productiveness.
This I, Cromwell, did. But for your story.

SOLDIER.

Into the chapel they have but now borne
Combustibles, and placed a match to secure

SCENE VI.] CROMWELL. 117

The conflagration of the palace before midnight,
While they, with arms prepared, shall shut you up
Within the flames.

CROMWELL.

Oh! horrible, most horrible. Ireton,
Take this ring. Seize them at once; let instant death
Be theirs, if that his tale prove true.

IRETON.

I have them, one and all. Fleetwood and Desborough
Now await your will.   [*Exit.*

CROMWELL.

My gallant guard, take this—a trifling gift.
Your self-approval be your best reward.
But for myself, I'll make you captain in my guard,
With treble pay. Attend on General Ireton
In this melancholy task.   [*Exit soldier.*
Who would be great, if blood must be its price?
Or I must let these bloodhounds tear me
Limb from limb, or wade myself in blood.
Charles, Charles, thou art avenged! Could I,
I would not wake you into life.
                    I almost wish
To lay me by thy side. I will once more
Look on thee in thy rest.
             [*Takes the light, and retires slowly.*

SCENE SEVENTH.

Vault—King Charles's Tomb.

ELIZABETH CROMWELL *enters, dressed in white, with flowers, and, singing, strews them round, and lays them on the tomb.*

Thou sleepest in peace, thou murdered innocence!
I told my Charles I would do this. Nightly I've decked
His couch with flowers most fair, year after year.
Alas! poor king—father to my heart's Lord.
This tender office ere long, I feel, must fall
To other hands. Sleep on—sleep on—sleep on!
A step—who comes? It is my father—what does he here?
I must be gone.

[ELIZABETH *flits round to one side, then across the back, and escapes.*

CROMWELL *enters.*

I heard a voice—methought a seraph's voice,
And perfumed air did greet me as I came.
Do angels watch his bier? What! flowers
Blooming all about his marble couch—the tenderest
Springing from it. He sleeps in peace,
Or sure these sweet attendants all would fail
And fade away—*they* are the ministering spirits
Of the blest. If such *his* happy end,
Why may I not look for a release
From all life's cares and toils?
Was his hand bloodless?
Mine's incarnadined! They who sought his fall,
And now seek mine—these demi-devils—
That they might gain their ends, sure forged the tale
That my son's death was planned and urged

By him, that they might damn my soul.
King, kinsman, royal master, rouse from thy slumbers,
And smile on me forgiveness! Think of the agony
A father feels, his butchered son before him.

Opens the lid of tomb.]

What! can it be that envious time has leashed
Its ravenous worms, that thus thou lookest
As when thou livedst, and on thy face that smile
Thou worest, uttering thy last "Remember!"
Men doubt thy meaning—alas! I read it well;
For ne'er have I forgotten thee. By day, by night,
At feast, at fast—waking or dreaming, in court
Or camp, in peaceful council or dread carnage—
There, before me, ever rose thy august head,
And, bleeding, lisped "Remember." [*A shriek.*
Hark, that piercing shriek!—that seraph's voice—my child's—
It is my child's. She comes—what would she here?

ELIZABETH *enters wildly.*

Blood, blood, blood—nothing but blood!
My dearest brother's, my most honored king's;
And now my reverend, reverenced friend's
Must swell the turgid stream. Who are you
Have usurped my place, and keep your vigils
By this sainted form? Hence, hence, hence!
This is my fond prerogative, given me
By my loving lord, that should have been—
The king that yet shall be. Come, come, I pray thee,
Come! I know thee not; and yet, there is a majesty
In thy mien betokens power and compels my reverence.
Come, come; *thou* yet mayst save him. Come, this way,
This way. [*She, retiring, beckons to him.*

CROMWELL, *following.*

Oh! woful sight. It hath o'erpowered me.

Scene changes to banqueting hall. ELIZABETH *enters, beckoning to* CROMWELL, *who follows.*

My child, my child, what means this frenzy?
Whither, say, whither wouldst thou lead me?
What, what wouldst thou?

ELIZABETH, *looking wildly.*

Blood, blood! No, no, not blood; that thou canst give me.
But life, dear life—the life, once taken, gone
Forever, never, never to be returned.
Awakening to consciousness.]
Father! is't thou, my father? my fond, my doting father?
My mind has wandered; but I know you now.
The child of thy tender love kneels for a boon—
The boon of an old man's life—a life worth
But a few brief years at best. Thou knowest
What 'tis to die. I saw you there—I know 'twas you—
Where death sweet office long hath given me.

CROMWELL.

Ah me! ah me! How all my honors shrink
To nothingness, my glories fade from sight,
And memory pictures horrors to my view!
What is it thou askest, my fair, though faded child?

ELIZABETH.

Ah! now thou art my father. Tender tones,
Long, long unheard, though never yet forgotten,
Are ushered in by smiles—my father's smiles,
The smiles were sweetest to my infant heart,
Though, to my woman's, strangers. Why wert thou

Ever great? Was to be goodness not enough for you?
Give me his life—my friend's—old Dr. Hewett's.
He has been guilty of no crime, I know.

CROMWELL.

Crime! thou sweet innocent. *Thy* life was doomed.
Was there no crime in that? Thy mother's, sister's,
Brothers', father's—all! He would have made
Whitehall—one hecatomb.

ELIZABETH.

Oh, horrible! Art sure? I thought that he loved me.
I loved him ever.

CROMWELL.

    Most sure. Thy uncle, Desborough—
Thy brothers, Fleetwood, Ingoldsby, and Ireton,
Took him and others in the very act,
        And now they die—

Thunder heard.]
Hark! how the elements are rent at bare recital
Of their dread intent! The lightning quivers
Through these vaulted domes, and horrid echoes
Chase from room to room.

ELIZABETH.

Their shrieks! their dying shrieks! Ah me! ah me!
Father, I have borne much—could have borne more;
But this *his* treachery takes such horrid form,
I shrink at thought of it. My heart!
My Charles! my brain!

LADY CROMWELL, LADY LAMBERT, INGOLDSBY, *enter as she
  is swooning in* CROMWELL'S *arms.*

LADY CROMWELL.

My child! my child!   [*They place her on a couch.*

CROMWELL, *sinking down by the couch.*

My child! my child! Support her, Heaven,
And preserve her senses.
                    Ha! Ingoldsby, what news?
Thunder heard again.]

INGOLDSBY.

                The elements are racked;
Disjoined, our loftiest buildings topple to the dust;
St. Paul's spire, reeling, groans. The rooks
And daws make black the air, and even
The tiny martlet quails the heart
With its shrill cries, driven from its ancestral
Moss-grown home.

CROMWELL.

What day is this, that man and nature,
Thus conjoined, do rack earth to its foundations?

LADY CROMWELL.

My lord, it is your day, your own auspicious day—
THE THIRD DAY OF SEPTEMBER!

CROMWELL.

Ah! is it so?   [*Turning to* DOCTOR.
        How does my child?

ELIZABETH *murmuring low words.*]

DOCTOR.

The wild delirium feasts upon her brain,
And burns up every sense, save some dark,
Dread memories. She raves of Charles—of blood.

CROMWELL.

My dearest daughter and fair nature—both
Whom I've best loved and worshipped, next to God—

Both crazed and mad!
         Ah! my old sickness comes upon me.
       "O Lord! thy miserable servant
Bows to thy will in all humility,
And craves thy grace. Bless thou this people.
Thou hast made me a mean instrument
To do them some good, and Thee, I trust,
Some service. Many there are have set
Too high a value on me, though others wish,
And would be glad of, my decease.
However thou dost dispose of me, my Lord,
Continue to do good to and abide
With them. Give them consistency of judgment—
One heart and mutual love, to go on
With the work of reformation, and make
The name of *Christ*, a name at which every knee
Shall bend and every head shall bow,
Glorious throughout the world. Teach those
Who look too much upon thy instruments,
To more upon *Thyself* depend. Pardon all those
(They are thy people) would trample upon the dust
Of this poor worm, for our blessed Redeemer's sake."*

  IRETON *enters, taking his hand.*]
         How now, my Ireton,
How is my child?

            IRETON.
         She is dead!

       CROMWELL, *caressing* ELIZABETH.
Dead! nay, nay.
         Gone! gone! gone home!
                  I too shall go.
Her sainted spirit heralds mine.
         * Guizot.

         My friends—
Let Richard be my heir. Guard ye him well.
At my interment, *I pray you*, have no vain ceremonials.
'Tis but the form that dies.
Publish to the world that Cromwell's last words
Were, that
      "Where the Spirit of the Lord is,
There is Liberty,"
        And that 'tis cradled
In New England now, to grow a Hercules
Shall bestride all earth.
So Cromwell's teachings yet shall rule the world.
Mankind shall say, in times to come, that here died
"The best thing ever England did."*

A fearful peal of thunder and flash of lightning. IRETON
     struck dead.

Hark to that fearful peal,
       As though heaven crashed
 Seeing IRETON.]
Thy knell, my Ireton.
      Thus only couldst *thou* die.

A brilliant light from above thrown upon CROMWELL, *kneeling by* ELIZABETH. *His head drops on her form.*

The Gates of Glory open stand,
       And I am summoned.†

     TABLEAU.

    Curtain falls slowly.

---

* Carlyle.
† The Court of France went into mourning, wearing dark-blue velvet.
—*Guizot.*

THOMAS A' BECKET.

THOMAS A'BECKET.

A TRAGEDY, IN FIVE ACTS.

PERSONS OF THE DRAMA.

THOMAS A'BECKET.
SIR JOHN OF SALISBURY, } His friends.
SIR PETER OF BLOIS,
ALBERT and HUGH, his attendants.
HENRY II. of England.
LORD FITZURSE, Henry's favorite.
LORDS DE BROC, DE MOREVILLE, DE TRACY.
SIR RICHARD BRITO.
REGINALD DE WARRENNE.
GERVASE DE CORNHILL.
EARLS LEICESTER and CORNWALL.
BISHOPS OF LONDON, SALISBURY, WORCESTER, WINCHESTER, and YORK.
SIR RICHARD DE HASTINGS, Grand Prior of England's Knights Templars, then 70 years of age.
PHILIP OF ROME, Legate.
SIR GUY DE LUSIGNAN, Knight of Flanders.
KNIGHTS OF FRANCE.
LUCILLE, Niece of A'Becket.
MATILDE, Cousin to Lucille.
LORDS and LADIES.

TIME:

Reign of Henry II. of England, A. D. 1163–1170. Scene lies in England, Flanders, and France.

A'BECKET.

ACT I.

SCENE FIRST.

Sea-shore after a storm—Fragments of a wreck.

Sir Richard Brito *and* Lord Fitzurse *enter from opposite sides.*

BRITO.
What means this haste, my Lord?

FITZURSE.
                        Hast thou not heard?
A'Becket and the King are foes.

BRITO.
A'Becket and the King! those late dear friends!
They cannot long be foes: A'Becket is too great
Not to forgive his wrongs; the King too weak,
In these wild troublous times, in men of mighty intellect.
He feels it, Sir; we feel it, Sir, though we do hate
The man who so o'ertops us. You, in the brief recital,
Teach this fact—saying, "A'Becket and the King
Are sworn foes"—see, how the priest comes first;
So stands he in the thoughts of every man.

FITZURSE.
And yet I've heard that he was humbly born,
But rose so fast, that, like the young fledgling,
Soars too high at first—singeing his wings

He weakened them, and now, full grown,
They will not bear him up—hunter and hawker
As he is—this churlish priest, born for the torment
Of the Anglo-Norman race. A tradesman's son,
No more—

BRITO.

   A tradesman's son! Know, my young Lord,
His father was a warrior too, as honest, Sir,
As brave—and honesty makes any trade
An honor; and more, his mother, tho' of another clime,
Owned gentle blood. When a mere boy,
He was sent to Rome by Theobald, Archbishop
Then of England, and straightway from His Holiness
Bore letters, prohibiting the crowning
Of the late King Stephen's son—thus firmly
Seating Henry on his throne:—thereafter
Soon appointed England's High Chancellor
And prince Henry's preceptor. Courtier complete,
Unbounded revenues, with seven hundred knights
And twelve hundred horsemen in his pay—
A regal state—he made the campaign
To Toulouse. Next he was to Paris sent, to treat
Of an alliance between the young daughter
Of France's king and our Prince Henry. Ay, and re-
  turned
With her to England. *He never failed.*
A tradesman's son, you say—his craft he ne'er forgot.
Then Theobald died—whom to the primacy
Could Henry raise but him, the great A'Becket?
First primate sprung from Anglo-Saxon race;
Honored and treasured by all of Saxon blood;
Received by Welsh with the most loud acclaim,
Their first Lord Primate under Norman rule—
For though I hate him, I must own him great.

The King till now did love him well—
                    What is the cause
Of strife?

FITZURSE.
                Unto the Pope he hath complained
Of the laity's infringement of the Church's rights,
And his assent refusing to the Constitutions
Of Clarendon, has fled to France. The King
At Northampton holds his court to-morrow;
His counsellors are all summoned.

BRITO.
This I for many a day have feared.
Go you not to the chase? our Liege at noon
Rides forth. Yet stay—who have we here? Lord Salisbury,
Storm-worn and sad!

Enter LORD JOHN *of* SALISBURY.
                You here, my Lord, in this dark hour?
Methought the air of France ere this did fan your brow.
What news from Lord A'Becket?

SALISBURY.
                None, none; but adverse winds
Have raged since England's Primate set sail
For France. How fares our Liege to-day?

BRITO.
                        Right well.
He's for the chase at noon, whither I haste
To wait on him—let's on, Fitzurse—Farewell, Lord Salisbury!
                [BRITO *and* FITZURSE *Exeunt.*

SALISBURY.
Farewell, most valiant lords—mad King, sad minister;
Oh! where will this day's business end, his favorite

Long, now fallen and fled! These Norman lords
Ne'er loved the Saxon priest—but his great genius
Bowed them to his will. Queen Eleanor
Never loved her King—hates him—
While she lives, she'll never cease to work their ill.
Meet helpmate has she proved to England's King;
Her uncle's mistress and the Turk's light of love—
For this, repudiated by Louis "the young."
Our Norman King, to rule her wide domains,
After six weeks made her his queen,
Bartering his honor and his happiness.
I see her hand in this; she wooed A'Becket's love,
And won his deep despite—return like this,
No woman e'er forgave.
                              Here have I sought
Since yesternight for those would brave the fury
Of the storm, and bear these letters to my wronged friend,
England's great Primate—great in his youth
In feats of arms, learned in legendary lore,
Foremost in the court and camp, and first in Henry's favor
Till he bade him wear the Primate's robes—
Then he foretold this hour! It's now three days
Since he set sail for France, in all which time
A tempest fierce hath raged, with winds adverse
To him—as though fate would not he should leave
His land. But lo! a sail! Mayhap it bears him back.
I'll to their aid.   [*Exeunt.*

SIR PETER *of* BLOIS *enters, his garments wet and soiled.*

SIR PETER.

A'Becket shipwrecked on his native shore!
He who hath piloted through so many a storm!
It augurs ill for him. Is there no end
To his great cares? Alas! I fear me, none,

For e'en the elements seem opposed to him.
No sooner had we left this mighty realm,
Albion's white cliffs slumbering in virgin beauty,
Than, robed in mist, all faded from our view,
And fierce old ocean, with a lion's roar,
Struck panic 'mid the seamen. So we who hoped
In France to feast to-day, must break our fast
In turmoil and in strife.

Salisbury enters.

Who comes? What! you, my friend?

SALISBURY.

Welcome, thrice welcome, tho' in such sad plight!
Thank Heaven, you have weathered out the storm.
How fare you, Sir, and our great friend, A'Becket?

BLOIS.

As well as ever, though in wisdom wiser.
We left the port with favoring gales,
But soon the scene was changed; an angry sea
Tossed our poor bark, like bittern, o'er its waves,
While she with true heart breasted all their force,
And still obedient to the helmsman's rule,
After three days' fierce conflict with the storm,
Though stranded on yon shore, is sound as ever,
Ready again to cope with them.
This was for us, my friend. It bids us brave
The storms of fate, though we are backward driven
By their force. What did you here?

SALISBURY.

I waited
Till the storm should lull, these papers to dispatch to you.
The King had just rode forth unto the chase,
When news was ta'en him, A'Becket and his friends
Had fled to France. Thereon he ordered

1*

A great council to be held at Northampton,
And questioned why he left—asking
If the same realm could not contain them both.

BLOIS.

No, Sir John, never while things are thus;
A'Becket must yield or combat with him manfully;
The last it *must* be. There is no choice but this.

[Pauses.

Heard I aright? Gone forth unto the chase?
How can he wear a heart so light in hour
Like this? 'Tis ever thus among the great
In power, that one man's sorrow proves
Some other's joy. So he now revels—riots
In his misery. Who have been with you
Since I left?

SALISBURY.

Young Lords Fitzurse and Brito.

BLOIS.

Fitzurse! You entertained him as a friend;
Though in the service of a foe, his heart
Inclines to us.

SALISBURY.

Even so methinks, my Lord;
But come—let's to A'Becket's home, where all
Do anxiously wait news of him.

BLOIS.

We will—when there, we must prepare a numerous suite
To wait on him to Northampton. 'Twere well
To make a goodly show of friends. *[Exeunt.*

SCENE SECOND.
Gothic Hall.

A'BECKET—*alone.*

So much for being willing slave to power!
Had I but sought my pleasure and my weal,
Forgetting his, whose shadow I have been,
Not his thought my thought, his every wish my act,
All had been well!
     But no, not so; I, to enhance
His glory, wealth, and power, to jealous envy
Have exposed myself, and now must fall
Even like Lucifer, lost in the radiance
I have heralded!
     Be firm, my heart, be firm!
'Tis envy speaks!
     The tale while told sounds loudly,
But palls when probed, bringing dishonor
On the babbler's head!
     'Tis weightless as the story
The old man tells, walking in second childishness.
Why should I be moved? Silence, thou petty voice,
I will not deign to note their idle words.
But, ha! a step—
     No gentle, sylphlike step;
I hoped my child's. They do approach—
 Retires one side.]   I'll note them here.

  FITZURSE *enters, looking round.*

FITZURSE.
How reverend is the air pervades these halls!
How like their great inhabitant, time furrowed!
Firm they stand, ready to cope with fiercest elements.

Oh! 'tis a noble house! fit home for such a heart;
Would it were tuned to softer measures,
That his step might move in harmony
With his king's. Gone, gone to France. I would
It were not so—for something tells me that my fate
And thine, great soul! are linked together.
A voice! a step!   [A'BECKET *comes forward.*
    What! thou, our Lord Archbishop!
Welcome, my reverend father, to your own land!
No home like this for you.

     A'BECKET.
 Much moved.]   Thanks, thanks, my son.
My Liege—How fares my Liege?

     FITZURSE.
    Well; save in wanting you.

     A'BECKET.
My King! my King! to think it should be thus!
But he required I should assume this office—
And I obeyed amid the formal greetings
Of the Lord Bishops, who ever hated me.
Then with my office I straightway changed
My robes, my habits, and my home; fasting
Where I had feasted; no more proud Norman's favorite;
Saxon born, I was the people's friend.
    But stay, whom have we here?

  MATILDE *and* LUCILLE *enter, with cloaks on.*
   MATILDE, *embracing him.*
    My uncle, my dear uncle!

     A'BECKET.
What! bravest thou the storm?

     FITZURSE.
    Angelic maids!

A'BECKET, *embracing Lucille.*

Thou too, my fair Lucille! What did you there?

LUCILLE.

I sought, with dear Matilde, tidings of you, my Lord.

FITZURSE, *aside.*

And then, to wend to heaven.

A'BECKET.

My blessings be with you.
Daughters, my Lord Fitzurse!

FITZURSE.

Fair ladies, at your service.

FITZURSE, MATILDE, *and* LUCILLE *retire one side; on the other enter* RICHARD DE HASTINGS *and* PHILIP OF ROME, *with attendants and great show of friends.*

HASTINGS.

Our service, my Lord Archbishop.

A'BECKET.

Aside.] This Norman Lord!
To them.] You're welcome, Sirs.
Pray, what may be your errand?
A noble one it should be, that is borne
By the Grand Prior of England's Knights Templars.

HASTINGS.

'Tis from your King I come; grieved deeply
By your hasty course, and much moved withal,
His language is, " That his loyal subjects
Ever observe his will;"—that he requires
Your consent to these the Constitutions
Of Clarendon. [*Produces scroll.*
Then reads—]
" Which do provide, that all control of church as well as

state, should be intrusted to the civil courts. Her clerks, accused of any crime, be tried by them. No clergy leave the realm without consent of King. That excommunicates should not be bound to give security for their continuance in some fixed abode. That all appeals, in causes spiritual, be carried from the Primate to the King, making his judgment final. That the Archbishops, Bishops, and other spiritual dignitaries should be regarded as Barons of the realm, possess their privileges and be subjected to the burdens of that rank—to attend the King in his Great Councils and assist at all trials criminal. The revenues of vacant Sees to belong to the King; and that the clergy no longer pretend to the right of enforcing payment of debts contracted by oath or promise, but should leave these lawsuits, equally with other, to the determination of the civil courts; and that the sons of villeins be not clerks ordained without their lord's consent."

A'BECKET.

Requires he this? My Lords, you know not what you ask;
Go, raze our churches, chapels, convents, ay, our homes,
Expel the clergy from his vast domains,
And you could do no worse!
       Nor is his message
Couched in gentle words, although, my Lord,
In your delivery it loses its sharper part;
Still would I that you had not borne it.
Your office is not raised in my esteem—
Degraded to the messenger of an angry King,
For passion urges this, and as kings are
Above their fellow-men, so should they be
Above their frailties; but I would learn
What further he designs.

HASTINGS.

Pray, be not moved, my noble Lord Archbishop:
First, he commands you, his late Primate—

A'BECKET, *hastily.*

His late Primate! who may he be?
Who was the Primate is the Primate still.

HASTINGS.

Such was his word, and he requires you surrender
Instantly the Castles of Eye and Berkham,
With all their honors, and deliver up
The culprit, now in your hands, charged
With such grave offence, in wedding
Lord Rupert's daughter.

A'BECKET.

Unequal birth his only fault—would at some mightier's gate
No graver lay! does he so soon forget fam'd Rosamond,
So fair! so frail! the only daughter of De Clifford,
Our great Saxon Lord, the prop and stay
Of his old age, degraded to the leman
Of his Norman King, to whom he was too faithful?
Accursed was the day when Harold fell,
For sin hath shadowed all our ways since then!
But stay, bear this from A'Becket of Canterbury
To Henry of England, King but by accident
Of birth: say that I neither will surrender aught,
Nor yield unto his will.
                      Whence is his power
That he should trample upon me, in all
His equal, save in honors?

PHILIP OF ROME.

My Lord Archbishop, pray be advised;
Beware a breach with King so powerful.

A'BECKET.

Philip of Rome, we, Anglo-Saxon born,
Are free by nature, as the wind that blows;

We bow no suppliant knee to power,
Save 'tis the *power of mind!*
The poorest hind may bear the proudest head
That walks unsceptred through the land.
Genius may rear her throne beneath the hovel's roof,
And there her worshippers in crowds will kneel.
I am the people's friend, the lordlings' foe,
When arrogance marks their steps—go, Sirs,
And tell the King I will not yield!

HASTINGS.

I fear, Archbishop, this is ill advised;
He is enraged with what has passed already.

A'BECKET, *much moved.*

Well, let him be enraged: what's that to me?
Why should I heed his anger? Leave him awhile,
And he'll grow calm and cool. The hardest steel
Not long retains its heat; the mettled steed
Will soonest tamely yield, outworn by his own spirit.

HASTINGS.

Those honors, my dear Lord, they are of mighty value.
Pray be advised! We would not have you lose
Your high estate, and all its great attendants.

A'BECKET, *aside.*

They are moved, the coward hearts! 'Tis for themselves
They fear. My privileges curtailed, where are their own?
   Aloud.]
My high estate! my honors! Who can disrobe me of them?
They were born with me, with me shall die! My office
I would resign as easily as I lay aside
This robe—[*aside.*] In faith, I find that it is somewhat
   worn,
I would a newer, if not plainer guise.

HASTINGS.

All England, Sir, would mourn your loss.

A'BECKET.

And so she should, for England holds me in her chains;
I am the veriest slave that ever lived.
No mother ever felt more pangs, than I
For England—there's not a churl in all the land,
But I am bound to him by bands of adamant,
My heart-strings webbed in his—

      King's gifts I value not.

To PHILIP OF ROME.]
What say you, Prelate?

PHILIP OF ROME.
    Give him his way.

A'BECKET.
       Never!

So help me Heaven!

Enter EARLS *of* LEICESTER *and* CORNWALL.

    What would ye, noble Sirs?

CORNWALL.

That you should let King Henry have his will.

A'BECKET.

You too, my Lords! I had hoped else than this.
In you I had confided, till the waters rose
E'en to their highest height.
 Aside.]   Ah! well I know
A dove's upon the wing, comes from a storm-proof ark.
 Aloud.]
I may not give him way—for nothing then will satisfy.
The Barons all are his—the Bishops, overawed,
Dare not oppose his will. Leicester and Cornwall,
Ye know not what you do.

HASTINGS *casts himself on his knees before* A'BECKET.

HASTINGS.

       Father, upon my knees,
I do beseeech you yield. I never knelt before
To any man.

A'BECKET.

       Arise, and never kneel again,
Save unto God.   [HASTINGS *rises*.
     What judgment tells me's wrong,
Entreaties never will make right.

HASTINGS.

If you regard your or your Church's safety,
Provoke him not—'twere vain, my Lord—fruitless,
All opposition. He, on his purpose bent,
Will have revenge on all who dare oppose.

A'BECKET.

My Lord, you know me not. I have no fears—
To yield my will, of all things, most I dread.
A dangerous precedent it would be
Both to myself and King; for unto me
Succeeding trials would each easier seem,
And I should yield, until my resolution
All was lost—while unto him 'twould be
Removal of the sole restraint upon his lawless will.
My Lords, I love my King (we were as brothers
Till this hapless hour), and cannot see him leap
Into the gulf of his mad hot desires.
         [*Lords confer aside.*

A'BECKET, *aside.*

Should I now yield, what will my country gain?
Yet is it wise, beggared to be of power,—
That which, of all things, least I'd bear to lose?
I cannot, will not, whatsoe'er the cost.

HASTINGS.

My Lord, you are alone in this.

A'BECKET.

My Lord!
'Tis virtue! and I would rather be alone
With her, than compassed round by all the hosts
Of vice. Of all my friends, are there none left?
Not one. [*Aside.*] The wise man to the whirlwind bows
His head.
[*Aloud*] I will attend the Court.
Farewell! farewell!

[*Exit Lords on one side*—A'BECKET *and friends on the other side.*]

SCENE THIRD.

Grand Council Room at Northampton—Throne with steps—Range of seats for Lords.

BRITO.

Where are your thoughts, Fitzurse?

FITZURSE.

In heaven.

BRITO.

In heaven! that's strange, indeed, in you.
What took them there?

FITZURSE.

The sight of one newly come thence
To earth—the fairest being ever eye beheld.

BRITO.

Indeed; whose house may't be is worthy such
A visitant?

FITZURSE.

Thou'lt rival me, I fear.

BRITO.

Indeed, not I; who is this paragon?

FITZURSE.

None other than A'Becket's niece.

BRITO.

        A'Becket's niece!
Banish that thought, my Lord. The King will frown
On this new fancy.

FITZURSE.

        Well! let him frown!
I live not in the fear of kingly ire.

BRITO.

Love makes you bold, young Lord. Oh, clip its wings
Before it takes too wild a flight—
       Lo, where he comes,
And angered too, 'twould seem.

FITZURSE.

'Tis with A'Becket. [*Aside.*] Oh cruel, cursed fate!
That my youth's follies do compel this service
To the King, while fair Lucille, A'Becket's niece,
Reigns my heart's queen. [*Aloud.*] My Liege.
 Enter HENRY *and his Court. He ascends the throne.*

HENRY.

Where stays this priest? Summon him hither on the instant—
Kings wait not on their subjects' pleasure.

FITZURSE.

He comes, my Liege, clothed in his robes of office
As Lord Archbishop—bearing the silver cross.

HENRY.

Why comes he thus?

FITZURSE.

       It is St. Stephen's Day.

HENRY.

So hath it been for years, yet never came he thus.
Bishop of London, preside you here.
        My Lords temporal,
Attend on me—the judgment we will await
Within—or I to be the King shall cease,
Or he to be Archbishop.

As HENRY *leaves the throne* A'BECKET *enters, holding the silver cross before him, and takes his seat in silence; his friends behind him, all magnificently attired.*

LONDON.

My Lord Archbishop, why do you come
Thus armed with the silver cross?

LORD.
        'Tis in defiance
Of our Liege, your coming thus into his Court.
But he has a sword whose point is sharper far
Than that of your pastoral staff.

A'BECKET.

Where is my King? He should preside to-day;
'Tis so prescribed by " Customs of the Realm."

LONDON.

Displeased with your approach in such unseemly mode,
He doth pass judgment in the inner Court.

A'BECKET.

Unseemly mode! the Church protects her own—
She is my Counsellor—unto her I trust.
Justice hath fled this realm.   [LEICESTER *enters.*

LEICESTER.
      My Lord, enraged, he swears
He'll be revenged. Oh pray, have pity
On yourself and brethren. Provoke him now
No more.

A'BECKET.

What words are these before the Great Council
Of the realm!

Aside.] Nay, rather let him not provoke me more.

CORNWALL *enters.*

CORNWALL.

It is determined, by the King's privy council,
You be impeached of perjury and high treason.
The first, in that you observe not the Constitutions
Of Clarendon—the last, in that you disobey
His orders.

A'BECKET.

What! have I then no friends?

CORNWALL.

You have your King, for this he doth reject,
And but demands that you shall subject stand
Unto the Court's judgment, in the pecuniary charges.

A'BECKET.

This, too, I do refuse—the judgment
Of no temporal court will I obey.

FITZURSE *enters.*]   What more?

FITZURSE.

My Lord, the King's permission
By the Bishops is besought, that, on the score of perjury,
They to Rome, against you, may appeal. To this
He doth consent.

A'BECKET.

The Bishops, say you?
Am I then prejudged without a hearing?
'Tis enough, I mark what you do say.

Aside.]

Ay, mark it well. 'Tis fitting, very fitting,
You, whose features wear *her* lineaments,

Whom Henry wronged, as me, he wrongeth now,
Should bear this message of his tyranny—
Thus searing our wrongs upon my heart.
Alas! poor Rosamond!

     LEICESTER.

    The Peers, besides, do you pronounce
Guilty of perjury and high treason;
But still, the alternative allow
Of rendering your accounts, and settling
Any balance now against you.
        Do this, my Lord,
Or hear from me your sentence.

   A'BECKET, *starting and rising.*

My sentence, ere you've tried me? Why, I
Can charges bring will crush you with their sounding,
Though ye are backed by hosts of friends,
While I've but one—my well-known "Truth,"
Which is far stronger in its single strength
Than all King Henry's power.
        Tho' I have ventured
On an unquiet sea, I'll brave its utmost fury.
The adder is not malignant, yet, too closely press'd,
May turn and sting the heel.
My sentence! Ye vain, proud Lords, ye have not words
In your vocabulary to frame my fitting judgment;
Ye minions of a King who has roused a lion
That he dare not face!
My sentence, Sirs, is written in the skies;
It is recorded on the azure vault of heaven;
Its letters the glittering stars—heralds
Of my future glories.
        As easy might
You angry sea, whose wildest waves,

E'en in its fiercest rage, are stayed by this rock-bound
    shore,
Strive to wash out what is recorded there—
I have no measure for such meanness!

ALL.
Do you hear him?

A'BECKET *turns to go, when a clamor is raised against
    him. He steps back and says—*
What noise is this? Oh, were it not forbidden
By my orders, with arms I would defend myself.

*The doors of the apartment in which the King is sitting
are now thrown open, and* A'BECKET *discovers a body
of Knights, with their garments tucked up and their
swords drawn, when* HENRY *approaches him hastily,
and exclaims—*

HENRY.
So! so! Sir Priest. What! this unto ourselves?
My Lords, we deem it fitting we should revive
The customs and usages of our grandsire.
What think ye, Sirs?

LORDS.
We do assent.

A'BECKET.
And we—saving the honor of God,
And of the Holy Church. .

HENRY.
There is venom
In that reservation. We will no more with thee.
Here is a special messenger from the Pope,
In answer to my prayer. He, with letters
Apostolical, enjoins all prelates, and more
Especially you of Canterbury, to accept and
Observe all the King of England's laws.

Choose here upon the instant—Compliance,
Exile, or death.

           A'BECKET, *pointing to heaven.*

My Liege, my hour has not yet come.
  Aside.]   All armed,
And ready for the act? A forced compliance
Will not bind "the rights of our order"—and as on them
Hangs the sole hope the Anglo-Saxon people have
Against this Norman monarch's fierce assaults,
I'll wear these robes, proof-armor in their cause,
And with religion on our side, the sole true friend
Of Liberty, I will assert—maintain their rights.
I will consent—straightway to France, and thence
To His High Holiness, appeal from this.
  Aloud to the Court.]
                        Prepare these Constitutions.

                HENRY.
                      This is well.
                ALL
Long live our King and Bishop.

                END OF ACT I.

ACT II.

SCENE FIRST.
France—An Anteroom—Gold and Blue.

MATILDE *enters with* LUCILLE.

MATILDE.

In faith, Lucille, our refuge here in France
Doth seem more like triumphal entry of hero fam'd
Than fallen favorites' flight—such troops of friends
Attend us on our way. Oh, banish, sweet,
From thy once radiant brow the sombre hue
Now rests there. You'll make me sad, dear girl.
Indeed you will.

LUCILLE.
   Never, dear cousin, with a willing heart.

MATILDE.

Willing or no, it matters not, Lucille,
My heart is ever mirror unto thine.
So cheer thee, love—thy suitors would not know
The face they once adored. What's the romance
The gay Lord Fitzurse [*Lucille starts*] sang, when last
  we feasted
By sweet Avon's side? Sing me one line, 'twill bring
To memory all those scenes of joy in which we revell'd,
And, as gay lark's song heralds the smile of dawn,
Wake from its dreams thy mournful pensive eye.
These knights of France are rich in all may win
The heart of beauty, and well I know
Full many a lance will break for thee,
Lucille.

LUCILLE.

And break in vain!

MATILDE.

Why so? How? Sighs and tears!
What is the cause of this? Of late I've mark'd
You're much alone, in shady walks, or where
The silver moon sheds her pale light. What is't?
Dost love? Thou'rt moved! Who is the knight whose
    badge
Thy heart doth wear? Tell me, sweet girl; I know
Thou lovest!

LUCILLE.

'Tis true, and am beloved.
Nor were I sad, but he in whom I live
Now mourns by Avon's bank his absent love.
His name, Matilde, I long have long'd to tell,
But that my heart's so jealous of his worth,
I would not e'en the air of heaven
Should know its precious secret.

MATILDE.

Know I its lord?
If so, how sweet we shall commune together,
Unfolding to each other our hearts' treasures;
For I a secret have, dearer to me than life.
It shall be thine—thine given me in turn.

LUCILLE.

Is't so? Fitzurse—his name.

MATILDE.

The noble, generous youth
We love so much? He who cours'd o'er the heath
Of Hounslow to our support?

LUCILLE.

The same.

MATILDE.

Why, thou hast known him but one little month.

LUCILLE.

One little month? So full of joys it was,
That, when I count them o'er, all else of life
Seems but one little speck, except, except
The last few days, which are as centuries.
Dost wonder that I am sad?

MATILDE.

Nay, dearest, rather wonder I that floods
Of tears marked not our swift departure,
When, all so unprepared, thy heart was rooted
From the soil it loved, to pine away afar.
But cheer thee now, thou shalt not miss him long;
He shall be summoned to attend our train.

LUCILLE.

Thanks, thanks, my dear Matilde; but he, you know,
Doth wait upon the King.

MATILDE.

Nay, nay, you say the Queen of Beauty
Rules his heart. She owns not a divided service.
If Fitzurse loves thee, what is Henry's will
Weighed against Love's commands? All things
Oppose its ardent calls, are but as rushes in its path.
He'll straightway come to France.

LUCILLE.

Then wilt thou see my face decked, like the morn
Of May, in the fair flowers thou so lovest, Matilde;
My heart will be as blithe as linnet's,
And the whole livelong day thou'lt hear my song;
My steps the gentle fawn's shall all outvie;
And in my smile, mirrored, shall be thine own.

The sweetest ever seen by man,
In their richest beauty.   Thy lover is—

MATILDE.

The Lord of Blois.   He whose wit is soul
Of merry meetings, and from whose sage discourse
Wisdom itself might learn.
                      But soon they'll come—
Our aged uncle and my own true knight.   *[Exeunt.*

SCENE SECOND.

Stone-Vaulted Hall.

A'BECKET.

This then is my reward for years of toil!
Oh! thou poor King, semblance of majesty!
To use armed force against a cowled monk!
My pity doth outweigh my hate for thee.
How soft the air of France!   The breeze that did accord
With words of hate, with voice of love doth harmonize.
Bright omen this—herald of joys to come;
Her King must smile, for many is the favor
I have rendered him; nor will brave Philip frown,
For him I have served in diverse manners.
But what of that?   Mankind of woman born
Never knew gratitude, since the first mother
Of us all rebelled and ate forbidden fruit,
Though Eden teemed with all most fair and good.
No, no, 'tis not to this I'll look; jealous they grow
Of England's King, and I will nurse this plant
Till it o'ershadows every other thought.
Rome's Pontiff, too, doth feel but little love
For him who so invades his rights.

Enter JOHN OF SALISBURY.

                                                      Who comes?

SALISBURY.

Your pardon, Father, if that I intrude.

A'BECKET.

Welcome, my son; when to our friends at home
You write, use Saxon names, lest that our letters
Intercepted, disguise be needful for their safety.

SALISBURY.

I shall, my Lord; but now a knight of Flanders
Attends your leisure. He comes intrusted
With kind messages.

A'BECKET.

Is't so? Give him a hearty welcome,
And, when refreshed, escort him to my room.

SALISBURY.

France, too, doth join in her regards. My Lord of Blois
Now greets her messengers.

A'BECKET.

            France too! Methinks the sun does shine
To-day! Go you with haste and give them welcome.
                                      [*Exit* SALISBURY.
Flanders and France! one more and all Fate's frowns
Are flown; thus she, who seemed a very shrew
To me, angelic maid will be. Ere they arrive
I'll summon my Lucille, for suffering beauty
More doth move the heart than ever did
The care-marked face of age. Albert! ho! Albert!
  Enter ALBERT.]
Bid my lady nieces attend me here,
As messengers from France and Flanders
Have arrived, and I would they should welcome
Them.   [*Exit* ALBERT.

Farewell, pale care! welcome, rose-cheeked joy!
Once more, as in my boyhood's hour, my heart
Doth gayly beat.
                    Louis of France, my heartfelt thanks
To you; and Philip of Flanders, success
Attend you ever—this hour shall Henry rue.

Enter MATILDE, LUCILLE, *and* PETER OF BLOIS.

MATILDE.

How fares my uncle?

A'BECKET.

            Well, dearest child; and thou, the same?
But this were needless, for thy smile assents
In terms more speaking than thy tongue could lisp.
My fair Lucille! Thou art not well, my child—
But soon the air of France will call its wonted color
To thy cheek.
                    Do those Lords attend?

BLOIS.

They do.

A'BECKET.

            Say I await them here.
                    [*Exit* BLOIS.

My daughters dear, season your welcome
As best becomes ye. I'd take by storm
These noble hearts, for first impressions
Are like first bounds of steeds, that start
Upon a race, which, feebly made, compel
Much after toil, else they ne'er reach the goal.
They come.

BLOIS *ushers in* LORDS OF FRANCE AND FLANDERS.

BLOIS.

From Flanders and from France, my Lord,
These gallant knights bring messages of love.

A'BECKET.

Welcome, welcome, gentlemen.
                              Sir Guy de Lusignan!
Nobles of France, he is well known to you,
For Fame did with one breath proclaim you all
Her own.
   To LUSIGNAN.]
                     My youth's fond playfellow!
Accept my welcome, and my thanks—thanks
From a heart o'erflowing—for this remembrance
Of thy sunshine's friend.

SIR GUY.

                              Friends in misfortune
Are the only friends the great man e'er should boast.
There ever are a thousand motes live in his sunbeams,
But when shadows fall, they darkling fade away.
Most noble Primate, our service unto you,
And our King's welcome.

A'BECKET.

            Thanks, my Lord, thanks to him
And you. My niece Lucille; Matilde, her friend
And cousin.

LORD OF FRANCE.

   Ever at your service, Ladies fair.
   Aside.]
How passing beautiful!
   Aloud.]   As large as is
The welcome of our hearts, which knows no bounds,
So would our King and we, that you should find
Our fortunes and our favors. Our Liege,
To Henry's embassy's complaint of violation
Of the Treaty of Montmerail, replied,
"Go, tell your King, that if he holds unto the customs

Of his grandsire, I well may hold to right
Hereditary, of succoring the exiled of all climes."

A'BECKET.

Indeed! indeed! 'Twas nobly said. Were I to live
Twice man's allotted time, I should not have
E'en hours enough wherein to thank his gracious Majesty
For such unbounded kindness shown me.

The knights and ladies retire to the back of the stage and
FITZURSE *enters.*

A'BECKET.

What! thou, my Lord Fitzurse?
  Aside.]   I love this youth!
And yet, alas! why so? His mother!
                      No! no! 'tis past, 'tis past.
  Aloud.] Welcome, my son.

FITZURSE, *kneeling.*

                How fare you, reverend Father?
Thy niece and cousin, all well, when so much evil
Is abroad?

A'BECKET.

            All well, my son—and you? Oh! thine
Is, indeed, true love!

FITZURSE, *aside.*

Ha! knows he that? Oh, would it were!

A'BECKET.

When in my power, you refused high rank,
Thus, in my poverty, to join my train.

FITZURSE.

I wanted but thy love. Thy offices,
Many, more able, needed. I but made room
For one of the hungry crowd, that he might gorge
Himself with power, that dish which all who eat,

Lest they are favor'd with its choicest parts,
Soon sickened, fall its prey.
                        Henry on wrong heaps wrong:
Four hundred of thy truest friends are banished
From his realm, and Peter pence is stopped.

A'BECKET.

May Heaven pardon him as I do now!
How greatness brings sad havoc in its fall
On all who prop it up.

FITZURSE.
                        Not this alone;
He hath sequestered the revenues of Canterbury,
And even thy domestics banished.

A'BECKET.

Revenged himself upon the innocent!
Oh, grimed heart! More fiendish than was Nero
In his rage! To think that he I've served so long,
From tender youth to age, should thus repay me.
Oh, wretched man and yet more wretched King!
My servants, say'st thou? In what have they wronged him,
Save in the service they have rendered me?
But he rewards the faithful with ingratitude.
I will to England hasten, and surrender up
My life ('tis all I've left) to him.

FITZURSE.
                        Nay, nay, my Lord!
That were both rash and vain.

A'BECKET.
                        My friends! my friends!
Think, think of them! Are they to suffer
For wrongs done by me? Justice hath fled his realm,
And devils rule his heart. Had I remained
In England, this had not been.

Oh, curse of greatness!
But thus the branches die, when falls the oak!
Had I the voice of Rome, I'd shake the realm
Until it tottered on the verge of ruin,
And his proud sceptred head lay in my courser's way.
Peace, peace, my heart, but grow not instant old
With this assault of Fortune! Bear up, bear all;
Still hast thou manhood's vigor, with the wisdom
Born of sixty wintry years.
             Attend me here, my son.
You who have flown to aid when fortune frowns,
Shall be the first on whom her favor'll light.
You'll find some friends in yonder room.
Farewell, and when you're weary of life's trifles,
Come to my closet; there you'll find its cares,
Spread with no niggard hand.

FITZURSE.

Bear up, my Lord, bear up; this unto Henry
Were the happiest hour he ever yet hath lived,
Could he but see your grief.

A'BECKET.

             My grief! grief and A'Becket
Are as far apart, as are the sun
And his antipodes!
                This is not grief
But rage, cooled in the air of practised self-control.
Oh, could you look into my heart's curtained chambers,
You would witness scenes would daunt your very soul!
A citadel stormed outwardly by foes,
The hosts within, maddened by suffering,
Turned upon themselves.

FITZURSE.

             Oh, Father! give not way.

A'BECKET.

Give not way! I know my part; forbearance
For a season wins control; when once I hold
The reins, Henry of England, beware my rule;
The jewelled sceptre shall be all thou'lt wear
Of royalty; that will I leave you, that my revenge
May the more bitter be, reminding you, poor King,
Of what you once had been, and might yet be.

FITZURSE, *aside*.

This to the King, you'd never hold those reins.

A'BECKET.

I, I had rather be your crawling slave,
Toil at the galleys from the first breath of morn
Till day hath sunk to slumbers, than live but king
In name, held in such light esteem, the very air
Would refuse to bear my words beyond the walls
That heard them. Down Fate's long vista I have looked
And seen what I have spoken.
                    Mark me, my boy:
My mother gave me this.   -
                    She was the daughter
Of a Saracenic chief. My father
Warred with hers. After a conflict fierce,
Overcome by him and prisoner taken,
Long lay he ill, tended but by my mother,
Then a maid of beauty, spotless as her virtue.
Ministering to all his wants, foreseen
Long ere conceived—she learnt to love him,
And he loved her—for what will sooner melt
The heart of man than beauty, kneeling by the couch
Where pain has laid his stricken frame.
After some months, the tears that nursed those hours
Of grief, were changed to smiles should gladden

All life's days; and theirs were in their spring.
One great and brave, the other fond and fair.
Ransomed, he asked her hand; her father frowned;
But 'twas in vain—their troth was plighted.
They swore to wed. He left for England.
Scarce had he reached her shores, when at his feet
Knelt a fair youth, "London" and "Gilbert" on his tongue
('Twas all the English that he knew), admittance
Craving to his service. Knowing 'twas her,
His heart alone adored, for love is ne'er deceived
However disguised the form—he raised her—
Clasped her to his breast—she was his own.

  * * * * * *

Within a little chapel by the sea-shore stands,
Mantled in ivy, veiled by rarest flowers
From the world's gaze profane, they gave their hands—
No hearts had they to give. Blest in each other,
Long in love they lived; and when he died,
The blow which felled the oak struck to the dust
The flower. There, by sweet Avon's side, where stands
A weeping willow, lie interred all
That was left to earth—their spirits dwell in Heaven.
     Oh ye who watched my infancy,
Upon my age look down in love: mail me
In virtue, that the shafts of vice may pass
Me blunt and harmless. Grant that my arm may wield
Her truncheon, while her banner floats high o'er
My victorious brow.
     But I detain you, Sir.
Go to my anteroom—there may my niece
And cousin both be found.
    I will with you. [*Exeunt.*

SCENE THIRD.

An Anteroom in Palace.

MATILDE, LUCILLE; KNIGHTS OF FRANCE *and* FLANDERS *advancing.*

FRANCE.

Ladies fair, we trust that us and ours you use
As best promotes your pleasures. Many's the charm
Of France—all yours, if you'll but ask it.

MATILDE.

Thanks, heartfelt thanks, most noble Lords; so rich,
So bounteous is your clime, that, were I not
Of England, I fain would be of France.
The very air of heaven is generous here;
The flowers, the fruits, so lavish all their sweets,
Ambrosial is each breath.

FRANCE.

     Nay, nay, unworthy she of praise
So sweet; believe me, 'tis that she borrows
From thy charms, that all's so passing fair.

MATILDE.

The rose could scarce desert us here in France,
So finished are you in your speech, my Lord.

FRANCE.

In the moon's ray alone, the dew-drop glistens
Longest. May we for many a day boast
The bright light thy sweet smiles give our land.
Who may this be approaches? A gallant gentleman!

MATILDE.

A noble Lord, the pride of all who know him.

Fitzurse enters.

FITZURSE.

To Matilde.] Fair lady, by your leave.
[*Kisses her hand.*
Your servant, gentlemen.

MATILDE.

My Lord Fitzurse, you're welcome.
Presenting Lucille.] My lovely cousin!

FITZURSE *to her.*

My Morning Star! [*Kisses her hand.*
Oh, what a golden day
Herein is promised me!

LUCILLE.

Fitzurse, my noble Lord!
The others retire.] [*They walk apart.*

FITZURSE.

My fair Lucille—Sun of my life, what, what
Hath ravaged my rich garden thus—its flowers
All faded—all its pure springs dried up—where
Are the roses rich, bloomed richest on thy cheek?
The lilies fair which made thy neck their bed?
Their breath alone remains. And those bright orbs
Which once did put the stars to shame, now seem
But wells of grief. Cheer up, cheer up, sweet friend;
Call from thy soul the light once wont to glisten
In thy tearless eye. You'll make me sad, dear girl,
In faith you will. Ah! now you smile, and now I know
My own Lucille. What is't hath changed you thus?

LUCILLE.

Thy absence, my dear Lord, and loving doubts
Lest we no more should meet. Ah! that alone
Were grief enough to make stones weep; but as the sun
Their sweet distilments draws from flowery meads,

So shall thy presence from my verdant heart
Reap harvest of such joys, thy eye will love
To linger on the scene, on which it once so fondly gazed.

FITZURSE.

True, Love, though banished from our cherished home,
We'll deck in joy our thoughts—and smiles the garb
Shall be, the face shall wear—all lands the same to love.

LUCILLE.

In truth we will, dear Lord—but pray, how came you here?

FITZURSE.

My heart had learnt to beat most healthful time
To the soft music of Lucille's sweet voice.
That missed—all others sounded "harsh and out of tune."
So I came here to France.

LUCILLE.

     Then Henry hath not frowned
On you—no, no, that could not be.

FITZURSE.

        Nor is;
But I have frowned on him—spurned the base rule
That tramples thus on worth; genius to slander's shafts
Hath fallen prey, and wisdom fled his realm.
The ides of March brought not more ills upon the sons
Of Rome, than this on England hath.

LUCILLE.

Oh, say not so, for she our country is—
But see, these knights of Flanders and of France
Have ta'en their leave—they are most courtly lords;
To them I'm much beholden.

FITZURSE.

     Thence, much am I;
Come, dearest love, and we'll amid this castle's varied
  scenes,
While away a few short hours.   *[Exeunt.*

SCENE FOURTH.

Court at Sens—A Grand Hall.

Enter HENRY *and* DE BROC.

HENRY.

I have advices tell me the Primate threatens me.
He threaten me! Why, what a slave am I!
A monkish cowl more terror strikes into my heart
Than twice ten thousand men, all mailed in steel!
Still, should he issue interdict, farewell
To all my power—this will suspend all forms
Religious—marriage, baptism, burial—No priest
Can then officiate in public or in private.
'Twill break the bonds of loyalty. I'll stay his course.
De Broc! my Lord De Broc! Give instant orders
That all England's ports be watched, with this command,
That any one, or man or child, matron or maid,
Who shall bear over, promulgate, or obey,
Letters of Interdict, receiveth instant death,—
No clergy's benefit allowed. Announce
That if the Cistercian Order, now at Pontigny,
Continue to protect this traitor, their Order
Be expelled from my domains. [*Exit* DE BROC.
   Enter FITZURSE.] Ha! my Fitzurse!

FITZURSE, *kneeling.*

My Liege.

HENRY, *sarcastically.*

How fares our loving Primate?

FITZURSE.

Well, my Liege—France, Flanders, and the Pope outvie
   each other
In favors shown him.

HENRY.

Is't so, in fact?

FITZURSE.

In fact, my Liege.

HENRY.

What can we do?

FITZURSE.

Make peace with him.

HENRY.

Make peace, but how? Must I cringe to him?

FITZURSE.

No, my Liege, use France. He will a mediator be.
There must be peace, else your whole realm's disjoined.
Better 'twere made in a friendly way, than you be forced
To it.

HENRY.

True, true; we will consult with France
As to the better mode. A'Becket knows not
You are in my service?

FITZURSE.

No, deems me fallen from favor.

HENRY.

Let it be so, but heed him well. Attend me! [*Exeunt.*

SCENE FIFTH.
"Gothic."

A'BECKET *and* BLOIS.

BLOIS.

Your orders are fulfilled, my Lord—
Yet may not Henry injure you still more?

A'BECKET.

He injure me? Each wrong he does me falls
As sand, a handful thrown aloft, covering whole acres
With its particles. Such my revenge shall be—
A myriad ills for every wrong he does my country
And my friends.
    At Sens, henceforth, I'll dwell in peace,
Out of the range of his hostility,
While he'll live troubled with the fear of me.
His Holiness hath bidden me, "in this my poverty,"
To be "Consoler of the poor." To Henry, begging,
He refused a conference, and me appoints
His Legate unto England. Most generous act!
Said I not that all worked well? Trust, trust to years;
We better read the hearts of men than ye
Of tender youth.

BLOIS.
    'Tis true, my Lord.

A'BECKET.
One Alexander, and but one, was to the old world known;
So shall Rome's sacred 'scutcheon his name bear,
Greatest of all her Pontiffs. Such men are offspring
Of a thousand years—none, none like him
Shall the next ten centuries see. Ah! here
Albert comes. More news? Methinks this day
Is big with it.
 Enter ALBERT.] [A'BECKET, *taking letter, reads.*
    What is this? What is this?
Henry inhibits all appeals, or unto the Pope
Or me; declares it treason to introduce
Our interdicts into his kingdom, and obliges all
Who in England dwell, to swear observance
Of these orders, on pain of most dread sufferings.
This, this is monstrous; it were as well that water

Were forbidden! I'll fill the world with it!
This is the cause of God! Go you, and unto Louis
Write this, also to Philip of Flanders:
"That I suspend the spiritual thunder
Over Henry's head, to fall, less timely repentance comes."
This will him deprive of all his continental territories,
And endanger his power in England.
Write this, and messengers dispatch to Rome
With news of what I do.
       I'll be myself once more.
I'll nothing with this King! He yet shall sue
To me! All mediations shall but faster forge
The bars keep Henry from my love.
 Enter JOHN OF SALISBURY.]
         Ha! my friend
Of Salisbury, what news hast thou?

    JOHN OF SALISBURY.
         John of Oxford
Hath for himself obtained absolution,
And resigned his Deanery to the Pope,
But, by his appointment, straightway received it back.

    A'BECKET.
Indeed! This looks not well for us! What arts
Were used to influence His Holiness?
What more?

    SALISBURY.
A Bull from the Pope, my Lord, the decree
Annulling, did confiscate your goods,
But with his prohibition 'gainst excommunicating
Any person in England, or interdicting that realm.
While he his wish doth indicate, exhorting you
To moderation and humility.

A'BECKET.
                        To moderation
And humility? I'll see my friend of France—
Louis will ne'er desert me.
                    Whence comes this change?
To moderation and humility!
And what is this but moderation
And humility? These cloistered courts
After my princely halls, and but two friends
For all my regal train—
I would for myself be humble, very humble,
Humble as the dust.
              My exaltation were my sure reward,
But my poor friends—my country!

END OF ACT II.

ACT III.

SCENE FIRST.

"Stone"—A'Becket's apartment in Monastery at St. Colomba.

Enter LORDS DE BROC *and* DE TRACY.

DE TRACY.
Is this the love France bears to England,
Such princely entertainment to her foes?

DE BROC.
'Twas ever thus, his seeming modesty
Was but the semblance of austerity.

A beggar's robe upon a princely couch
Proved well this upstart's vanity.

DE TRACY.

Peace, peace! He comes——

DE BROC.

Well! let him, 'tis but to blind
The vulgar he's thus clothed, they never see
Aught but the ante-room, and that's the same,
A picture of sad poverty. He knoweth well
How best to catch the vulgar crowd. My Lord,
There's danger here to us and to our rights!

DE TRACY.

Once on the shore of England, 'twill go hard
But we shall tame his spirit; escape
Were not so easy, had we guarded well.

DE BROC.

We'll have no peace while Becket lives to plot.

DE TRACY.

True, true! There's something in the air of France!
How proud grows Lord Fitzurse!

DE BROC.

Fair and false! false and fair!
He counts upon A'Becket's niece's wide domains.
I sent some flowers to his lady love,
Of fragrance rich and rare, with lines composed
By our most sweet queen, in the envelope
Came from Lord Fitzurse—(she knew the hand,
For he's a dainty scholar) together—
With his last words to us,—
    Sarcastically.] His friends should advance his suit.
Lo! here the Archbishop comes.

Enter A'BECKET.

DE BROC.
Our gracious Lord Archbishop!

A'BECKET, *aside.*
Our Lord Archbishop!—no thanks to you I'm so.
Aloud.]
What would ye, Sirs, with me?

DE BROC.
A friendly conference.

A'BECKET.
I'll send my kinsman to you, Sirs: I hold
No private conference—there's a wide gulf
Between the Saxon Primate and the Norman lords.

DE TRACY.
You do mistake us much, my Lord. We come as friends.

A'BECKET.
So came the serpent, who beguiled poor Eve,
Promising knowledge, which but proved her ruin.

DE BROC.
Not so, my Lord. Peruse this letter, 'tis from England's
    King.
    Aside to DE TRACY.]
Mark him, my friend!

A'BECKET *reads—then says—*
Indeed, 'tis well—'tis well.
Accept my welcome, most noble Lords,
And pardon an old man's petulance,
In that I did receive you, formally—
Sit ye, and we'll discuss this business.
Ho! Albert.   [*Enter* ALBERT.
        Bid them prepare repasts for fifty knights,—
Friends have arrived from France.   [*Exit* ALBERT.
            How does his gracious majesty?

DE TRACY.

Well in all things save one—he bade us say,
And that, the loss of your society.
With this, that with the past its ills were flown,
Therefore, in oblivion buried, let all
Vexed questions be, and begs your quick return.

A'BECKET.

      Bury the past, my Lords!
Do we forget the avalanche has hurled
Our stately mansions to the dust, and cast
Unto the winds our prosperous fortunes?
Henry asks much—besides, here have I
Plenty, honor, ease; while I in England,
At best, should find but lack of love, dishonor,
Penury.—No, no, my Lords; not to use
Harsher phrase, this is ungenerous!

DE BROC.

Nay, nay, my Lord; you and your friends shall be restored
To all your livings; and all the benefices
That have been filled during your absence
Shall be vacated, until supplied by you.
He asks but this, that you absolve his ministers.

A'BECKET.

We will confer on this. Albert, attend these lords.
You must be quite o'erworn with your ride.
I thank you for your love, shown in your haste
To greet me. Doves had scarce flown faster.

DE TRACY.

Our service to you, Father.   [*Exeunt.*

A'BECKET.

Falsehood here, falsehood everywhere, methinks
The very air is filled with it. I scent naught else.
Return to England and he'll repair the past!

Restore myself and friends our proud estates—
Can he restore the time of which he has robbed me?
Why, what a fool he thinks me! Will do all this—
All this, ay more, so say these lords. Catch me
With promises, and birds with lime, when on them
Ye can lay it, Sirs! There's something more in this;
Insult to injury. I'll none of it. When I may land
On England's shore, backed by my thousands,
Then I may return, but never on the strength
Of Henry's promise—which, like the Upas,
Wins the gazer's eye, but to the trusting touch
Is poisonous.
And more: there are my private heart-seated wrongs
Which stalk around me, though there's lapse of years.
'Twas he who robbed me of my youth's fond hopes,
Dishonoring her who was my only pride!
No, no, not so; I will be just even in my hate:
Hers was the sin to me—not his—he knew not of my
    love.
Oh! I forget—my heart and head grow old—
I forgave him then, and took England for my bride.
Away. ye selfish thoughts! Ye must be strangers
To the breast of greatness.

Enter MATILDE *and* SALISBURY.

A'BECKET.

My child, here is news from England.
Henry craves our return. [*Aside.*] I'll sound her
    woman's wit.

MATILDE.

    You will not go, dear father.

SALISBURY.

Most surely not.

A'BECKET.

He promises to restore myself and friends
Unto our former honors.

SALISBURY.

His promises, my Lord—

A'BECKET.

Are—

SALISBURY.

But sportsmen's calls to lure their prey.

MATILDE.

You will not go?

A'BECKET.

Should I be afraid, my child?
A'Becket ne'er knew fear, for he is mailed
In the garb of faith!

SALISBURY.

Father, it is not that you fear, but you mistrust;
You know he is treacherous, as hyena fierce,
And you'd not venture in his den.
Prudence is a manly virtue!

Go not, my Lord.
Here are your truest friends, consult with them.

Enter FITZURSE *on one side,* LUCILLE *on the other.*

A'BECKET.

Lucille, my child! my Lord Fitzurse—ye whom
I much do love—ye whom I call mine own,
Give me your voices. England here writes
(Her lords have just arrived), and begs
Our quick return, promising to all our friends
Their former state.

LUCILLE.

Father, you'll not return!
Aside.] Why came Lord Fitzurse here?

A'BECKET.
Do you counsel thus?

LUCILLE, *kneeling to him.*
Upon my bended knee, I do beseech you, Sir,
That letter! [A'BECKET *gives it her.*
  Aside.] The same hand as that to Henry's embassy.
Love cannot blind me to the fact, 'tis his,—
Fitzurse's!—Bear up, my heart! I'll note him well.

A'BECKET.
And what, Fitzurse, say you?

SALISBURY.
  I, would not trust his promise.

FITZURSE.
                I, would, my Lord;
Honor and safety unto all he vouches.

LUCILLE *to* FITZURSE.
Would you, my Lord?

FITZURSE.
    I would, fair lady.

LUCILLE.
               His promise!
Oh! Father, do not go, save hostages
Be left with France for your security.

A'BECKET.
Well thought, my child!

SALISBURY.
    And deeds, confirming all your rights,
Be sent.

A'BECKET.
So be it. Salisbury, meet me at hour of nine;
Lest Henry trifles, we'll safe bind at once.
Each now, to their several pleasures.
    Exeunt all, except FITZURSE *and* LUCILLE.

FITZURSE.

Sweet flower of Spring, all will be well!
I heard from Henry by this embassy:
There is full power to comply with what
A'Becket asks.

LUCILLE.

My Lord, you, from King Henry, advices have!
Why spake you as you did, when others raised their
    doubts?

FITZURSE.

I gave my answer unto all they asked.

LUCILLE.

My Lord! My Lord! You gave your answer!
A friend had opened to his friend his heart;
So he his thoughts had read. A follower
Should have done so. I would not trust this King,
Nor—

FITZURSE.
                  Nor what?

LUCILLE.

No matter—

FITZURSE.

Dost thou reprove?

LUCILLE.
                You heard from Henry!
How could you hold communion with A'Becket's foe?

FITZURSE *aside*.

Am I love's slave, that I am questioned thus?
   Aloud.]
Dost thou reprove, fair maid?

LUCILLE.
                As does your heart,
Does mine; but oh, what grief, if that it must do so.
   Aside.] To love, to doubt! Oh, wretched fate is mine!

FITZURSE.

For me, Lucille, these words?

LUCILLE.

For you, my Lord;
Or any man, whose smiling face
Is but the glittering sheath, covers a heart
Would stab its dearest friend.   [FITZURSE *starts.*
You met these lords in private
Ere they had seen mine uncle; a secret conference
Held with them; these facts concealed, when in good faith
Consulted.   [FITZURSE *offers to take her hand.*
Nay, Sir, your hand's unclean, fresh from the traitor's act.

FITZURSE.

Lucille!

LUCILLE.

Who would be false to him, is false to me!

FITZURSE.

Why this? How know you that I conference held?

LUCILLE.

Your silence to my charge when made!
    Aside.]
I will not wound him, with these dreadful lines—
His letter to the King—assassins of my young heart's
    hopes.
I've said enough, unless his heart is stone.

FITZURSE.

'Twas in your uncle's cause, and thine; besides,
I saw them but a moment.

LUCILLE.

Would'st thou prevaricate and gloss it o'er to me,
My Lord?—you met them, Sir, my uncle's foes,
In private, 'tis enough—false unto him,
You'd be unfair to me. "Candor" is the motto

Blazoned on true love's shield! Farewell!
I am much grieved to find you lack this virtue.
Who would have thought you thus could mar
The noblest gifts of nature?
       Farewell, farewell!
My love is changed to pity. Leave me, Sir!

    FITZURSE.

Lady, you will repent you of this hour.
        Farewell! [*Going.*

    LUCILLE.

My Lord, I do repent me of this hour,
And many hours past! May Heaven pardon you,
As I do now!

    FITZURSE.

Farewell, fair Lady, since it must be so.
You will relent.

    LUCILLE.

  Never! never!

    FITZURSE.

      Farewell! [*Exits.*

    LUCILLE.

Are there in store for me more bolts like this?
If so, would Heaven they'd fall at once
And crush me.

   A'BECKET *enters.*

    My child, what moves you thus?
Where is Fitzurse?

    LUCILLE.

  Fitzurse! Fitzurse! He's false to you, to me,
To the whole world; for all who knew him
Held him as candor's child. Trust him not,
Father, trust him not! [*Giving a letter.*
     Thy letter and these lines,
'Twas the same hand penned both.

A'BECKET *reads.*

Ha—
"A'Becket's friend, who fair Lucille doth woo,
Is Henry's friend, A'Becket's direst foe.
Her bridal rites will prove A'Becket's grave,
When fair Lucille becomes, Lord Fitzurse's slave."
Where found you this? [*Aside.*] 'Tis from Queen Eleanor!

LUCILLE, *taking flowers from her bosom.*

These flowers bore the thorn.
I cannot nurse you longer.   [*Drops them gently.*

A'BECKET.

Poison oft lurks beneath earth's fairest fruits!
What more knowest thou?

LUCILLE.

He saw these lords this morn;
Held private conference, ere you met them, Sir.

A'BECKET.

Indeed, was't so? nor spake when I did question him?
How false! How foul! Cheer thee, my child, all sorrows
Have their balm! Go, seek Matilde, I'll summon
Salisbury.   [*Exit* LUCILLE.
I cannot believe, without the weightiest proofs,
That he is false to me.
            Yet it is his heritage.
Him whom I guarded, though unbeknown,
From tenderest infancy to full-grown pride.
I saw the germs of greatness in the boy,
And trusted they would bloom in manhood.
Thus ever fail our fondest hopes.
            My poor, poor child!
Why falls this blow on her? Her, whom I thought
Secure as cloistered nun from love-born griefs.

SALISBURY *enters unseen by* A'BECKET.

How vain is man's heedfulness! Poor girl! poor girl!
But thus it is with all—how fitful is life!
To-day, in manly pride, as dares the bark
The ocean's changefulness, the gallant youth struts,
Conscious of his power; but soon, as sinks
Beneath that ocean's frowns the groaning hulk,
His crest is lowered by the storm which strikes,
Sooner or later, all who hope to soar
High o'er the world's wild waves.
       Youth is hope's season,
Though the seed that's sown, oft yields but sorry harvest.
Life is a dream, naught real but the hour.
Unstable as the stream, earth's offerings,
The sweetest to the taste are joys unhoped.
The bitterest sorrow comes when unforeseen.
Hard seems life's yoke, yet easy 'tis to bear,
If mated, but with faith.

SALISBURY.

How wonderfully wise! He's wrapt in thought
On man's futility. I must disturb his musing.
Father!

A'BECKET.

      My son, what news?

SALISBURY.

Your terms made known to Henry's embassy,
They, having well feasted, would not o'erwait
The night, but posted back again. Methinks,
My Lord, he'll grant you any thing, so urgent
Were their words.

A'BECKET.

    'Tis well; but hast thou heard
What passed between the King of France

And he who is miscalled England's?
Thus says a later embassy, just arrived.

SALISBURY.

A later embassy!

A'BECKET.

E'en so. Hear thou their words—
Attended by his friends and counsellors,
His sovereignty proudly worn, Henry approached
Unbending; his salutation formal,
And his words as cold as winds that come
From Norseland. 'Twas not the part of France
His breath should be the breeze from balmy Southland
    blows.
But as exposed, most hostile things produce
A genial spark—even from the meeting
Of their distant spirits, a flame of love
Sprang forth. Right royally forgetting and forgiving,
He to those honors of which I was so unjustly reft,
With many more, restored me.
                  We will to England soon,
When unto you, high office I'll intrust.

SALISBURY.

Bright ray of Peace! May Heaven be thanked!

A'BECKET.

E'en so—and by its mercies we are called
In action to proclaim unto the world
Our gratefulness. Much is there to be done;
The lawless nobles must be curbed, licentious
Is the very air of England. Gold, glittering gold,
And an unseemly pride, are all these nobles
Glory in. Their vassals are oppressed,
And the High Church neglected.
    3*

This for thine ear alone.   It must, shall, be reformed.
[*Enter* LUCILLE.
What would you, child?

LUCILLE.

The King, our Liege, arrived to-day in France
This letter bearing, his lords an audience crave.
   Gives a letter.]
Fearing treachery lurked beneath, I bore it
Here myself. What says his Majesty?

A'BECKET, *after reading.*

We are recalled to all our honors!
The King reposes now some few miles hence,
His lords of high degree attend me here.
Salisbury, go you and sound them well,
Note all their actions, even their garb observe.
The leopard's skin is most in vogue
With our nobility, and 'neath its beauties
Oft a poniard gleams. I fear not, but mistrust.
Their purpose known to you, you'll find me here.
   [*Exit* SALISBURY.
Lucille, my child, pray lay aside this grief,
Thou mayst have heavier trials yet in store.

LUCILLE.

If so, I'll bear them—as I will bear this—
Am I not A'Becket's niece? his child?

A'BECKET.

   Well said, my idol girl—
Yet stay—thy beauties now full blown, many there are
In England who will strive to pluck the flower
From the parent stem—and at thy age the heart
Beats not alone with throbbings born within,
But, like the sweet airs heard in verdant vales,
Whispers in melodies in ten thousand born.

LUCILLE.

I've done with love—an o'ermastered argosie—
I've sunk my young heart's countless wealth
In the deep bosom of forgetfulness—
Mine uncle dear, hast thou not watched
O'er infancy's frail flowers, smiled on their budding,
And what you are pleased to call their full-blown
Beauties, tended, with parent carefulness?

A'BECKET.

A father's love, no more.

LUCILLE.
     Yes, more; a mother's!
Were you not both to me?

A'BECKET.
      And thou to me, a child.
The purest, dearest moments granted me
In a long life, I owe to thee, Lucille.
I never knew a parent's love. Though I am risen
To greatness, 'twas heart-born grief marshalled me
To honor; since then I have never halted
In my rapid course; no matter how opposed,
All things I made, rungs in ambition's ladder;
In my whole course of life o'erleaping
Where I could not level to my will, and once,
But once, have fallen—and that was, as the flame
On sudden dies, to shine with greater brightness.
We will prepare for England.   [LUCILLE *retires.*
 Enter SALISBURY] What say these lords?

SALISBURY.

All that, to the ear, is fair.

A'BECKET.
      But to the thought
Most foul—I read your meaning—speak, my friend.

SALISBURY.

With every wish for your success—much joy
That you to England will return—smiles, words
Such as are used by courtiers, they lauded
Henry to the skies, for what he did perforce.
Making him centre unto them, his satellites,
No more, no more!

A'BECKET.

     So greatness ever is attended.
Upon the lion's heels thus treads the jackall,
And what he leaves, delights to feed on.
You met them graciously! Salisbury,
If they can, they will sting—we must draw their fangs.
Wait they below.?

SALISBURY.

     They do, my Lord.

A'BECKET.

We will receive them here.
  Exit SALISBURY *and enter* ALBERT.
Albert, I may have work for you, await without;
Your arms are ready? Cordin and Bassett
With you? I'll knock, should you be needed.

Enter SALISBURY, DE TRACY, DE MOREVILLE, *and* SIR RICHARD BRITO.

A'BECKET.

     Welcome, Gentlemen!

DE TRACY.

    To the Archbishop of Canterbury
Our service—welcome to the Primacy once more!

A'BECKET.

Thanks, Gentlemen; thanks!

DE MOREVILLE.

        The King commends himself to you;
He would that you, with your fair nieces both,
Should grace his court to-night, for soon he goes
To Normandy.

A'BECKET.

        Say to my Liege we will attend
His pleasure. This hour heralds days of joy
To come, rich in the service we may render him;
And believe me, Gentlemen, that handmaids meet
My children fair will be.

BRITO.

Well know we that, my Lord, for hearts, ne'er owned
The power of love before, unto their beauty
Bend the suppliant knee.

A'BECKET.

        To maiden influence
Noble hearts e'er yield a grateful homage;
Their beauty shows not only to the eye.

BRITO.

So have we learnt, and happy shall we be
When we may welcome them to English homes;
We will await you in King Henry's palace.

A'BECKET.

Thanks, my Lord, thanks to all! Peace be with you.
    Farewell!   [*Exeunt.*
So much for their nobility!
Didst note, my Salisbury, how constrained their words,
Their actions forced, uneasy—guilty souls
They bear about with them—trust them?
                      You know me better—
Besides, I have old claims on them—a wrong
A'Becket will forgive, but not forget.

SALISBURY.

Such wrongs you never can: use them, but watch them.

A'BECKET.

We will: prepare a fitting escort to the Court
To-night—to-morrow we'll to England.
But what should faith professed, prove false?
Louis bade me not trust, save that the kiss
Of peace were given—this he will refuse—
Bear this forthwith unto the Bishops of London
And Salisbury, and to the world make known
My sentence of excommunication against them.
Now will I fix upon foundation firm
As that whereon Albion's white cliffs are based
My Empire and my honors. England's glory
And the Church's power—her people's welfare
And her nobles' pride—shall be A'Becket's care.

END OF ACT III.

ACT IV.

SCENE FIRST.

A large Hall in De Tracy's Castle, England.

Enter FITZURSE.

FITZURSE.
    New wonder on new wonder—
       A'Becket
And the King at peace! No thanks to me for this.
The churlish priest ere now had been but dust,
Had Henry ta'en my counsel.

  DE TRACY *enters.*
         De Tracy,
Hast heard the news? They say, last night, strange things
Were seen—water was cast upon a burning pile
And brighter made the flames; with the furred cat
The house-infesting vermin couched;
And the watchful guardian of my house fawned
On the thief assailed it!

DE TRACY.
      'Tis strange, indeed!

FITZURSE.
Yet stranger still is what hath happ'd to-day.

DE TRACY.
      How so?

FITZURSE.
A'Becket and the King are palm in palm.

DE TRACY.
     Bright omen, Fitz., for you!

FITZURSE.
                  Indeed!

DE TRACY.

May not his fair niece partake the nature of the times?

FITZURSE.

The sun which gladdens nature's face, ne'er changes
His fixed course. The moon, which softly smiles
Upon a darkened world, may gild, not chase, the gloom.
No change e'er comes o'er these which most delight
The world's sad wayfarer. How may the fair Lucille,
Then, turn aside and smile where she hath frowned?
No, no, De Tracy! [*Aside.*] He shall not read my heart.

DE TRACY.
                  In charity.

FITZURSE.

In charity! Should Fitzurse prize the hand
Without the heart? The sun is golden,
But without its heat, what would its radiance be?
'Twould catch the eye, but on the senses pall.
De Tracy, I have lived in court and camp;
Wealth, honor, want, despite, have been my lot;
With all there was a void—a lack of something
Which I knew not of. When griefs afflicted
And when joys assailed, alike 'twas felt,
My friend—a loneliness. I knew not whence
It came, till fair Lucille I saw.

DE TRACY.
                 Why then
Too proud to take the hand?

FITZURSE.
                The hand without the heart!

DE TRACY.

When lovely woman so regards a man
That she'll to him intrust her lot and fortune,
Is it not worth more, when springing from esteem,
Than when it shoots to life, like the fair flower
That blooms at dawn, to close ere noonday comes?
The plant of slowest growth is longest lived,
Its shoots the farthest and is firmest fixed!

FITZURSE.

It may be so—but love without romance!

DE TRACY.

Have done with fancy! She's a fickle dame!
Her votaries decks in colors false and fleeting.
Your nature has too much of the bright clime
Wherein your youth was passed. The wave which sparkles
May a poison bear, when raised unto the lip;
While sluggish waters will the fainting form
Awake to life and strength!
     If fair Lucille but smiles!

FITZURSE.

Alas! how can she?

DE TRACY.

  Deem that she prizes justly your true worth,
Now longer, better known.   Here are De Moreville
And Sir Richard Brito.
 Enter DE MOREVILLE *and* SIR RICHARD BRITO.
Welcome, Gentlemen! My Lord Fitzurse,
Sir Richard Brito and De Moreville here
Have ever found a home. We once were a merry crew;

Let's be as merry as the times permit.
Ho! boy, there!—wine. [*To* FITZURSE.] Come, Sir, be
  one of us.

FITZURSE.

With all my heart! Here's to you, Gentlemen!
Why, 'tis as good as is your speech, De Tracy—
A free and generous wine.

DE TRACY.

                            Thanks, noble friend!
Here's unto all, long life and happiness!
Why hangs, Fitzurse, this cloud upon your face?
Your manly spirit should o'erlook the ills
Of life, and smile at frowning fortune.
Clear, clear thy brow, and let it shine as does
The mountain's top, high o'er the thunder-storm.

FITZURSE.

It shall. Yet gives not the mist enshrouds the mount
From view, a richer beauty to it, when 'tis seen?

DE TRACY.

Ay, truly! But a truce to jesting; what ill
Afflicts you?

FITZURSE *to* DE MOREVILLE.

          Thou hast heard the news? A'Becket
And the King at peace!

DE MOREVILLE.

              At peace! Is't from that quarter
That this storm-cloud comes? Strange! strange, indeed!
A'Becket has a niece, my Lord. [FITZURSE, *impatient*.
  To DE TRACY.] You've seen the fair Lucille?

DE TRACY.

                      When but a child.

DE MOREVILLE.

The loveliest flower boasts not the richest bud.

FITZURSE.

Most true! Yet, is not Lucille beautiful?
Aside.]
I hoped, A'Becket outworn with grief,
Lucille, our Liege's ward, I might have won her.
Her wealth would prop my falling fortunes,
Though her disprize should chill my heart.

DE MOREVILLE.

The fairest maid e'er seen! Fair Venus' prototype!
You loved her once?

FITZURSE.

           And if I'd live must win her.
Will not A'Becket strive so to please our King,
As in his favor henceforth e'er to live?
Henry's command might find a willing ear,
Were the past brought to mind.

BRITO.

Wouldst thou threaten the great A'Becket?
You know him not, my Lord. His surplice clothes
As stout a heart as ever armor cased.
Shrinks the firm-based rock from wave
That may overwhelm it? Who'd dare so much
As name the word, to threat? His glance
Would fall on him like Heaven's thunderbolt;
His stately mien, awe-filling, strike him mute!
I am a soldier, one who has borne arms
From youth to age, and yet would brave the serried ranks
Rather than face that tongue's keen irony.
Oh! be advised by me.

DE MOREVILLE.

           Sir Richard well doth speak.
King Henry's favorite and A'Becket's friend,
Your suit were easily gained, never as his foe.

Render the Primate favors—he'll not frown;
And then, in gratitude, his niece's thoughts
Will turn to you; her heart float down the silver stream
Of peace, and fancy bear it through its flowery brakes,
To the glittering source whence all her new joys spring.
De Tracy, thinkst not so?

DE TRACY.

                You counsel well, my Lord—
And yet, Fitzurse, the hand without the heart!

FITZURSE.

That matters not! I'll wear her, if not win her!
The ray that woos the verdant mead, dispels
The mist enshrouds it from its heat.
So shall my heart's fond love the tear that dims
Lucille's bright eye, and 'neath its warmth new beauties
    bring
To light. Now let's to Court, my Lords!

BRITO.

                Wouldst wrest
The flower from the parent stem, where it would bloom
For many a day, to see it fade and fall
Within the hour?

FITZURSE.

A'Becket rules this realm but as I rule her heart!

DE MOREVILLE.

                Believe me, my Lord,
Its rich gem gone, the casket's not worth having!

FITZURSE.

Leave that to me, my arms shall be its setting.
I'm for the Court.   [*Exit.*

DE TRACY.
                    So I! So all!
There shall we see if he is Fortune's child—
I'll save this maid, unless she loves, from love so wild.
                              [*Exeunt.*

SCENE SECOND.
Porch to the King's Ante-room.

HERALD.
The Lord Archbishop comes!

HENRY.
             We will descend and greet him
As our brother. [*To* FITZURSE.] Note him, young
    Lord!
A'BECKET *enters in great state, he and his suite mounted.*
Welcome, my Lord Archbishop, to my Court!

A'BECKET, *dismounting.*
My service to your Majesty.

HENRY.
We gave this audience that, your wishes learnt,
Once more we might be friends—we have no need
Of words—what is your wish?

A'BECKET.
             First, that, being your subject,
You free pardon grant for all that's past.

HENRY.
                  'Tis thine.

A'BECKET.
Then, as being England's Primate,
That you restore to me the Church of Canterbury,
All its possessions, and your royal favor,

With promise on my part of love and honor,
And whatsoever may be performed by an Archbishop
Unto his sovereign.

HENRY.

'Tis granted all—all's thine—
Herewith unto my favor I receive you
And your friends. Go, for a time, with me
To Normandy, where we may labor for our subjects' good.

A'BECKET.

Long absent from my friends and country, Sire,
'Twould please me, had I leave, straightway to sail
For England.

HENRY.

Your pleasure is mine, my Lord, to England
Let it be. My Court in Normandy is ever thine,
When it shall please your Holiness.

A'BECKET.

Thanks, my Liege; thanks!

HENRY.

" Would you but do as I desire, all things
Should be intrusted to your care."

A'BECKET.

It shall be so.

HENRY.

'Tis well! At Rouen you will find meet preparations made;
And her Archbishop your escort to England.
Now unto Court; where we in harmony,
Amid our assembled friends, will close the day.
Bring here our steeds. [*Exeunt attendants.*

The horses are brought; A'BECKET *prepares to mount,
when the King holds his stirrup.*

A'BECKET.

Nay, pardon me, my Liege; this is not meet!

HENRY.

The monarch of the realm makes all things meet;
Mount, my Lord Primate!

A'BECKET.

Nay, nay, my Liege!

HENRY.

I will be King, even in my courtesies.

A'BECKET.

So be it. [*Kisses the King's hand and mounts.*

HENRY.

On to the Court, my friends!

[*All mount and ride off.*

SCENE THIRD.

The Court.

Lords and Gentlemen in waiting. Enter FITZURSE, DE TRACY, DE MOREVILLE, *and* SIR RICHARD BRITO.

FITZURSE.

Lo! where they come! How loving, palm in palm!

DE TRACY.

'Tis so! Stand back, my Lords! The King!

Enter KING HENRY, *and* A'BECKET, *and attendants.*

HENRY.

My Lords and Gentlemen, receive once more
My reverend counsellor and loving friend,
Thomas A'Becket, Primate of England,
Of Canterbury Archbishop, unto our favor,
And all those honors so justly his, herein restored.
Respect him, as you love me.

ALL.

Welcome to the Lord Primate!

A'BECKET.

Thanks unto all! Thanks unto your Majesty,
That you have so o'erstepped the bounds
Of kingly condescension, thus to the Court
Presenting me. [*Aside.*] Pour oil on ruffled waves,
For when the storm's just o'er, their swell is highest.
    Aloud.]
Though time has changed the mortal part of him
Here unto you returned, the immortal soul
Has grown most strong in sacred learning;
Holding communion with those happier climes
Where virtue only reigns. That realm alone
Higher is than England's, and on the faults
And failings of mankind looks with more kindly eye.
My noble Lords, here see I those
I called my friends, and found my foes!
But, with my blessing on you all, accept
From me free pardon of the past.
Let the volume of your hate be sealed,
So far as aught's recorded against me;
Mine did I long since hurl far down the past's abyss.
Look to the motives which did move me once,
The means I used you'll find were just.

LORDS.

He would uphold the past! Treason to our King!

A'BECKET.

Peace awhile! Let not ill-tempered haste
Dash into atoms the frail cup of love I offer
To your lips. Here is no treason! I would that Church and State
Were as twin brothers, linked in amity;

United, they shall stand till time's no more;
Divided, they must fall ere set of sun.
Discontent among the Lords.]
My Liege, command that silence reign, else our good
    purpose fails;
And all that's done be but as words written
On the sea-shore's sands.

HENRY.

Peace, my Lords, peace! Who speaks,
His King offends.
My Lord High Primate asks
Attentive ears.

A'BECKET.

In our honored King, my Lords, the father
Of this great realm, you see the pride, the power
Of England—in me, the instrument of Heaven;
An humble agent of its blessed will.
What were our King disrobed, dethroned?
What were the priest, stripped of his sacred office?
Foes are there who'd delight in Henry's fall!
Foes are there who do long for my dishonor!
The heart must entertain and harbor vice,
Ere the seducer's voice can steal
Into its curtained chambers, and rob it of its jewel.
Remember this; be true unto yourselves,
Your King, your country. You'll find Truth's legions
Are your best resource. All are but men—yet he
Who worthiest bears his charge, adds honor to his
    honors.
Your ear, my King.

DE MOREVILLE, *aside.*

How bold a tongue he has!

BRITO.

Said I not so?

DE TRACY.

     And yet, how gilded is his speech;
It falls upon the ear as on the eye the sun;
So dazzling it doth dim, and bears the mind
Along, unconscious of the course it takes.

FITZURSE.

He's very dangerous—his speech is serpent-like—
It charms but to destroy! Were he but dumb
I then could master him. I fear this peace is short.

DE TRACY.

Ha! the King's brow doth cloud.

A'BECKET.

     The kiss of peace refused!
My Liege, why so?

HENRY.

    A vow I made precludes its gift.

A'BECKET.

The conference, then, is o'er. The bond,
Without the seal, were valueless. My Liege!
My Liege! think well of this. 'Tis a slight gift—
A gift when given not gone, so rich the return
'Twill yield. My King, retract thy vow; the Church
Permits. A'Becket then is yours—we must be friends.
 Aside.] I must not sue. I, who so soon enthroned
Shall be, high over all earth's kings.
      Still my country speaks.
 To HENRY.]
Your realm demands it, a people's groans mourn
Their sad miseries; and a distracted land—
Most eloquent counsellor in my cause—
Pleads loud for it.

HENRY.

            It may not be. What England says
Must be—our word, our bond.

FITZURSE.

                        My Liege, the price
That's paid cancels the bond. Here, see the smiling face
Of lovely peace; there, dire war's frowning brow,
With all its attendant horrors.

HENRY.

                    You counsel peace,
Young Lord, who ever were for war? You lack not
   courage!
Has he sought to bribe you, my tried follower?

A'BECKET, *scornfully*.

                              To bribe!

FITZURSE.

To bribe! Could I be bribed, my brow had never worn
This deep gash which now it bears, a valued trophy
Of the day I met the blow, were else my King's.

HENRY.

            True, true, I've wronged you!

A'BECKET, *aside*.

            Not the first wrong you've done him.
Fouled in his birth, not even though King,
Canst thou cleanse him.

HENRY.

            Take here my thanks, young Lord!
While thus reminded of a deed, till now forgotten—
One you should be proud of, wear this sword,
For years my constant friend! As I have worn it
So I'll wear you; ever my counsellor
Both in Court and camp. When your King finds
True merit, he rewards it. Is it not so, A'Becket?

A'BECKET.

I thought so once, my Liege, and much it pains me,
That this hour should be a witness against that thought.

HENRY.

It shall not be so.   The kiss of peace may not be yours,
A vow made in an hasty hour precludes it.
But come unto my heart.   [*They embrace.*
My Lords, this day does unto England bear
Unheard of blessings.   A prosperous people
Are the greatest riches which a land can boast.
  To A'BECKET.]
Herein do I restore you to my love,
As I already have unto your honors.
I must away to Normandy.   Preserve my realm
In peace.   Farewell to all!

A'BECKET.

              Farewell! most gracious Majesty!
May Heaven's choicest blessings be with you,
And honor, love, and a long life be yours.

HENRY.

Thanks unto all!   Farewell!
  Exeunt the KING *and his attendants except* FITZURSE.

A'BECKET.

My friends, we will prepare for our return
To Canterbury.   [FITZURSE *approaches.*
              Young Lord, you have well spoken;
And though I had preferred some other's voice,
My thanks are due to you.

FITZURSE.

Father, receive it as an act
Was due from one has wronged you much,

Owes you great favors. May I not claim your pardon
For the past, since you have said that all foregone is for-
    gotten?

A'BECKET.

Pardon, I may not grant. You have my prayers
That you will ever walk in honor's footsteps.
Whate'er the toil in tracing them, they at least
Will lead to pleasure and to peace.

FITZURSE.

It shall be so. When may I wait on you?

A'BECKET.

When I return to England.

FITZURSE.

        Not before? my suit is urgent.

A'BECKET.

And my cares are many.

FITZURSE.

        None, none so great as mine—
A young heart's hopes.

A'BECKET.

Rash youth, touch not upon that chord,
Whole seas of misery are in those words!

FITZURSE.

Hast known love? Thou knowest what I do feel.
Past words, past thought, for reason holds no sway,
When love gives birth to hope!

A'BECKET.

        Love! profane not with thy lips
That holy word. 'Twas made for angels!
Mortals know it not!

FITZURSE.

What mean these words?

A'BECKET.

Impatient, wayward, and wilful from thy youth,
I hoped thou wouldst to honor grow.
Unknown to you, I nursed you in your infancy,
Watched o'er your boyhood, and when to manhood grown,
Sought to instill all generous sentiments.
You know not how I loved you!
I had a niece, the only being who did bear my blood,
Sole surviving daughter of a sister loved
Only as angels are; as bright, as good,
As beautiful as they.

       You wooed her.
Deeming you were the soul of honor, your faults
The faults of generous youth—your suit I favored.
The lady's eyes found grace was in your form,
And gave admittance in her guileless heart
To your too potent wooing.

       And I was glad,
For you I had preferred to all the glittering throng
Who wooed my niece. I looked on this
As the sheet-anchor of my declining years.
I thought that my solicitude for you
Would be rewarded by your tender care
Of her I loved so well—that she would be
Incentive unto you to every noble deed—
And thus together you would walk in honor.
But no! not so! The lurking devil showed
His cloven foot. Your angel read deceit
Upon your brow, and handed me this letter.

FITZURSE.

Ha! is it so? What fiend was't gave it her?
Give! give it me! that I may track him down!

A'BECKET.

Nay, it matters not! Thou ownest its truth
By thy hasty words—the heart that's new in crime
Betrays itself. Thou canst not wear the coronet
Had been thine. Dishonor now is seared
Upon thy brow.

FITZURSE, *touching his sword.*

To me!

A'BECKET.

Darest threaten!
The curse of Rome—

FITZURSE, *kneeling.*

Stay! stay! those dreadful words!

A'BECKET.

I do relent. I will not curse thee, tho' thou merit it.
The serpent's curse was on thee from thy birth!
Thy wrongs array thee 'gainst thy fellow-men!
Kneel then! though thou mayest sting my heel
('Tis all thou canst do), I will not bruise thy head.
    FITZURSE *kneels.*]
Kneel at this whitened sepulchre of lofty aspirations
And repent. It is the holy teaching of my Church,
Repentance never comes too late to any man.

END OF ACT IV.

ACT V.

SCENE FIRST.

Hall in Palace at Canterbury—A'Becket alone.

A'BECKET.

Land of my birth! my weal, my woe! all hail!
All hail! You yet shall be my grave! My grave?
And have I toiled through life for this?—for this
Alone?
Is this the whole of man's brief tale, the sum
Of his mortality?
Of dust we're born, like dust we're buffeted
By fortune's fickle winds, at most but fourscore years or so,
And then to dust return. Oh! sickening thought!
The loathsome grave and its vile myriads
Disgust man with his nature!
But that a higher destiny awaits
The soul immortal, here doth own at best
A slight brief tenancy, how worse than valueless
Were life, that principle which still doth live
Through all the changes of mortality—
This it must be! yea! yea! 'tis this that makes
Us struggle through the ills on us attend,
From cradled infancy to the grave of age.

LUCILLE *enters.*

Ah! my fair Lucille! What? tears in your old home?
Give not way to grief! 'tis the medicine
Of the soul, wisely administered,
By an unerring hand.

LUCILLE.

I know this well, dear Father, and its truth
I feel—but my grief is so heavy! 'Tis dreadful
Thus to have the heart's first flowers crushed
In their bloom! To have the name, I once so fondly hoped
That I should proudly bear, dishonor's synonym!
Alas! my poor, weak woman heart! I thought
I had o'ermastered thee, but thou o'ermasterest me!
Thy tendrils are too firmly fixed within my breast,
For even the direst wrongs to root it out.

A'BECKET.

True 'tis, my child, that it is dreadful;
But the hand that wounds will heal.

LUCILLE.

Oh, would it might! For since that most dread hour
When I first learnt his perfidy—Ah me,
That I should call it so!—Not even one instant
Have I been alone. My grief is everywhere—
Its melancholy notes I hear at dawn,
High o'er the lark's; the woods by day,
But with its plaintive melody are filled;
And when night comes, her hideous birds
Haunt me, where'er I wander—and then
When sleep's sweet hours draw nigh, most frightful dreams
Hover about my couch in hosts. Oh, Father!
Life is dreadful at such cost!

A'BECKET.

                Join the gay crowd,
My child. Call to memory's chambers
Blithesome thoughts; their fragrance will refresh
Your wounded spirit, and healing bring thy soul.
Time is the grand disposer of events—the hour
Of joy will come!

LUCILLE.
>> The hour of joy!

A'BECKET.
>> That was my word—
Remember, you are A'Becket's niece.

LUCILLE.
>> I will,
And be *his* child. I'll think those scenes of pleasure,—
Long since flown—sounded depths, I thought were fathomless,
And seek for rock-based charms.

A'BECKET.
'Twere well! But leave me, child!
>> One who hath wronged me much
Craves a brief interview, and comes e'en now.

LUCILLE.
Is it Fitzurse, that you'd not have me here?
Forgive him! Oh, forgive him, Father, for my sake!
Alas! that ever I should have betrayed
The Lord I loved!—but was he not unworthy?
How wretched must he be, his fair fame gone!
Spare him! oh! spare him, Father!

A'BECKET.
>> Be comforted, my child.
I will! I will! [*Kissing her.*] There! there! be comforted!
I'll leave him to himself—Let conscience be his monitor.
>> [*Exit* LUCILLE.
Alas! sweet maid, child of misfortune!
Untimely born, you cost a widow'd mother's life.
But here he comes. How can I e'er forget the past?
By him this fair field ravaged—all its flowers felled!
 Enter FITZURSE.] What would you, Sir? be brief

FITZURSE.
Then, to be brief, your pardon.

A'BECKET.
Take it, with this request,
That we may meet no more.

FITZURSE.
There is a name I fain would lisp.

A'BECKET.
Nay, name it not, it is too pure for lips
Like thine.

FITZURSE.
Oh! say, she is well!

A'BECKET.
As well as one
So deeply wronged can be. Farewell! farewell!
You have my pardon. Pray, leave me now. You call
To memory life's heaviest hours, which I would fain forget.

FITZURSE.
Oh! grant that I may labor in your cause;
Restore myself unto your favor; regain your niece's love.

A'BECKET.
Art mad?

FITZURSE.
I trust not, Father. May I not see her?

A'BECKET.
Go gaze upon the lily the whirlwind hath crushed;
You'll see her image without paining her.
Leave me, Sir! [*Stands lost in thought.*

FITZURSE, *aside.*
Alas! why had King Henry's will more weight
Than my dishonor?

Aloud.] 'Tis well! I will! Farewell!
Ruler of England, and Lord Primate, too!
If Fitzurse lives, this hour you shall rue. [*Exit.*

Enter SALISBURY.

SALISBURY.

My Lord, those Bishops did refuse to take the oath,
And straightway sailed for Normandy.

A'BECKET.

Is't so? Now comes a storm!

SALISBURY.

The young prince doth refuse
To meet you, and commands that you remain
Within the Church's verge.

A'BECKET.

From Prince Henry, this?
I had not believed it, came it not from you;
He ever was to me a son!

SALISBURY.

All those of note
Who welcomed your return, are summoned
To give bail, upon a charge of base sedition!

A'BECKET.

This from King Henry? Well, I can thunder too!
I'll issue an excommunication
Against his dearest friends: the Lords De Vere,
Clifford, and Montreuil. See this done upon the instant.

Exit SALISBURY. *Enter* ALBERT, *ushering in* REGINALD DE WARENNE *and* GERVASE DE CORNHILL.

Welcome! my noble Lords, what is your pleasure?

REGINALD.

Straight as your question is our reply:
We come as ministers of the King, demanding why

On York's Archbishop you have passed
Sentence of suspension, and against London
And Salisbury, excommunication?

A'BECKET.

We recognize no right, either in yourselves,
Or him, whose ministers ye claim to be,
My reasons to demand for this, or any other act!

REGINALD.

Is it come to this? Indeed, our Henry is but King
In name! Mean you, my Lord, to bring both fire and
    sword
Upon our afflicted land?

A'BECKET.

              My acts will answer that.

CORNHILL.

The Lords De Broc, and Nigel de Sackville,
What of them and their many friends?

A'BECKET.

But this—since by their acts they've brought
Heaven's thunder upon their heads; they must find
In other place than this, the power shall shield
Them from its fury.
            Go ask their injured tenantry
What they deserve! Nay, nay, nay, nay, not ask;
But look upon the ruined father
And his polluted child! You'll find there's many such.
Let this be my reply: the interest of my land
Is my first thought. Henceforth know, noble Lords,
That as the populace of England need a friend
To guard them from oppression,
            That friend they have in me!

REGINALD.

By this we know your feelings towards ourselves;
And nothing's left to say, but fare-you-well! [*Exeunt.*

A'BECKET.

Farewell to you! What mean these haughty nobles?
Shall their cold words, or their unmanly threats
Turn me from duty's path—even tho' the cries
Of injured innocence fell not each instant
On my ear? Oh! poor nobility, thou wronged name!
Thy nature has descended to the serf;
There! there alone, we find you, *robed in rags!*
Henry will know me now, for York, the chronicler
Of each day's pettiest acts, has fled to Baieux;
Where England's King, like the huge monarch
Of all creeping things, will, squeezing
For the pleasure of the hour, make him but one day's feast.
Fie on such men! Ho! Albert, ho! [*Enter* ALBERT.
    Bear this to Lord Salisbury instantly.
Command immediate execution of my will.
 Exit ALBERT.]
Fitzurse is dangerous. Banishment or the grave,
His choice!

Enter SALISBURY, *in haste.*

SALISBURY.
     Father, why this?

A'BECKET.

'Tis my will, my son!

SALISBURY.
     Fitzurse hath friends!

A'BECKET.

So hath A'Becket. Albert, bid my Lord of Blois
Come hither!

SALISBURY.

Father, pray hear me! He once was held
By you in honor. For no known offence has fallen
From your favor!

A'BECKET.

Men's offences are not always known
To the world!

SALISBURY.

Most true, my Lord!
But, upon what pretence
May I fulfil your order?

A'BECKET.

On what pretence?
On none! Hast lived so long with me and not know
This? But you are slothful in this business.
I must have those about me who will act
My very thoughts!

SALISBURY.

And is this my reward?

A'BECKET.

For what?

SALISBURY.

Unbounded love for you! Great sufferings,
And service from my boyhood until now!
Father, I will away, and bid him hence;
You're over anxious; this would make you
Ungenerous.

A'BECKET.

Poor boy! it is enough. I've worn you
Ever by my side, as the warrior wears his sword;
A graceful weapon, thinking the blade true steel,

But on the contest, finding it poor stuff,
Casts it away!
                I wish no meanly tempered weapon
For my use!

SALISBURY.

        Pardon, my Father, I spoke not thus
In aught save reverence. I would not you should do
What the world might scan. Men's deeds live after
    them!

A'BECKET.

True, true, you're right, my friend! They do! they do!
At least some men's do. I was too hasty.
Give me the order; mine I would have printed
In the type of justice! for what is therein clothed,
Shall until Doomsday live! Bid him to me.
  Exit SALISBURY.]   [*Enter* BLOIS.

BLOIS.

Father, news has arrived, Fitzurse has fled
The realm in rage! denouncing you and yours,
And swearing vengeance!

A'BECKET.

                Indeed! and whither?

BLOIS.

I fear to Baieux.

A'BECKET.

          To Baieux! To horse! to horse!
There's danger in his thunder! Speed to the nearest
    port!
Here, take this seal! Arrest him on the instant!
Oh! would that I were young again! I'd post myself,
But that this poor mortality is too feeble grown
To bear my soul's desires; messengers
I will dispatch to every sea-port town,

With orders to arrest him, though at cost of life!
He, of all men, I fear—for he is false!
And falsehood is more deadly in its touch
Than dagger's venomed point.
 Enter SALISBURY.]   Salisbury, what now?

SALISBURY.

Fitzurse has fled to Henry!

A'BECKET.

How know you this?

SALISBURY.

     Your trusty Hugh is here.
   Enter HUGH.

A'BECKET.

How know you this?

HUGH.

    I saw him take a fisher's boat,
And, cursing you, bid them spread all sail
And steer for France. He knew me not.
Deeming his errand hostile unto you,
My Lord—a marc the bribe—I straight despatched,
With those I knew to trust, the fastest craft
That England's waters boast, with orders to arrest him.

A'BECKET.

Well done, my son! But were your orders sealed?

HUGH.

They were. When last you went to France you gave me this,
Your seal.—[*Showing ring.*]

A'BECKET.

Well thought in thee; bring me the earliest news of him.
Farewell, my sons! Pray leave me all awhile,
I am o'erwrought to-day.   [*Exeunt.*

                         Fitzurse fied to Baieux!
Dread news for me! his voice has too much power
With our King.
                         Ye noiseless ministers,
Who do in silence watch o'er the troubled spirits
Of this world! oh, guard with me this hour!
Dread horror strikes deep into my careworn heart.
Must I give o'er—all frustrated my schemes!
All efforts vain!   Toiled have I oft
By aid of Heaven's hosts from dawn to dawn,
Ever, but brief and faint like glow-worm's glimmer
Hath proved my rest.
                         Pleasures I've tasted—
So the worldlings say—they were as dear-bought,
And when won, as trite, as galley slave's reward.
Rest! rest!—there is no rest for me!   Ambition,
Bitter, bitter are thy fruits!   Man fights for bubbles,
And but bubbles gains.
                         This is the song of all—
And yet 'tis dear, as dear as is his mistress' voice,
Heard by the lover in his midnight dreams.
Ambition! avarice! glory! love!
Ye all but golden lures, do shine and sparkle
Like night's spirits on your way, marking a course
Uncertain at the best.   Phantoms which all men chase,
Yet all elude.   A brief short hour of joy
Of life's long days, is all that I have known.

Enter LUCILLE—A'BECKET *entranced.*

Beautiful spirit! thou who leddest my heart,
'Mid heavenly harmonies, to those rich-gemmed courts
Where loving spirits meet, bring comfort, courage,
And a firm resolve from thy blessed realms to me,
That I may bear the trials of this hour, and rule,

Where others reign. Ah! my fair child, is't thou?
Did I then but dream?

LUCILLE.

Alas, you did! for I am yet but mortal.

A'BECKET.

Nay, say not so. Consider, sweet, those words
But as the air, passes unheeded by.

LUCILLE.

Why so, dear Father?
Should we then shame to own our loves?

A'BECKET.

Not so;
But rather keep them to ourselves, as gems
The miser stores, unknown to the world, to feast
Upon in solitude.
Come, child, within.
 A trump heard.] There's news,
I hear, from France—will need my care.
Attend on me
To-morrow. Good-night! good-night!

LUCILLE.

Grant me but this—forgiveness for Fitzurse,
For though I would not wed him,
I have my heart
O'ertasked, and fancy I may have wronged him.

A'BECKET.

Nay! nay! it is too true! too true!
Hereafter we will speak of this. Good-night,
Sweet child! Kind angels hover o'er thee! [*Exeunt.*

SCENE SECOND.
Hall in Baieux Palace.

Enter HENRY *and* ARCHBISHOP OF YORK.

HENRY.

My Lord Archbishop, what brings you here from York?

YORK.

Suspended by the Primate of your realm,
I could but flee to you.

HENRY.

Suspended! on what grounds?

YORK.

Grounds, my Liege? did this A'Becket e'er require
Grounds? His will! his will! my Liege—no more.

HENRY.

Are you alone the sufferer by this act?

YORK.

No! would to Heaven I were! London
And Salisbury both have fled the realm
And hasten hither. Their excommunication
Reached them also.

HENRY.

Impossible! Is't true?
How know you this?

YORK.

From their own lips I heard it.

HENRY.

What would this churlish priest? What needs he more?

YORK.

Methinks, your crown. You'll ne'er know peace, my Liege,
While this A'Becket lives.

HENRY.

Raze from the calendar the day he came to life:
Blot from my statute-book his seals. Oh, Heavens!
Am I but king in name?

Enter DE TRACY, DE MOREVILLE, *and* SIR RICHARD BRITO.

HENRY.

What news, my Lords, from England?

DE TRACY.

   My Liege, your Primate doth refuse
The Lords De Broc and Sackville to restore.

HENRY.

Indeed! Must I endure all this?
       " Are ye all cowards,
Who do eat my bread? Is there not one
Will free me from this turbulent priest?"
I will to England straight. Attend on me,
My Lords.
[*Exeunt all except* DE MOREVILLE, DE TRACY, *and* BRITO.

DE MOREVILLE.

Heard'st thou that, De Tracy?

DE TRACY.

Ay, and will act on it! Sir Hugh De Moreville,
You've no love for A'Becket?

DE MOREVILLE.

    Not I; nor you, Sir Richard.

BRITO.

Not a jot, my Lord! but I do love my King.

DE MOREVILLE.

Say rather, yourself—fall he, fall you.
We'll meet at Saltswood, and should you Fitzurse see,

Bring him with you.   His wrongs demand revenge.
Your hands—
     Here do we swear to rid him of this Priest.
              [*Exeunt.*

SCENE THIRD.

Wood near the Archbishop's Palace.

FITZURSE *enters.*

Why bend my footsteps hither, on their way to death?
When last they trod these shady woods, her voice
Fell like the music of harmonious streams,
Taking their sinuous way through flowery brakes.
Then spring was in her bloom, and my glad heart
Melodiously sang, tuned to the key
Her choristers warbled in.   Now all
In winter's icy garb is clad, and the heart's blood
Then flowed so warm and fast to every note
Of suffering—now is all curdled
By my many wrongs, and throbs but with the hope
Of keen revenge.   Come on! come on!
Though thou shouldst strike a benefactor's heart!
Come to thy work! thy longed-for work!
Be steady thou, my hand! no paltering now!
Did he not stay me on my way to France,
And force return to England?   Now I will wait on him.

Enter DE MOREVILLE.

Well met, De Moreville!   What meaneth this, old friend?
Your looks estranged, and on your brow I read
The workings of a troubled spirit.

DE MOREVILLE.
                        The poor old man!
A'Becket is doomed!

FITZURSE.
The poor old man! A'Becket doomed!
                        What of that?
Yet how so? Why should I feel for him?
                        He never felt
For me, in all my sufferings.

DE MOREVILLE.
                        What sufferings?

FITZURSE.
Sufferings! The sharp pangs of the young heart—
The heart that feels more keenly in one hour
Than age's in a year! Remember, my dear Lord,
You broached this business first to me;
Whate'er had been my thought, it knew no word—
    no act.

DE MOREVILLE.
True, true, but thou art warm! I come prepared,
And with me other of our friends, to do
The deed our King shall thank us for.
                        Wilt thou be one of us?

FITZURSE.
I will!
    ALBERT *passes by*.]   Ho! there!
                        Say to your master
The Lord Fitzurse craves his ear.
    Enter DE BROC.]   Well met, my Lord;
Come not De Tracy and Sir Richard with you?
    To DE MOREVILLE.]   They did appoint this hour.

DE MOREVILLE.

        They did, but should they fail!

FITZURSE.

They'll never fail! You're pale, De Moreville;
Dost thou fear?

DE MOREVILLE.

De Moreville fear! Lo! where they come.

Enter DE TRACY *and* SIR RICHARD.

DE TRACY.

My Lords, are ye prepared?

FITZURSE.

        We but await your coming.
Who shall demand the conference?

BRITO.

        Yourself!
You have most cause for hate, most reason
For the deed.

FITZURSE.

        True, true, I have most reason.
Revenge doth urge me on! while ye have
But your King's dark hints.

BRITO.

        Which unto me's enough.

Enter ALBERT.

ALBERT.

My Lord awaits you, Sir.

FITZURSE.

I will attend on him.

        Wait ye without.

Exeunt.]

SCENE FOURTH.
Palace at Canterbury—A'Becket's Room.

A'BECKET.

Why comes he back? I do mistrust the man!
How heavy is the air—it bodes a storm!
My children all away! would they were here!
No news from Rome to-day! nor Henry's Court!
'Tis strange! 'tis very strange! Things all seem
Out of tune—even my heart beats
In less healthful time than is its wont;
But I am old, and cannot look in age
For that which youth may boast. Lo! where he comes
With stealthy step; why not with manly tread?—
That herald of an honest heart! I will not fear
Him, nor his friends, come they in hosts!

FITZURSE, *bowing.*

      Most Holy Father;
The King——

A'BECKET.

He would have known better than to have sent
You to me! Would you deceive me? When saw you
The King? Dost thou not fear my rage?

FITZURSE.

There's terror in the whirlwind's, but I see it not;
Why, then, should I fear yours?

A'BECKET.

     Audacious youth!
What would you, Sir? Your errand, quickly—here, on
  this spot—
And instantly; though I had rather it should be
From any tongue, than thine!
    A traitor's voice so angers me!

FITZURSE.

York, London, and Salisbury, at Henry's feet
Have fallen.

A'BECKET.

There let them lie! What's that to me?
Yet speak.

FITZURSE.

The King commands they be restored to honor.

A'BECKET.

And you have borne this message! What, should I not
  comply?

FITZURSE.

His anger!

A'BECKET.

Thunder is heard.]

His anger! Hearest thou that blast?
Aside.] What bodes this wintry thunder?

FITZURSE.

I do.

A'BECKET.

On it, that Monarch's anger rides,

Whom I alone do fear.

FITZURSE.

To Henry, this?

A'BECKET.

To Henry! ay, to Henry!
I've spoken it to Heaven; why not to Henry?

FITZURSE, *aside.*

There is but this——

A'BECKET.

What sayst? Speak out! You fear
To bear my answer to this mock king! Poor slave,

I pity thee! Oh! the worst master of the slave
Is—slave!

FITZURSE.
   To me?

A'BECKET.
      Ay, Sir! To you!
Enough; leave me! I am weary of this;
You have my answer!

FITZURSE.
        A slave!

A'BECKET.
That was my word! Leave me!

FITZURSE, *aside.*
Now will I do it. No, no, once more I'll see Lucille;
There'll be an hour for this.   [*Exit.*

Enter MATILDE *and* LUCILLE.

A'BECKET.
My child! my child! my children, both!
Thus e'er come Heaven's rays in gloomiest hours!
All safe! I feared for you; so wild the storm!
My heart is softer than it was of yore;
So grows the oak with age.

MATILDE.
      You are troubled, father;
What new grief?

A'BECKET.
      One I once loved was here,
But oh! he's fallen, like the roseate cloud
That sinks away in darkness; the admiration
Of my wondering eye, begrimed and black with sin.

LUCILLE.
But others come, as roseate as was this.

A'BECKET.

This from thee, sweet child of sorrow? I had not sought
From thy fair brow, philosophy! But grief
Is a chastener to the virtuous heart,
From which, when bruised, as from the rose
When crushed, the richest perfume springs.
I must prepare for vespers. Rest ye here.
 Enter FITZURSE.]   [*Exit* A'BECKET *and* MATILDE.

LUCILLE.
     Fitzurse!

FITZURSE.
      The same.

LUCILLE.

Aside.] I must bear up. [*To* FITZURSE.] In name, but
  not in nature.
What do you here? And are they, then, your friends—
Those men with scowling brows, and lips which woo
The smiles they may not wear? for Nature
Never will be so belied, as paint
Upon the foul heart's face those charms the virtuous only
  wear!
But speak; what would you?
       I fear, no good.

FITZURSE, *kneeling.*

Earth's best gift, your love?

LUCILLE.

Arise, Sir! leave me! lest my frown shall strike
Upon thy steeled bosom, with such fanged darts,
Thy soul shall flee their power, and it shall fall
But on a lifeless corse.

FITZURSE
     Lucille!

LUCILLE.
                    That tone!
The wind thus sweetly whispers, that doth bear
The gale.   Ah, me!   Ah, me!

FITZURSE.
                    One word, and I'll no more:
Your love or uncle's life!

LUCILLE.
                    Villain!   Help! ho!

Enter A'BECKET, SALISBURY, BLOIS, *and others.*

A'BECKET.
What means this, Sir?   How came you here?
Salisbury, guard thou Lucille.

FITZURSE.
                    Recall thy word—her hand!

A'BECKET.
Never!   How dare you this?

FITZURSE.
                    This! ay, more!

A'BECKET.
Presumptuous man!   You know the past!
How dare you threaten?

        FITZURSE *lays his hand on his sword.*
                    Threaten! beware, Sir!
Lest I more than threaten!

A'BECKET.
                    Audacious youth!
The wrath of Heaven be on you!   Begone, Sir!
Leave me!   my hour has not yet come!

        FITZURSE *aside.*
But will ere night—at vespers.   They are too strong for
    me.   [*Exit.*

BLOIS.

Villain! I'll after him!

A'BECKET.

Nay, nay, my son!
There is no fear for us. The Church's shield will ward
All earthly blows; and when Heaven's falls,
It will, whate'er our heed.
        Let's on to vespers.
My daughters, come with me; there's something
Sacred in a virgin's charms, since the first birth
Of time. So sacred, he whose warrior
I am enrolled, called one *His mother*.   [*Exeunt.*

SCENE FIFTH.
Vespers—The Chapel.

Enter A'BECKET, SALISBURY, BLOIS, MATILDE, LUCILLE,
   and attendants.

BLOIS.

Close ye the portals! spare nor bolt nor bar!

A'BECKET.
        Nay, nay, my son!

BLOIS.
    Oh, Father! be advised this once!
Villany lurks around! No shrine so sacred
But it will pollute with its foul breath.

MATILDE.
    Oh, Father! hear my prayer!

LUCILLE.
    And mine! Upon my knees,
Dear Father, grant me but this? Oh, be advised!

A'BECKET.

Fear not, my children! To your love I would yield,
" But 'tis not meet that we should fortify
God's temple, like a castle."
        We need no gates,
No bulwarks, and no arms! If He wills we shall live,
We will not die—if die, 'tis but for once!
And who would live, when by his Father called
Unto that home, so rich in every joy?
Hark to the vesper hymn! How like
A voice from Heaven it comes!
        My blessings be with you!

Low music—they kneel.]

*He ascends the steps of the High Altar. Enter the five
conspirators and twelve companions.*

DE BROC.

Where is the traitor, Thomas A'Becket?
 No answer.]   Where is the Archbishop?

A'BECKET, *turning round.*

" Here am I, no traitor, but a priest,
Ready to suffer in the name of Him
Who redeemed me." But what do ye here in arms?

DE BROC.

Take off the censures from the Prelates,
Or instant death!

A'BECKET.

    Never! so help me Heaven!
Put up your swords! Who dares insult his God?
Fitzurse, stand back! I have done you many a kindness;
Touch me not! by Heaven's arm alone I'll fall,
Never by thine! Think ye that I fear you?

Kneel at this altar, which ye have so foul'd,
Lest that your souls alone may cleanse these stains,
And make atonement for this sacrilege.

FITZURSE.

Fly then! oh, fly!   My oath! my oath!

A'BECKET.
         No, never!
I am prepared to die.

DE BROC, *striking at him.*
         Fly! or you are dead!
Or else be borne, a prisoner, to the King!

FITZURSE *strikes him.*

LUCILLE.
Hold! what, thou, Fitzurse!

FITZURSE.
         There—die!

The blow glances from A'BECKET *on* LUCILLE, *who has rushed to shield him, as she exclaims—*
         Fitzurse!

FITZURSE.
What have I done?

 A'BECKET *supports her as she falls, saying:*
       Stand off!   What hast thou done?
My child! my child! earth was not dear to thee.
Thus will we unto Heaven.   [*Still supporting her.
Unto the attendants.*]
        My children, sheathe your swords,
Fitzurse, sheathe thine, and let these do the deed!
Thy mother drank my heart's life in our tender youth;
There is none left for thee.   Fair Rosamond
Had been my bride; an honored, virgin bride,

Had not thy father, Henry, our King, won her
From her truth, and steeped her in dishonor.

FITZURSE.

Fair Rosamond my mother! [*Looking at his sword.*

A'BECKET.

Alas! it is too true.

FITZURSE, *to his sword.*

      Come! do thy work!
Thou wert his gift who gave me life; that gone
With her fair fame—my unknown mother's,
Whom I have worshipped as a saint in heaven,
I sheathe thee in my heart! Her life's blood on thy blade;
With thee I wed, Lucille!
 Stabs himself and falls at LUCILLE's *feet.*]
      Now are we one! [*Dies.*

A'BECKET.

Oh! that my loved Liege, Henry, should have known
This hour! How do youth's sins track man unto the
  grave!
 Turning to Conspirators.)
He'll curse ye, Sirs, who have done this foul deed;
And cast ye to dishonor! while, with repentant ashes
On his head—bare-footed, scourges on his back—
He'll walk, and prostrate lie before the shrine
Of him who now doth fall but to be canonized;
And when his hour shall come; (but this, I charge you,
Under pain of Saint A'Becket's ire,
Ne'er to disclose till then!)
      His queen, vile Eleanor,
Inciting foes! for she will ne'er forgive his frailties!
His realm disjoined! Sons disobedient!
In rebellion, all; with none but hired menials
Near his infected couch, this mighty monarch

In vile rags shall die! No regal state, no honor, and no
 love!—
Not e'en the love of one poor heart, for him
Whose every love was lust, and love of self!—
Yet, had I lived, I would have saved him
From this last dishonor.
Come, murder, have thy way! My life fast ebbs.
To God, St. Mary, and the Saints who are
The patrons of the Church, and to St. Denis,
I do commend myself and the Church's cause.
You've done your worst!
Ye Norman Lords, here dies the Anglo-Saxons' hope;
To rise hereafter in a far Western land,
Whence like the sun, with Freedom's glorious rays,
It shall illume the Wide, Wide World!
 They kneel around.] [*He dies.*

FINIS.

CANONICUS.

CANONICUS:

A TRAGEDY, IN FIVE ACTS.

PERSONS OF THE DRAMA.

CANONICUS, Chief of the Narragansetts.
MASSASSOIT, Chief of the Mohegans.
SAMOSET, Chief of the Whampanoags.
HOBOGOMOC, Chief of the Nansetts.
WOPOWOAG, Chief.
SASACUS, Chief of the Pequods.
SAMOSACUS, Son of Canonicus.
MUNTUMO, Son of Massassoit.
MOINA, Niece of Canonicus.
NYANA, Daughter of Sasacus.
JONES, a Quaker.
CARVER BRADFORD,
WILLIAM STANDISH,
HENRY CARVER,
MARY ALDEN,
} Pilgrims.

Scene—PLYMOUTH ROCK, etc., NEIGHBORING FORESTS—A.D. 1620.

CANONICUS.

ACT I.

Scene First.

Indian Council Fire—Indians seated around it.

MASSASSOIT.

The moon pales in the west, as feeble with his year's wanderings and journeyings, the sun leaves his tent in the east. The brook's murmur is hushed, and in its face the young fawns of our tribe see their beauty decked in the diamond waters. The Ice-spirit is abroad, and the Snow-king soon will come and cast his white mantle over all. Brothers, it behooves me, old in years and in service, to see that our homes be made secure, now that Nature's war-shout is heard and that our young warriors find the bear, the elk, and the deer; while our squaws seek the eels, fish, and clams. The corn is in the husk—have it gathered!

SAMOSET.

Well spoken, Great Chief of the Mohegans; winter's whisperings I hear. Hark, a step, firm and strong. *Lay ye low.* [*They put their ears to the ground.*]

MASSASSOIT.

It is a great warrior comes. There is blood of foes fills the air! Ha! the tramp of Canonicus, chief of the Narragansetts. [CANONICUS *enters.*] Great Brother, our council fire, as our hearts, languished you away, but now its flames will brighten, as shall our spirits. Thirty tribes by their bravest sons here are met. They bring tales of great wrongs from Acanadas—creeping snakes, who have stolen our hunting-grounds and driven off our game. Stolen our corn, we away, and even broken faith after all their promises.

CANONICUS.

Is it so? Canonicus knows no fear. Canonicus has warriors. Aye, fifteen hundred braves. They have stout arms and fierce hearts. Where the Great Spirit guides, they will go to victory or death. Let us march, each with his stoutest youths. The forest saplings we shall need— withy and tough as the green tree whence came our bows. Let our arrows be of the white-oak, stony-headed, hard like our hearts to our foes; firm fixed as our hearts to our friends. They have pale-faces with them, whose winged arrows, sightless as the wind, kill ere their bow's twang is heard. In an ambush we must lay, when the camp-fire is found, and ere the break of day leave none to tell the tale. Poison waters their drink; their braves sleep like turtles in winter.

SAMOSET.

'Tis well spoken, great chief. The Whampanoags love not the pale faces. Their winged canoes, twenty moons gone, stole our bravest youths. One Samosacus, your son, would have been chief of your tribe. But he is gone!

CANONICUS.

Aye, my son, my son. Canonicus may not weep, except they be tears of blood. What now sees my dim eye on the great waters? A dancing wave! or a gull! So long have I gazed there with my heart's eyes for him, in vain, in vain,—Canonicus thinks each ripple may be his son.

MASSASSOIT.

'Tis a winged canoe; like a snow-flake it shows, then falls and fades away—anon and anon.

CANONICUS.

Ha! Moina comes. [MOINA *enters.*] Moina, my fair child! Daughter of the spray-spirit of Amoskeag. What tale hast thou for thy loved one's father's ear?

MOINA.

As the maiden handmaid of the sun sank to slumber with her lord, Moina sat by the sea-shore, far out on yon high rock, when she spied a sparkling wave or a ripple on the sea, or snow-gull's feather as she thought; when lo, a winged canoe; aye, many wings she bears, e'en like a flock of birds darkening thereabouts the air; and on its decks warriors strong, all shining in the moonbeams, coming fast toward the shore.

CANONICUS.

And what thy thought, my child?

MOINA.

Samosacus sailed in such. Samosacus may be there. Samosacus may return.

CANONICUS.

He will, my brave girl. You yet shall be his bride. Let Canonicus gaze on the sea. [*Advancing to shore.*] A dancing feather, it bounds before the winds of the rising sun. Now it nears. It has many wings, and warriors crowd its decks; 'tis the pale-faced friends of our foes. Quench these flames, and let six young braves be as the wolf pursuing the timid deer; all-seeing, yet unseen. Each and all then to their wigwams; and at dawn, at Manomet we will hear of their night's watchings, and then move on our foes, near Kennebec's fierce waters. [*Exeunt.*

[*Pilgrims' boats land.* CARVER, BRADFORD, WINSLOW, STANDISH, *and Pilgrims.*]

STANDISH.

Ha! an Indian camping-ground. Be wary, men. They may be friends. If so, 'tis well; if foes, we must meet them bravely; we must not fail. Should we, our cause is lost, our colony at an end.

CARVER.

Captain, to you, as military leader, a man of large experience, we must listen and obey. While I am the Governor chosen of our chosen few—in all 101, with forty-one men only, all loyal subjects of our Sovereign James ———. "We have undertaken for the glory of God, and advancement of the Christian faith, to plant the first colony in the northern part of Virginia, and do covenant and combine ourselves together into a civil body politic, for our better order and preservation, and by virtue hereof shall enact, constitute, and frame such just and equal laws, as shall be thought most convenient for the general good of the colony, due precaution being taken." I would counsel that we rear our standard here upon this rock, where now a hospitable fire greets us [*Fires relume*] after our five months' weary and chill voyage—a happy augury.

BRADFORD.

Be it so! And let us in grateful remembrance of kind friends, far away, give it the name of Plymouth, and invoke God's blessing on our cause.

[*They rear the standard, and all kneel around in silent prayer. The Indians* (6) *steal around, and seeing them at their devotions, retire quietly.*]

CARVER [*rising*].

Here, on this ice-clad rock, we do devote our hearts, our souls, our bodies, to God's cause; to the advancement of the Christian faith and universal freedom.

Hark, an Indian whoop! and here they come.

MASSASSOIT [*advancing*].

Welcome, pale-faces — few in number; the Indian hordes, mighty in strength and power, would be your friends.

CARVER.

Thanks, brave chieftain. We would find you friends. We come as such. We bring you medicine from the Great Spirit, and gifts of lasting good to all. For many moons upon the deep, our corn, our meat is scanty. We would have these. Beads for your wampums and trinkets we will give.

MASSASSOIT.

Thanks, Great Chief; though we need them not, yet our young braves and maidens gladden in them. Freely will we give you of what we have in store. Fierce winds are now at hand, and snow-flakes thicker than the sands of the shore are upon us. Rear your wigwams; Massassoit will send you aid, and in the meantime seek his friends. [*Indians exeunt.*

STANDISH.

He boasts of his power. Let him not seek to take advantage, for we have that here [*his gun*] shall strike such terror in their hearts, that they shall freely give all that we ask.

CARVER.

Captain, we come in the name of the Prince of Peace. Our best reliance is on the guidance of our God. Already this friendly Indian, coming as he does, shows his love. Cast not away this favor by unworthy acts.

STANDISH.

Governor, unworthy acts to me, Miles Standish, your Captain. . . . . Nay, nay; excuse a soldier, one who cannot forget his bluntness.

CARVER.

Miles Standish, you are our Captain. Your trade were best forgotten until a foe appears. I am your Governor, selected by our people. Let no testiness disturb our harmony here at the outset. Foes enough we will have. We must be true unto ourselves. Your hand, sir, here before our assembled company. We are friends.

STANDISH.

In heart and hand! The day wears, and the clouds thicken; let us haste and prepare our homes. [*Exeunt.*

Scene Second.

Indian Camping-Ground at Manomet.

CANONICUS.

Pale-faces at our wigwams' doors. Pale-faces at our Council fires. Pale-faces friends. So says Massassoit. Old chief, age dims thine eye; thy heart was ever gentle; too gentle for the chief of the great Mohegans. Canonicus sees these pale-faces, as the evil spirits who haunt our swamps at nightfall. "Will-o'-the-wisps," their song so musical, yet so fatal—the arrow may not harm them; they track our steps, tho' never so silent they be, but there is poison in their breath to the brave sons of the forest, and death in their stealthy tread. I'll none of the pale-faces—they are like these——

Samosacus, my son, speared the eel and dragged the oyster and clam from his soft bed, and bore it to their winged canoe, now twenty moons gone; and they sailed far away with him. Did they but bear him back, I would not be their foe—though never their friend. [MOINA *enters.*] Moina, my fair girl. Hast thou news? What says Massassoit?

MOINA.

He is not here! Samosacus has not come; I sought the medicine-man of our tribe, and he bids me dream six moons more of love and he will come. Samosacus, my husband.

CANONICUS.

Says he thus much? It is well. Go and dream. My heart is firm. Canonicus never faltered. Massassoit may be their friend. Canonicus will know them not. Our young braves have gone to seek the Acanadas. Canonicus would go, but there is now greater danger nearer home. [HOBOCOMOC *enters.*] Hobocomoc, you saw their camp; what of them?

HOBOCOMOC.

Men of peace, by their guise—save some few. Men of prayer by their acts—more like squaws. They build them wigwams—will prove their graves. They build them and then will go to their graves. So fast they die.

CANONICUS.

What needs we should fear. The Great Spirit watches over us. Their warriors are how many?

HOBOCOMOC.

As the stars seen at noonday!

CANONICUS.

So few! Have they food? Have they shelter?

HOBOCOMOC.

But scanty at the best—but slight for these wild storms.

CANONICUS.

Bear them corn and deer's meat in plenty. Take fifty braves; tell them Canonicus will not be their friend; but he would feed even a starving foe—that our Great Spirit teaches this.

MASSASSOIT [*enters*].

Great Chief of the Narragansetts, the pale-faces crave thy friendship!

CANONICUS.

Does the proud antlered monarch of the herd seek the lair of the wolf? Canonicus sent Samosacus, his well-beloved son, with a gift to the winged canoe, and they bore him away. Canonicus learns their wants, and sends his braves with gifts of meat and corn. Canonicus will watch over them; an offended father, but he will be their friend. They are like himself; they are flesh and blood, the Great Spirit made all; they shall not suffer for want of shelter, of food, be they not our foes. Canonicus has spoken. But hark! the shouts of our returning braves.

[CANONICUS *and* MASSASSOIT *seated on couch of skins. Indian Braves enter with trophies of Victory.*]

WOPOWOAG.

The Acanadas sleep. More in number than the suns of many years, they bite the dust. Their bones bleach the plains. Their blood colors the waters of the Kennebec, and their scalps are at thy feet, Great Chief of the Narragansetts. [*Laying down trophies.*]

CANONICUS.

Pale-faces were with them?

WOPOWOAG.

Are with them, great chief. Their iron bows are ours. They lie with our crafty foes.

CANONICUS.

You heard no tales—no further tales of gatherings in the forests—of the coming of fresh foes?

WOPOWOAG.

We have left scarce enough to bury those we met. Years must come ere they will war against the salt-waves' sons.

CANONICUS.

Were all slain?

WOPOWOAG.

All, save one, Canonicus. He called upon your name in the fight; the hatchet would have finished the winged arrow's work; but the Spirit in thy name stayed the blow. He is here.

CANONICUS.

Bring the pale-face before me! [*White man brought in.*] Pale-face, though of our foes, Canonicus revenges not himself upon the vanquished. Speak—thy tale.

JONES.

A sailor, with one Merton, we landed on these shores twenty months past. We sought for food. An Indian Chief came in a bark canoe.

CANONICUS.

My son. He lives.

JONES.

He was welcomed upon our deck. His fish and clams were well paid for; he was kindly used—a gale came up and we were driven off to sea, and steered away for England. Samosacus was the guest of lords and kings. He slept at Windsor, and was made rich in jewels and in gold. He is feted and feasted.

CANONICUS.

What of that? That gives him not back to Canonicus —that brings him not to the arms of M..ina. You speak of your king—who is he? The pale-faces tell me he wears a crown—is seated on a golden throne—has rich attendants, glittering all in gems, and warriors at command. That at every step he is surrounded by an obsequious crew, who fawn if he but smiles, faint if he frowns. Is this to be a king?

Canonicus would have none of it. We, who are kings, the proudest monarchs that rule on earth, have for our proud throne, our Great Spirit's footstool, one step alone below Him. His star-gemmed heavens our canopy—the untrammelled sons of the forests our friends, our braves. We have no fear for them, they have our love, our trust; and we have theirs.

But what more of Samosacus? You say he is feted and feasted. Can they give him more than we? All the game of the forests, of the streams, is at our feasts. The limpid waters ever sparkling, as the Great Spirit made them our drink, ever freshening and pure. Can they give him more than this? But where is Samosacus?

JONES.

He bade me say: Should I return to his native land, that on the sixth moon from this he would be with his friends—that so England's great chief had promised.

CANONICUS.

Such was my dream. So spake Syosset, our Medicine Chief—and so Moina dreams. Release your captive, braves. He is our friend from this—his home with us— a bride, fairest of our daughters, shall be the reward for the great news he bears us. Now to the Great Spirit be our thanks upraised. [*Indian ceremony, and curtain falls.*

END OF ACT I.

ACT II.

SCENE FIRST.

Indians Assembled in Council.

CANONICUS *and Braves of the Narragansetts*—SAMOSET *and Braves of the Whampanoags.*

CANONICUS.

What news, now, of these pale-faces? What more do they? Their wigwams built against the winter's blast, the red man's meat and corn their food. Is it not so?

SAMOSET [*Chief of Whampanoags*].

Brother, it is so. And still they die like the leaves from the trees.

CANONICUS.

Have they no medicine-men? Bid Syosset go to them; he the most skilled of our tribe; and, Samoset, let yours go too. I doubt he of Massassoit is already there.

SAMOSET.

Even so—and he himself has gone together with some fifty braves to render aid.

CANONICUS.

Samoset, Chief of the Whampanoags. I like not this. The pale-face weak, our friend; strong, were our foe.

SAMOSET.

We meet them at the full sun to-day. I bade them welcome—as yet, find them friends? Come with me, Great Chief of the Narragansetts.

CANONICUS.

Canonicus will not go. Canonicus has spoken. They shall not starve. He will not be their friend. Canonicus is the red man's friend. [*Exit* CANONICUS *and Braves.*

SAMOSET.

They meet at the full moon. Braves, we must be with them. [*Exeunt.*

SCENE SECOND.

Forest and Sea view.—Moonlight.

Whites march in on one side in great state. Indians same on other side.

CARVER [*advances*].

Great King of the Mohegans, Massassoit, in the depths of winter, cast upon your shores, you were our friend, and so with great Samoset of the Whampanoags. You gave us welcome, gave us shelter, gave us food. Now in the first burst of spring, when the earth is full of promise and of hope, we would enter into a league of friendship which shall bind us all more firmly together. We come to bring him word, from our Great Spirit, the Father of us all, to teach the red man our arts; arts that shall make him happy, make him rich.

We ask but peace and unity, and liberty to worship God and live after our own simple ways.

MASSASSOIT.

Great Chief of the Pale-faces, we have heard. The Great Spirit bids us give the pale-faces welcome—be his friends. They may share our hunting-grounds and our shores. The forests furnish fuel, and the clear streams purest waters.

CARVER.

Red brother, this is true, from you and many others; but there are foes. Some open and avowed, some stealthy as the wolf. Some creeping like the snake. Massassoit and Samoset we know for friends. But who else have we as such?

MASSASSOIT.

Show the sign that shall bind, and we will soon find our friends. Massassoit sets his seal to it.

CARVER [*unrolling parchment*].

Here's our bond, signed and sealed. Fix your marks, 'tis all we ask.

MASSASSOIT [*lancing his arm*].

Thus I make it—with my blood—thus with my life.

SAMOSET.

And so does Samoset! Brother chieftains—friends to the pale-faces—our great king binds us all—so let each bind his tribe. [*Many chiefs sign.*]

MASSASSOIT.

Now let this be borne to the Chief of the Peconics. He sent threats to our pale-faced friends—bid him attend us here. Summon the Great Chief of the Narragansetts; him of the strong will and the stout arm: Great Canonicus. [*Exit two Braves.*

CARVER.

Well spoken, and better done, noble friend. May this day be but as that of many suns to come; and the paleface and red man be but one. Thinkest thou Canonicus will come? Him we honor, him we would have our friend. He has nobly done.

MASSASSOIT.

A red man's tread I hear far down in the vale, but 'tis faint and faltering. Not Canonicus, I know. His step is fixed and firm; now again, from the forest it comes—'tis Peconic your foe, then our foe—like a low-born dog, a cur, he steals along. [*Chief's escort* PECONIC—*painted ashes color.*]

You of the ashen face, of the Peconics, we bid you here. We the friends of the pale-face, we bid you here, their foe. Few words may we speak. You their friend, else our foe. Such, soon the singing birds of winter were more in number than thy tribe!

PECONIC.

Great king, such thy will, such must be ours. Massassoit has the heart of all. You have my hand. [*Signs the treaty.*]

MASSASSOIT.

Where now is our brother, Great Canonicus? Ha, I hear his step coming hither, it shakes the earth! [CANONICUS *enters.*]

CANONICUS [*looking round*].

He is here!

MASSASSOIT.

It is well!

CANONICUS.

Who are these? Our friends? Friends at the feast, friends at the fight! braves, all. What do ye here? Sell yourselves to the pale-faces? What need of bonds or of your hands? The pale-face, the red man's friend; the red man never could be his foe. Room enough for all; food enough for all, while the forest gives its beasts, and their branches its birds—while the sea-shore gives its shell-fish, and its waters its fins! The Great Spirit ordains this. Who dare disobey?

MASSASSOIT.

Thy hand then to this.

CANONICUS.

The Chief of the Narragansetts has given his word—there needs no hand—though the pale-face would it. Massassoit knows it needs it not.

CARVER.

We would have some sign.

CANONICUS.

Chief of the Pale-faces: when the pale-faces first came to our shore, and would have shelter, who or what bade Canonicus build them wigwams? who or what bade Canonicus send them corn and meats? who or what bade Canonicus forget that the pale-faces stole his son? The same Spirit will teach him to be their friends until they are his people's foe—to forget his private wrongs while they are friends to his.

CARVER.

We have given. We would have some pledge, some sign.

CANONICUS.

It is here. You know me as a friend. Read me in this, when as a foe. [*Takes from an Indian a bundle of arrows, wrapped in a rattlesnake skin, and hands it to* STANDISH. *Says :*] Twenty rattles had it living—a hundred deaths was in each. My heel crushed its head—so my arrows shall hearts of foes.

CARVER.

Boasting chief, we fear you not. [BRADFORD *whispers to* STANDISH, *who fills skin with powder, privately.*]

MASSASSOIT.

Brave son, we know you well! Canonicus was ever as the sun. True as that! we would not this!

CANONICUS.

Great Father, old in years. Your words are peace; strong in arm. Your son so wills it. Peace kept, he will keep it. Canonicus has spoken!

BRADFORD [*returning skin*].

Brave chief, we return thy skin! thy gift!

CANONICUS.

The red man knows it not—'tis not so he treats his friends.

BRADFORD.

The white man's power is now in this skin.

CANONICUS [*throwing it in flames*].

To the flames then be it given. So he forgets the pale-face's wrong. [*The powder flashes and is gone.*] So fades away on the wind thy power. See, the red man's shafts are still good. [*Pointing to arrows.*] Thou hast my sign.

End of Act II.

ACT III.

Scene First.

Canonicus and Braves assembled.—Forest Scene.

CANONICUS.

Nineteen moons gone, Samosacus not returned. Faithless pale-faces. Moina's heavy heart gives Canonicus a heavy hand. Still our white brother of our wigwam bids her hope. [Moina *enters.*]

Moina, my fond child, sweeter thy voice to my heart than the song of singing birds of spring. Soft as the murmur of the evening winds fall thy steps on my ear. What is thy wish?

MOINA.

Great Chief of the Narragansetts, father to my Samosacus, Moina, thy child, asks for justice and mercy for a pale-faced sister. In my wigwam now she lies, heart-stricken, features saddened and heavy, doomed by her stern brothers; turned from their homes, her kindred, her lover; a dark mantle o'er her shoulders, darkening even her very soul, with a "scarlet letter," bright and glaring, like the sun in angry cloud.

CANONICUS.

The "Scarlet Letter!" 'Tis the badge of sin, my daughter, fearful sin; too pure thy ear to know its portent! It is the white man's "Law."

MOINA.

Nay, nay, she has no sin; a bird of love from her heart is nestling in mine. I know she has not sinned. Woman wit reads woman's heart, best reads her wrongs.

CANONICUS.

Bid her here. [*Exit* MOINA.] We will hear her tale. Canonicus never turns a deaf ear on the calls of mercy and of justice. Here she comes, graceful as the woodland's fawn. [*Enter* MARY, JONES, *and* MOINA.]

Maiden, we are thy friends. Fear not, though thy face is pale and fair, to uncover before my braves. Thy sex is thy safeguard with mine of the Narragansetts. What thy woe? What thy wish? Give me thy tale. We will hearken; we will act.

JONES.

Great Chief, may I speak? Many moons have risen and sunk since a prisoner you took me in, fed me, and gave me clothes. I went to the white man on Plymouth Rock, as they call it, and they spurned me, and cast me out for a fancied wrong; saying, I was not of their faith; though I worshipped the same God and hoped in the same Saviour's love. *Quaker born*, they loved me not, would have me not. This is their mercy then. Justice—such is it ever; but the Chief of the Narragansetts is my friend, gave me all I asked.

CANONICUS.

Gives the same to a vanquished foe. Nothing more. But what is this to the fair daughter of your race, now before us?

JONES.

She loved, and was deceived. A man in power her undoer.

CANONICUS.

'Tis as ever runs the white man's tale. Gentle maiden's all the sin, though guileless and pure; in the artful woer no offense ever found. What wouldst thou, daughter?

MARY.

My babe, my guiltless babe. They tore it from my arms, my bosom. My boy! my boy!

CANONICUS.

Dry thy tears! Cease thy cry! Thou shalt have thy babe—thy boy. And thy lover, wouldst thou him?

MARY.

He has my heart, and I honored him. Though thus wronged, I would die for him!

CANONICUS.

Go, my braves—ten in number—to the pale-faces of Plymouth Rock. White Son will be thy spokesman. Say that, though Canonicus is bound by no pledge, save the pledge binds all mankind to their fellows, that he will meet their chiefs in council ere the sun is in the west, that Canonicus will be with them; 'tis to save their honor, it may be their lives. Canonicus has secret news for them.

Moina, prepare; thou and thy white sister go with us!

[*To* JONES]. White Son. Nineteen moons have passed. Samosacus is not here!

JONES.

One moon more must full and fade ere we question their faith. Our King never broke his word.

CANONICUS.

He has my honor. He never will! Now, hasten unto Plymouth Rock. As thy shadows we will be with thee.
[*Exeunt all.*

SCENE SECOND.
Plymouth Rock.
CARVER, STANDISH, JONES, *and other Indian Braves enter.*

JONES.

Governor, Canonicus, the Great Chief, sent us here to give you word he would soon be with you with great news, to save your honor, perhaps your lives.

CARVER.

Then at last he will wait on us. It is, friends, a mighty portent; it foreshadows the glory of the English rule. Thus tribe after tribe sue for peace with us; all were our friends save this proud Chief, and now even he craves a hearing.

STANDISH.

The terror of our arms has filled the land! Said I not, it would?

CARVER.

The justice of our rule, trust me, has done far more.

BRADFORD.

A smiling Providence, through all our ills, hath ever shone its face. There be our praise, our thanks.

Enter CANONICUS and Braves.

CARVER.

Welcome, Great Chief, to our Council Fire. Take the pipe of peace and feast with us.

CANONICUS.

Canonicus needs no pipe of peace. He never made or threatened war against the pale-face of the east. He comes as he came, through his braves, when first you trod his shores, and the Ice King raged and ravaged the land, to give you counsel, to give you care. There was danger to you then in the snow-cloud; there is fiercer danger in the storm-cloud of wrath that rides through the summer sky. Canonicus comes as a friend to give you warning. He bids you be just, be merciful. You may yet seek for both in a foe, and seek in vain—Canonicus' voice unheeded.

CARVER.

What mean you, great Chief; there is terror in your words, yet your actions are those of friendship?

CANONICUS.

Then hearken to my words, as the brave does the distant tramp. Low and close thine ear to my speech. You say you came in love to our shores. You fled from a land of fierce laws to a land of love; where free, you might worship your Great Spirit after your own form, and live in "union" and in "brotherly love."

BRADFORD.

Even so.

CANONICUS.

You tell us, this teaches to love thy neighbor as thyself. Is it not so?

CARVER.

It is.

CANONICUS.

To do unto others as you would be done by.

CARVER.

Most truly so.

CANONICUS.

Know you this man, a pale-face brother?

STANDISH.

It is the fellow Jones!

CANONICUS.

Great warrior, thy speech is unworthy thy rank. That sneer sits not well on thy manly lip. Greatness ne'er insults a fallen foe. Still, as thou wouldst seem to name some, what may be his offense?

STANDISH.

He is a Quaker!

CANONICUS.

Then not thy brother? Not thy neighbor? A Quaker, backed as thou art by armed warriors, thou lookest on him as though he were the mountain wolf; thine eye glares as the panther's on the deer he would devour. Such thy faith, canst thou ask the red man to be thy friend? Dost thou not teach him to be wary and watch thee as a foe? The lesson you teach we will learn, but may the Great Spirit of our Fathers keep us from its practice. Such thine, and you must fall. Canonicus bids you beware.

Moina, my fair child, where is thy friend? [MOINA *brings in* MARY.] Know ye this fair flower? the lily of the vale were not more beautiful.

CARVER.

Aye, Chief! She has broken our law.

CANONICUS.

Your law! Your law! Be it so. Was there no partner in her guilt? as you choose to name it. Where is he whom we would name her lover, her husband, her chief? Where is the pledge of their loves? Your Great Spirit gave the fair mother her babe; do you, but men, paleface men, dare take from her what He gives? Thou hast taught us He says, Vengeance is mine. If ye have no love, no mercy for the girl, give her her child, that it may shield ye from His wrath.

WILLIAMS.

Canonicus speaks well, Governor; I counsel that we restore the child.

[MARY *casts herself at his feet*, MOINA *with her.*]

MARY.

Give me my child, my darling babe!

CANONICUS.

Arise, Moina; never kneel to the pale-faces. I and mine are lords here. Peace, daughter, you shall yet have your child. Canonicus holds the pale-faces in his hand. They will not he should clutch it in anger.

Great Chief, you say she sinned. She sinned not alone; where is he she loved so well; loved as only woman loves?

STANDISH.

Off to the chase.

CANONICUS.

Pale-face, thou knowest it is not so. Canonicus reads thy thoughts—thou art too brave in spirit to lie. Truth is stamped upon thy brow, and frowns down upon thy lip as thou speakest. Bring him here, or Canonicus leaves this Council, with that untold, upon which hang your lives and those of all belonging to you. If you will not learn mercy, you shall learn justice, though Savage of the Forest, as you name me, be thy teacher. What means this mantle, this glaring litter on the gloomy ground? Is this mercy? Is this justice? Her undoer has no brand, is not driven forth from his home—has not been robbed of all dearer than life. Yet he is strong, and can bear the forest life. She is frail and feeble as a flower; and but for Moina, had failed long ago. Remember the lightning's flash rifts the oak, but the lily is unharmed.

[*A young man enters.* MARY *shrieks, and faints.* HENRY, my loved Lord!]

CANONICUS.

It is he! Young chief, what means this wrong?

HENRY.

It is not my doing.

CANONICUS.

Nay, nay; thy voice is faint. She is thy love, thy wife. Thou must take her to thy home with thy babe. Thy people's life is the price.

HENRY CARVER.

My father wills it not.

CANONICUS.

In this, thou hast no father upon earth. Hearken to Him who speaks from heaven. [*Thunders.*]

GOVERNOR CARVER.

Nay, nay; we will it not. She has sinned!

STANDISH.

Aye, fearfully sinned!

BRADFORD.

Shamefully sinned!

ROGER WILLIAMS.

Yet, been sinned against!

CANONICUS.

Well sayst thou, man of peace and of prayer! But be it as you say, Great Chiefs—even so—take this knife. [*He whispers to* MARY: "*Fear not.*" *He supports* MARY *with his left arm and holds the knife in his right.*] Now let him who has not sinned strike her! even to the heart! Canonicus holds the fawn for the slaughter!

HENRY CARVER.

My Mary; my dearest Mary. [*He springs forward, but is held by his father and* MILES STANDISH.]

CANONICUS.

Not one to strike! Not one fit to rid the earth of this foul blot! Not one of all, preachers and prayers as ye are—without sin.

Tear off this badge of shame, not to her, but to you men of years and of sin. If ever the Narragansett should war against ye, this after your manner shall be the ensign they will rear. Your hearts shall quail at its sight, thinking of your injustice, of the lesson taught you by the unlettered red man of the forest. Young chief, take thy bride. She is too pure, I know; but thou hast her love. Moina, she is faint—bring her babe; its feeble cry will reach the mother's heart and awake to life. [*Resign-ing* MARY *to him.*] Thy arm, young chief. [*Giving babe.*] Thy marriage bond! Her life is saved. Thy wounded honor healed. Great Chiefs, reverse your laws. Canonicus is obeyed—thy nation's saved. A thousand braves await your call. Thy foe, fierce Weston, is on the march against you, but his days are numbered. Canonicus has spoken. Mercy and justice have triumphed! Holy Father, Thy blessing! Kneel, my children!

ROGER WILLIAMS.

Take her, Henry! take him, Mary! ye are one!

END OF ACT III.

ACT IV.

A beautiful Scene near Canonicus' Wigwam—Moina sitting at the foot of a Waterfall.

MOINA.

Twenty moons have come and gone. Spring's flowers have bloomed and are buried. Summer's fruits are come again, and the autumn nuts shall fall, but Moina has no Samosacus to gather them for her. The fair daughter of the pale-face chief has her brave and her babe. Canonicus sought and found both for her, and gave her life. Why may he not bring Samosacus to me, who have loved now so long. The leaves rustle through the winds, murmuring through the tall grass, where the deer loves to feed. Now they come to quench their thirst, while Moina tells her tale to the music of the waters—they heed her not, fear her not, for she loves them as she loves all the Great Spirit made. The sun is high, and the heat fierce. Soon our young braves will seek these waves. Moina must away ere they come to spear the fish. Too long have I tarried, but my love fills all time. Moina knows no nights, no days; all are as one, Samosacus not returned. The young braves are here, and with them the young Muntumo, the proud, painted warrior of the Mohegans, who seeks my love, but it is gone!

[*Indians enter, and* MOINA *retiring, turns back.*]

MUNTUMO.

Why wilt thou away, fair Moina? We came to stalk the deer and spear the fish. Had we known 'twould fright thee away, it had not been so. Some other time we had sought them. What does the fair child of Canonicus by the murmuring stream? Would she the voice of love? Muntumo will sing her songs; tell her tales of the past; tales of the fight. Will wear twenty scalps in his girdle, and hunt the deer alone for her, if she will but sit in his wigwam and be his bride. 'Tis the son of Massassoit, Great Chief of the Mohegans, has come to sue for her love.

MOINA.

Moina hears it all. Moina is heavy-hearted. Brave Muntumo, Moina has no love to give. It is gone.

MUNTUMO.

Moina has no love! Yet she lingers by the banks of the Merrimac. She watches its clear, limpid waters come welling up from the rifled rock, go dashing down the hillsides, stealing under the dark, old forests; receiving into its transparent bosom each little brooklet, rivulet, and river that hastens from miles around to pay tribute to its conquering way, until at last a broad, sparkling, beautiful sheet of water pours its flowing wealth into old ocean's briny depths! And has Moina no ear for love, hearkening to all this?

MOINA.

Moina has love for all; not for one, proud, brave, Muntumo. Moina would light the fire in a wigwam of her own tribe.

MUNTUMO.

Light but mine, our tribes shall be one. Canonicus has no son.

MOINA.

Thou sayest not true. He has a son. Samosacus is away; now many moons gone. Samosacus will be here.

MUNTUMO.

Not Samosacus of thy tender years, of thy love. I read thy tale. Pale-face arts have spoiled thy boy. Moina loves an Indian brave, not the petted puppet of the pale-faces' show.

MOINA.

Moina loves but once. These waters have but one song, ceaseless, undying. So Moina. Thy love I prize, 'tis of one brave and good. Saugus the Chieftain, too, hath borne his gay present of murmuring sea-shells. It could not tempt my girlish heart. So I sighed his love away. Muntumo has my honor, he is great and good. Muntumo has my thanks, shall have my prayers.

MUNTUMO.

Samosacus will not come, fairest daughter of the forest —he dallies far away.

MOINA.

Nay, nay; not so. He will come. Hark that tramp; 'tis the tread of friends—Canonicus, Father, and ha, Samosacus! [*Enter* CANONICUS, SAMOSACUS, *and braves.*]
Samosacus! Samosacus! [*Sinks in his arms.*]

SAMOSACUS.

My Moina!

MOINA.

Great Father, this thy act. Thy heart of love works for all. Samosacus, thou dost not speak.

SAMOSACUS.

Thy beauty strikes me dumb, fair Moina, like the sun on awakening sight; thy brightness dazzles all. I see, I feel but thee. Father, thou hast cared her well.

MOINA.

But how came you here, and Moina not at the shore?

SAMOSACUS.

Many miles from this lies the winged canoe bore me home from England's shore; but of this, by and by, and the wonders met my sight. Samosacus has journeyed long his Moina to greet. Samosacus is weary.

MOINA.

Quaff these limpid waters, they will give thee strength. An Indian brave, thou knowest their power. Kneel with me at its fount—the lily shall be thy cup, gemmed all with dew! [MOINA *kneels, and gives water out of lily leaf.*]

CANONICUS.

Braves, add your voices by this bright water so glittering in the sun, making gay music in our homes; gladdening the hearts of all at return of Samosacus, our son.

MOINA.

Our pale-face brother spake the truth.

SAMOSACUS.

Thy pale-face brother, where is he? I knew this not.

CANONICUS.

A brave took him prisoner in the fight and brought him home. He spake of thee; called thy name, and we welcomed him. He told us of thy fate, after many moons of mourning, and said thou wouldst be here twenty moons gone, and he was true. The pale-faces call him "Quaker," call him Jones, and will have none of him.

SAMOSACUS.

Jones his name? He was my friend. There is another waits without. Roger Williams he is called; chosen servant of the Great Spirit. Driven out by the pale-faces, he journeyed south; our paths crossed. I spake in his tongue. He told me his tale. I brought him hither.

CANONICUS.

Thou hast done well! Persecution marks their steps—these Plymouth men! [*Enter* ROGER WILLIAMS, *with staff and bundle.*] Bid him hither!

Pale-face brother, thou hast my heart; here art welcome. Last moon thou wert in favor; what thy fault with thy pale-faced friends? What thy teaching, that thou art driven out?

WILLIAMS.

Great Chief of the Narragansetts, thou more than friend to my people, since thou hast dared to tell them wherein they erred; thou wilt not think the less of me when I say, my fault, my only fault is in that I preached, "that the civil magistrate should restrain crime, but never control opinion. Should punish guilt, but never violate the freedom of the soul." For this they have banished me from my home, from my friends; but the Great Spirit, who governs all, will guide me to another, where I shall gather together warm, true hearts, and found a State where the purest principles of civil and religious liberty shall prevail.

CANONICUS.

Well hast thou spoken. Well hast thou done, thou faithful minister of the Great Spirit. My braves shall guide thee to a home worthy of thy pure, rare nature; an island girded by the sea, long the sacred resting-place of the warriors of our tribe, who, great in battle, council, or in chase, at last yielded to the grim foe of all. This shall be yours, and those you may appoint, a recompense for your earnest action in Mary Carver's cause; as thou hast won it by service to her, the fairest of her fair race; so thine shall be the land from which shall spring the loveliest of their sex throughout this clime, nursed by the balmy breezes from the south.

Samosacus, our son, though just returned, shall be your escort, with fifty braves. Be wary, for the Pequods, starlike strong, are on their march. I and my braves with their great chiefs, Pokanoket and Massassoit, will haste to meet them.

SAMOSACUS.

Moina weeps. Samosacus just returned.

MOINA.

Truly Moina weeps, but they are tears of joy, that honor, such as this, should be for him.

CANONICUS.

Thy blessing on us ere we go, Father of the pale-face and the red man of the wood.

[*Indian war-dance; then they kneel, and* ROGER WILLIAMS *blesses them.*]

END OF ACT IV.

ACT V.

SCENE FIRST.

Indian Camp—Waterfall—Hour, Morning.

MOINA.

The bird of morn sweetly sang as Moina's eyes were kissed by the early light of dawn, and told her heart Samosacus would be home with many scalps of foes in his belt, and many prisoners in his train. He must have met the great chiefs of the Narragansetts and Mohegans with their white brothers as they call them, and joined them in battle against the Pequods and the tribe of Winslow. Ere he comes, I will deck me by the side of these glassy waters, for my bridal is at hand. [*She decks herself.*] The beauties of lovely maidens have been reflected in this glassy mirror. Mighty warriors have washed the paint from their faces, and the blood from their hands in its bright waters, and deeds of nobleness, of daring, of outrage have been planned on its brink. [MUNTUMO *enters.*]

Ha, Muntumo of the Mohegans, what wouldst thou in

the chamber of Moina? From day's early hours our tribe have given this spot to its daughters as their own. But thou art faint, and there is blood. What means this, brave Muntumo?

MUNTUMO.

Love for thee, fair Moina! The white man, Carver's son, used thy name with foul speech, detracted from thy fair fame.

MOINA.

He whose bride Moina saved? He whose babe, our Great Father Canonicus sought and found? He whose honor he healed, and whose sick heart he cured? He used Moina's name?

MUNTUMO.

He did, and though faint and weary with the long fever, I told him 'twas false. He struck me; I felled him to the earth with the little strength I had left, and he stabbed me to the heart. Snake with the forked-tongue, I left him stunned by my blow, and tottered here to die, that the warrior might sleep where his heart only lived; near her, the child of him he so honored, great Canonicus.

MOINA.

Nay, nay; thou shalt not die. Taste these waters [*gives drink from stream*], they are strong, full of life, and will give it thee. Thou shalt not die. Moina bathes thy brow. Thou art pale. [*She supports his head.*] Thou art faint. My childhood's friend, my childhood's lover, though I would it not. Art thou gone? there is no breath —there is no sigh!

[*She stoops to list his breathing.* SAMOSACUS *and his braves enter.*]

SAMOSACUS.

Ha, Moina! and my foe! Moina, dost thou well?

MOINA.

Muntumo is no more. The Great Father has called him home. Faint, he fell at my feet, and I bore him water. I bathed his brow. What meanest thou, Samosacus? Thou turnest away with a storm-cloud on thy face.

SAMOSACUS.

Thou bathest his brow! Thou kissedst his lips! In death your spirits mingled. Samosacus mourns thee gone. No Moina has he now.

MOINA.

Cruel brave, this is not so. Monia kissed him not! Moina had been thy foe, had she done but as she did. Thou hadst not loved her had she failed in the office and the hour when maidens shine most lovely—by the side of suffering, by the side of death! Thou sayest no Moina hast thou now. It is well. Jealous grown—wronging in thought—no Samosacus have I now. I loved him of my youth. Samosacus left my side—his pure nature changed. The pale-faces have turned his heart.

SAMOSACUS.

And the fate of war turned his eye, when lovely as the dawn of day, graceful as the swaying lily—the daughter of Sasacus, the Sachem of the Pequods—fairest Nyana, gave beauty to the scene.

MOINA.

Ha! is it so? May Samosacus be blessed. May Nyana be happy. There is no Moina more. Young braves bear Muntumo to the foot of the falling waters. He was great, he was good; his burial shall be in honor. Hark! a tramp is on the air. 'Tis Canonicus comes! [CANONICUS *enters.*] Dear father, at my feet, death-wounded by the poisoned fang of the double-tongued pale-face—whose fair bride, whose babe, whose honor you saved—fell Muntumo, with the tale that the pale-face slurred her name—the name of her who was their friend—Moina, thy child. He said that it was false, and the pale-face pierced his heart. His last words were of you. You must render him the last of earth's honors!

CANONICUS.

Brave Muntumo, art thou gone? Thy heart knew no guile; thy hand no blood, save blood of foe. Thy honor thou hast left to me, and thou shalt be avenged! Bear him near to me, young braves. May his life be your guide. Let thy maidens, Moina, join—rare the service we will show him.

Scene Second.

Plymouth Rock—A Council, Indians and Whites.

SAMOSACUS.

Great Governor of Plymouth Rock, now two years absent from my land, but just returned son of the Narragansett, I joined your warriors with our braves against the Pequods, and in my train have many prisoners. Some are maidens young and beautiful. Some are chieftains brave and strong; and one, the Sachem of the Pequods, brave Sasacus, fell beneath my blow. It was my part to claim his life had I listed. His daughter, the beautiful Nyana, smiled through her tears, and turned my arm. As my captive I claim his life, and to his native lands would give him back.

CARVER.

Never so! Our foes increase—such folly shown toward them.

STANDISH.

His death would best serve our cause.

SAMOSACUS.

Warrior, but for my father's alms, my father's counsel, my father's care, Plymouth Rock ere now had been no more. Think of that! His blood would do ye no good. His hate is all gone. His friendship may be yours. I ask but my rights!

CANONICUS.

Valiant son! I have heard thy speech. It is well. The pale-faces have no rights here. As our friends, we will guard their lives and their honors. [*To Whites.*] Ye seek the life of Sasacus. This may not be. He is a brave sachem, kind and merciful, and has a right to the same usage he gives others.

CARVER.

Canonicus, it is our law! He dies.

CANONICUS.

Your law! Is this the law your Great Spirit teaches? Far other lesson our Great Spirit has taught us!

CARVER.

Your Great Spirit! How know you that there is a Great Spirit?

CANONICUS.

See you these footprints in the sand? How know you that men have been here?

I look aloft into the boundless sky. I gaze upon the fathomless deep. I wonder at the countless beauties of earth, and at His thunder shrink with awe, and yet you ask how I know that there is a Great Spirit? There is—there is, I know. I feel there is, for does He not dwell within this narrow heart and yet fill all the world? Braves, bear Sasacus in honor to his home! My son, be he your charge. [*Exeunt.*

STANDISH.

Not so, brave chief. He must die. [*To a soldier.*] Go, watch their steps.

CANONICUS.

Governor of the pale-faces! say you so?

CARVER.

'Tis our law!

CANONICUS.

This is your law? What is your law, then, for foul murder done?

CARVER.

Death is its penalty!

CANONICUS.

When the pale-face does the deed?

CARVER.

Even so!

CANONICUS.

Bring hither young Carver, the governor's son. [HENRY CARVER *enters.*] Young man, there is blood upon thy hand! The blood of my friend, the brave Muntumo! I gave you your bride, your babe, and more—your honor. You sought to stain the honor of my child—the peerless Moina. Muntumo knew 'twas false. He spake it. You struck him. He felled you to the earth, and you stabbed him to the heart—he died! Was this well done? Pale-faces, thy law is death. Give me this boy's life for my friend's. 'Tis thy law!

CARVER.

Nay, nay. He did but avenge a blow!

CANONICUS.

Muntumo sought to avenge my fond child's good name, thus illy spoken! Whose offense was the greatest? The blow given her fame would last for life. That Muntumo gave thy son (though in answer to his first rendered) was washed out by gentle words and felt no more. Again will the Chief of the Narragansetts ask ye justice. He will pardon thy son for the sake of his bride—his babe—but he saves brave Sasacus, and sends him in safety home.

STANDISH.

Nay, nay; this shall not be. Rather a pale-face should die than this fierce chief be free. [*To* CARVER *aside.*] There is old Jones. He is no use now. Let him be hung instead. Besides, he merits it for other faults. This will appease the chiefs, and Sasacus be ours!

CARVER.

Be it so. Bring him disguised in Henry's clothes.

[*Exit* STANDISH *with guards and* HENRY.

CANONICUS [*aside*].

These wily chiefs! They say the red man is untrue, is like the snake! That they cannot trust him. They have one law for themselves, and one for the red man. Yet this is justice? Had Muntumo slain his son, Muntumo must have died. His son slew Muntumo—but only a son of the forest. 'Twas no offence; he is free; he lives.
[STANDISH *enters with guard, and old* JONES *disguised and blindfolded*].

STANDISH.

Canonicus, thy victim is here, bound hand and foot.

The rope is around his neck. A tree is near. Take him, and we take Sasacus.

CANONICUS [*looking around*].

[*Aside.*] A fraud! I see it all, and I will prove it such! [*Going up to culprit, he whispers,* "Fear not." *Aloud:*] Pale-face, thou must die. Thy minutes are numbered! Yet thy Medicine Father is not here! [*Turning to* CARVER.] Pale-face Chief, let one be sought. He must die in the faith you teach. Hast thou no mercy for thy son, thy eldest child, thy only son? We red men know not the cord. The arrow bears our death warrant.

[*To* CARVER.] Take you this rope; there grows a tree of a thousand summers. I would thy son have a forest monarch for his monument!

CARVER.

I cannot hang my son! Even your hard heart would ask not this!

CANONICUS.

Thou needst not hang him. Only adjust the rope; the rest were easily done.

CARVER [*doing it*].

This, I will do!

CANONICUS.

And this will I. [*Severing the rope.*] Pale-faces, I scorn ye. Ye who would add fraud to murder. Braves, this is our old friend Jones, in this man's son's attire. I knew it from the first. Bear the brave old man to his home with us. Death shall be the portion of all who disturb him—now blind and deaf, and without speech in his age and sufferings. Miles Standish, this is not good. Thy race is doomed. Such acts, then death. Pale-faced Chief, thy honor is gone. Canonicus would scorn to crush such a reptile with his foot. [*Exits.*] Sasacus is in safety now.

STANDISH.

Governor, this Canonicus will ruin our settlement. He befriends all our foes. We must be rid of him!

CARVER.

Yes, the sooner the better. Make Massassoit his foe.

BRADFORD.

'Twere easily done. Muntumo, his child, died with them. Send peace and presents, too, to the Pequod Chief. Sasacus will be won over.

CARVER.

Miles Standish, see it be done forthwith. [*Exeunt.*

SCENE THIRD.

Canonicus' Encampment—Early dawn.

[SAMOSACUS *and* NYANA *enter.*]

SAMOSACUS.

Fair Nyana of the Pequods. Thy father is saved! Brave Sasacus has his home, and his nation is at peace. Thou hast heard my tales of my warlike tribe, and of the bright waterfall makes music in my home—it is here. Thou hast heard my vows of love. Your father gives thee me. Wilt thou not be my bride, the light of my home? I will away to the chase and bear the game. I will to the wars and bear the trophies, if thou wilt but be my love!

NYANA.

With a heart like thy fountain, brimful of trusting love. A welcome bright ever in her eye, and warm in her cheek. Nyana will watch thy return to thy home. Nyana saw Samosacus, as she saw the sun of life. Nyana will be thine.

SAMOSACUS.

Come, then, to my wigwam, where the choicest skins are spread for thy rest, and ere the day is done I will proclaim thee my bride. [*Exeunt.*

[MOINA *enters decked as for a bridal, and sees them as they pass out.*]

MOINA.

The mellow dawn has broken once more. The bird of morn is on the wing; the loved music of the waters gently kisses Moina's cheek. Soon they will kiss her cheek, her wan, pale cheek; as she pillows it there, bathe her flushed, her burning brow. Cool this raging thirst at her heart, and bear her spirit pure like their spirit pure to the hunting-grounds of the blest. Samosacus loves Nyana. She is fair. Samosacus is dead to Moina; for Moina Muntumo died. Moina now dies for him! I will climb the gray rock, where the eagle only soars. Bathed in a flood of golden sunlight, upon its summit I will stand for the last time.

[*She ascends the rock—morning rays beaming upon her.*]

May the Great Spirit bless their bridal. May their race be without number. May their glories glow forever, and outshine all other tribes.

CANONICUS [*enters*].

Moina! My Moina! Canonicus heard thy voice—the only music to his heart! Where art thou now? Where art thou now? Ha! braves, see her there! Quick, seek the path, unseen by her, and bear her hither. She raves. She is mad—her voice hushed. My hearth-fire is quenched. Canonicus knows no home. Dear Moina, my child retrace thy steps; hasten hither.

MOINA.

Like the eagle in his swoop, Moina seeks the pool. His victim, the golden fish—hers, her wounded, broken spirit. Canonicus, Father, Moina comes!

[*She springs into the air and falls in the pool.* CANONICUS *rushes forward and drags her out almost lifeless.*]

CANONICUS.

My wounded deer. My gentle fawn. Pet dovelet of my warrior heart—thy hand is warm, thy brow is flushed, but thy tongue is mute, thine eye is dimmed. Here is no breath—thy bosom is still! Thou knowest no sorrow now. Thou art blessed. Faint grows my strength, firm grow my foes and many. My own house is not true. Samosacus won thy heart, for a fancy cast it away. He seeks a stranger bride for his home. He will find his death, his ruin! Ha, what means this warrior shout. There is a foe in our camp. Young braves, meet them there. Canonicus guards his child!

[MASSASSOIT *and warriors enter.*]

MASSASSOIT.

Muntumo, thy shade is here! Canonicus, thou slewest my son. So says my pale-face brother!

CANONICUS.

So saying—he lies!

MASSASSOIT.

Great Chief, you loved him not. He sought the fair Moina. He died at her feet. Samosacus was his foe.

CANONICUS.

A father's bleeding heart hearkens to every tale. Massassoit knows well the Narragansett Chief. He knows he cannot lie. 'Twas the foe of our race slew thy son.

MASSASSOIT.

'Twas ever so. You hated the pale-faces. They were good to the Mohegans! They gave long life to Massassoit, and he loved them. They are his friends. They bade him here find his son, his heir!

CANONICUS.

So you may. You away, I bore him here; laid in state until you should come. My braves are by his side—they guard his couch. Moina, my fair child, whom he loved, is with the flowers; the lilies were her death-couch—than their perfume, her breath more rare. Muntumo's last minutes she soothed. His last words were to her. Her last were for him. Braves, bring here Muntumo. One grave shall be for both. Old chieftain! my child! [*Displaying* MOINA.] Massassoit, rest you here. A double burial claims your honor.

[*The Indian funeral wail is heard.* SAMOSACUS *and braves enter, bearing* MUNTUMO, *and lay him on a hillock near* MOINA.]

SAMOSACUS.

Brave Muntumo; fair and dear Moina. Ye now are one. [*To* MUNTUMO]. I would my arrow had pierced thy heart. My anger slew my love. I took a strange bride, found her false; already has she fled my side!

CANONICUS.

Samosacus, thou seest thy deed! Was this worthy thee, worthy my son? Shall Canonicus call thee his? Blood-

stained art thou in his sight. Thou canst not paint so
thick but he will see thy face all gory with Moina's blood.
Thy strange bride will prove thee false; thy strength will
fail thee 'neath her arts, and thy name be writ in water.
Thou'lt leave no heir; thy race is done, and in thee dies
out mine. Hark, a warrior shout comes on the wind.
Stand firm, my braves, all. If 'tis foes, use thy arms; if
friends, they will share our griefs. Canonicus guards
Moina!

[*Enter band of Pequods and whites, guided by* NYANA, *who
retires unseen by Narragansetts.*]

STANDISH.

Canonicus, thou art our prisoner! Our avowed, our
open foe. You have sent aid to Roger Williams. You
have given him lands; have given a home!

CANONICUS.

Is this all?

STANDISH.

Strong in braves, you wounded our honor by subverting our laws. You taught evil lessons to our young. You
freed our foes. For thy reward, behold our friends [*the
Pequods*]. Dost thou not fear? [*Thunder heard.*]

CANONICUS.

Hear'st thou that voice? Aye, thou tremblest at the
sound. Canonicus knows its portent. In the voice of
truth, which he has ever worshipped, ever followed, Canonicus has no fear! Canonicus bows to no man!

SASACUS [*enters*].

Samosacus, where is my child? Young Manomet was
her brave! She had given him her love, and you stole
her from his side.

SAMOSACUS.

Great Sachem! Thou knowest 'tis false. My prisoners you were taken. I saved your life. Her beauty touched my heart. You bade me, could I win her love, to keep her my bride! I wooed her. I won her, as I thought. My Moina I feared was fickle, was false. She is dead. She is no more; and Nyana is gone!

NYANA [*springing forward*].

Not so, Narragansett—fierce foe of my house. Nyana is here, and Manomet has her love.

SAMOSACUS.

Nyana, art thou false? Thou stolest my heart; thou stolest my life. My vanquished foes, I gave ye freedom. Treacherous friends, I know ye no more.

SASACUS.

Lying youth! thy hunts are numbered. Pequod warriors, seize them all. Braves of pale-face chief, join your strength. Old wrongs shall here be settled. Massassoit, they slew thy son. Muntumo's spirit walks the gloomy shades.

CANONICUS.

This in my camp! Treacherous foes! This at the peaceful burial of our best beloved. Put up your arms and leave my home. Canonicus ever honored yours. You have no wrongs. He has many, but he calls them not from their graves. He buried them long ago, and would not wake them into life. Ha! an arrow in the air; what new foe in our camp? Braves, to arms. We'll meet them there, though more in numbers; we yet are strong. Massassoit, send thy braves; we ever fought side by side. [*Exit.*

MASSASSOIT.

Massassoit has grown old. He cannot hear. The pale-faces are his friends. Braves, join them; be firm and fixed. Muntumo is no more. Ye know his fate.

[*Clash of arms and battle-shouts. The Pequods, Mohegans, and whites against the Narragansetts; at length* SAMOSACUS *falls; while* CANONICUS *endeavors to shield him, young* CARVER *stealthily wounds* CANONICUS.]

CANONICUS.

Ha! is it thou? Where was thy bride? where was thy babe, thy honor, to stay, thy sword has drunk the life-blood of him who once loved thee well. [*To* MASSASSOIT.] Old chief, my voice is faint, and though thy ear grows deaf, and thine eye is dim, Canonicus bids thee beware of false friends. Many moons now gone, we were at peace, but the winged canoes touched our shores. 'Twas an ill-omened bird! The pale-faces sought our lands. They poisoned our waters, they wasted our forests, they slew our game, destroyed our shell-fish. Our corn has failed, and we are poor. Canonicus told you this. Canonicus loved them not, but still he was their friend. 'Tis for this they have stolen his life. 'Twas little worth; his Moina with the flowers. His Samosacus a stricken oak. His race is done, and so with thine aged chief. Muntumo no more. Bear him here by my side; lay Samosacus at our feet, with Moina, darling, in my arms; last of his race, Canonicus dies. But accursed be this spot to the pale-faces. The richest of a thousand hills, with the sweetest waters in the land, they shall weep themselves out for Moina in bitter tears, which evermore shall parch the thirsty lip.

A thousand deer have fattened here and fallen. Not a blade shall it ever bear, for the false pale-faces' use. My curse is on it.

Canonicus, the last of the Narragansetts, is avenged!
[*He swoons and dies, and curtain falls to slow music.*]

FINIS.

POEMS.

POEMS.

TO DEAR MOTHER.
1833.

Why will ye all be so gloomy and sad
When smiling, our dear mother earth looks so glad,
When the fish in the lake swims gaily on,
And the lark sings on high, her matin song.

Leave sorrow for winter—'tis the spring-time of year,
When earth's scenes are gay—their heavens are clear,
When the twittering birds teach their young how to fly,
And on their light pinions, soar off to the sky.

Then teach ye your young, by gladness and cheer,
Their lot, if a sad one, with light heart to bear,
That on virtue's wings they may safely fly,
And reach, at the last, a haven on high.

That as fall's piercing winds and winter's chill blasts
Fall sharp on the ear, while we know they'll not last,
And as spring-time will come and flowers will bloom,
So pleasures and griefs are man's lot to the tomb.

ON MOTHER'S DEATH.
September, 1873.

There's rare joy on high, aye, rich joy in Heaven,
Bright angels have welcom'd, their sister was given,

To cheer this dark earth, with its sins and its fears;
Lo! she's wreathed in smiles, while we're bathed in tears.

Mourn not, fond Sisters, Father, proud in love, kneel,
And bowing thy head, in humility feel,
Though 'reft from us here, the flower was given,
Blooms with rare beauty in the bright courts of Heaven.

So lovely by nature, so gentle to all,
Why marvel, the angels our dear Mother call,
Her voice of the spheres—ever gracious her ways;
She shone, upon earth, one of Heaven's bright rays.

Weep not, fond Father, but on those she loved
Lavish the tenderness you ever showed
To our dear mother, thy youth's chosen bride,
The cherished of Heaven, thy jewel, thy pride.

There's rare joy on high, aye, rich joy in Heaven,
Bright angels have welcom'd, their sister was given
To cheer this dark world, with its sins and its cares,
The wreath of her smiles gems penitent tears.

THE SHEPHERD.
1833.

The Shepherd, low reclining on the sward,
Surrounded by his gentle, bleating sheep,
Doth seem the very prince of indolence,
But nature's wonders never let him sleep.

Unto the mind of him, thus simple, seems
The world affords far many a happier dream

Than crowded paves, or converse of the great,
Which on man's brow but seldom casts a beam.

E'en then its rays do blister where they touch,
And in the whirl which rages in his brain,
He learns that honors are not easily won,
That riches, power, pride, are all in vain,
That none but waters from Heaven's pure springs flow,
Bring to the toiling spirit a healthful glow.

LINCOLN'S ACT OF FREEDOM.

His own, his presence—His an eagle eye,
Far peering into futurity.
His mind a marvel, as the age he lived.
His virtues great. His wondrous worth unknown.
Perfection rare, childlike simplicity,
He reared a fame, so monumental
That it fills the world : high over all
Save him, our Washington—his only Peer.
One wrung from despot, freedom for our land.
One burst the bonds of slavery bound her sons,
And with prophetic ken, made them the equals of all
    fellow-men.
The act which wrought it, was by Heaven inspired;
The sages of the land in council met,
Faltered in giving to the world, the words
Bore to oppressed, the boon of Freedom.
With eye uplifted, clasped hands, he prayed:
"Teach me, my God, what best to do"—is heard—
"Sages, I give it to the world"—he said,
Rebellion prostrate laid—
        Slavery forever dead.

LINCOLN.
April, 1865.

Around his bier they stand,
  Our Hero's chosen troop,
The leaders of his famous band:
  A sad, a silent group.

No whitened tent-sail now
  Flaps in the swelling gale,
But round his death-couch bow
  Hearts never known to quail.

The proudest trophy man
  Can ever boast on earth,
The highest honors ever worn
  Born of an earthly birth,—

All, all are his—his own,
  Earth hath no more to give;
He is marching on to his life-won home,
  Where only the "chosen" live.

HAMILTON.
1833.

Nevis, thou lonely sea-girt island, where
The softest music is old ocean's roar,
And the loud thunder, with sharp lightning's glare
In awful grandeur, fills the quaking air.
He was indeed thy child, firm as thy rock
Amidst the raging sea, fixed was his soul
In noblest principles—his nature even
As the elements are, pure as high heaven.

Their spirit dwelt in him; when but boy
He stretched his longing eyes out on the main,
And sought his home in a far distant land,
Where 'gainst oppression's justly hated hand,
Noble and free in nature, like their own wilds,
Brooking no tyrant's sway ; fore'er to strive,
No toil—all danger dare—no death, to die,
Men warred for their homes, and liberty.
He yet but boy, saw what it was they sought,
He told them where to seek—and taught them well,
That ne'er a smile was won by suppliant knee;
But that the heart must brave and noble be,
Upon whose brow the light of liberty
Brightly would shine. That vestal flame,
Unguarded, it would flicker, fade and fall,
And Tyrants' chains, ignoble souls enthrall.
His thoughts were like to the resistless wind,
Unseen, yet felt, wherever they were turned.
Like earth's great source of light, burnt with fierce flame,
Love in his bosom, for his country's fame.
Mighty his mind—his memory never failed,
A storehouse, where in seemly order laid
Rare gems, collected from all wealthiest mines,
Rich fruits of learning, from each age, each clime.
In nature, as the ermine pure, ever the same
To the world's mendicants, or the sons of fame.
When he was "taken off" his mourners were the world!
All nations wept. His murderer's name was told
Where'er he walked. The air, burden'd with his blood,
Speeding, to all, that dread deed did unfold.
A fugitive from his outraged land,
Seared on his brow the assassin's brand,
Burr's stealthy step was heard on great France's floor,
"Admit him," said Prince Talleyrand—but say—

"Hamilton is my household god"—
"His image guards my door." *
Abashed, Burr skulked away, never to cross it more.

NAPOLEON AND HAMILTON.

The mightiest men whom this great age hath known,
Were born in islands, 'neath an ardent sun;
In their rare natures—his pure essence burn'd.
Scarce in their teens when life had but begun,
One, sought by arms and war to rule the world;
The other, by great knowledge yet untold.
One lived the fear and terror of mankind,
And dying, left a bloody fame behind.
The other lived honored and loved by all,
Wept by the great and good, his early fall.
Both born in islands, girded by the deep;
Both roused the world from its lethargic sleep.
Napoleon lies in Les Invalides' tomb,
While bloody memories mourn his fearful doom;
Hamilton lives where praises never cease,
Crowned with the laurels of the arts of Peace.

SONNET.

"Contentment."   October, 1839.

As through the sky, thy even ways thou takest,
Lighted, but not impeded by the stars,

---

* When the great minister of France, Prince Talleyrand, took leave of Hamilton at his residence, "The Grange," Hamilton took from his mantel his miniature, and presented it to the Prince as his parting gift. This he so highly prized, that he ever kept it suspended over the mantel of his hall in his palace in Paris. Burr called there, but at this warning, skulked away, abashed.

So may I, most sweet moon, my journey make
'Mid men, whose wondrous deeds shall shine afar.
Unheeded and unenvied, may my days
Be on the bosom of contentment borne;
Not free from care, for then my "Maker's" ways
Might be forgot, and I indeed forlorn.
But as the lark doth usher in the day,
With thankful carols urging on mankind,
So might I know the true poetic lay
That cheereth on, and leaveth care behind:
Then would I deem that I was truly blest,
Then might I say, contentment I possessed.

SONNET.
To Grief.

Is there no haven from thy sea, oh grief?
Boundless and ceaseless as old ocean's roar
Are thy assaults? Is there no shore
Whereon my bark may lie and find relief
From thy fierce storms? Oh! beams there not above
Some Pilot Star whereon the eye in Faith
Fixed firmly, as voice within now saith,
May see a parent, find forbearing love?
Oh, thou Great Being—let Thy saving grace
Heal the deep wounds my anguished bosom wears,
And give me strength Thy gracious will to bear.
Teach me, O Lord, that I a worthy face
Present—that thus those seem so hard to me
May be accepted as kind gifts from Thee.

TO MY AUNT, SUSAN A. GIBBES.
1837.

Lady, I know not which the most to praise,
Thy gentle manners and thy winning ways,
Or the bright jewels which adorn the scene,
Where, with a mother's love, thou reignest supreme.

Rome's noble matron to Campania's dame,
Asking her jewels bright, felt pride, not shame,
To say she owned no baubles, rich and rare,
But that her sons were the sole gems she'd wear.

So may'st thou to the brow of beauty turn,
That brow, where deep-read sages yet may learn,
Or on the damask cheek where blooms the rose
Which fadeth only, when with jest it glows.

As on the face, seraphic of thy child,
Which doth in innocence long hours beguile,
That lovely prattler, in her face we see
What most we've learnt to love, dear Aunt, in thee.

All I have felt, and feel, I may not tell;
'Tis not the sparkling stream, you know full well,
Hideth the rarest gems, tho' oft I slothful seem,
Dear Aunt, for thee, do my heart's jewels gleam.

THE BUCKWHEAT FLOWER.

From thy sweet blossom doth the buzzing bee
    Draw purest of its much-loved honied juice,
The autumn air is fragrant made by thee;
    The yeoman revels in thy promised use.

Earth in her waning years now blooms again
  In the pure beauty of her spring-time days.
Ye vestal flowers, from your verdant fanes
  Win from departing warblers new-born lays.

Ye now call forth more music from the mill,
  Its wonted song else hush'd, as o'er the rocks
Returned to nature's ways, the sparkling rill
  Sweet measure marks for the gamboling flocks.

Nor doth thy usefulness here cease; to thee
  The cheek of beauty owes its rosy hue,
The arm of youth less powerful would be;
  That all things have their use, thou teachest is true.

TO MARY L——.

On hearing of her approaching nuptials, induced to wed against her will.

STAY, stay these horrid nuptials;
  Unholy rites are these;
Only where heart to heart is joined,
  Does wedlock Heaven please.

Oh! lady, thou art sad and pale!
  Fear harbors not with love,
Think you, if now thy heart doth quail,
  Thy future 'll joyous prove?

No, no, trust not that cheating hope,
  Look on thy heart and see,
If other image dearer still,
  Is cherished not by thee.

Oh! lady, life thou knowest not yet,
    Tho' sorrow thou hast known;
For where's the bird, whose wings unwet,
    O'er whom no cloud hath flown?

Many an hour shall take its hue
    From that in which thou'rt wed;
Oh, better than these heartless rites
    Be with the early dead.

As thou shalt take thy earthly lord,
    So shall thy journey be,
On love's wings, soaring far and wide,
    Serene be land and sea.

On storm-cloud borne, but ills and strife
    Shall mark thy darkened way,
'Tis but a gleam now lights thy life:
    One gleam, ere darksome day.

Wealth, vain and glittering wealth,
    Pomp and its heartless suite
May shine, may fawn, and win thy eye;
    Can it thy heart's need meet?

Much is there now to gild the scene,
    Words kind, smiles sweet, hopes bright,
But change's finger 'll touch, I ween,
    The fairest earthly sight.

Words kind, diamonds 'midst sands shall shine,
    Smiles sweet, as rays shall be,
To miners who've for ages delved
    Far underneath the sea.

Hopes bright thou'lt chase, but chase in vain,
　　As phantom barks they'll be;
Nought but phosphoric lights they'll shine
　　About thy gloomy sea.

Stay, stay these horrid nuptials,
　　There's one who loves thee well,
And who, I know, dwells in thy heart,
　　Let this thought break the spell.

For spell it is, full well I know,
　　Thy fancy is too bright,
To robe that dark-eyed man as once
　　Thou saidst, thy love was dight.

Then stay these horrid nuptials,
　　Thou must not wed to-night,
'Twere better bear his bitter curse,
　　Than live to loathe his sight.

Stay, stay these horrid nuptials,
　　They may not, must not be;
No, no, I'd rather hear that bell
　　Sound its last knell for thee.

Then would sweet flowers deck thy grave,
　　The rosemary there would bloom,
And friends would mourn a spirit blest,
　　When weeping o'er thy tomb.

Not sigh for hours, in grief spun out,
　　E'en to a sightless thread,
But cheered, that thou to "home" hadst flown,
　　Home of the happy dead.

TO MISS ——, A FAIR PIANIST.
Augusta Gibbes, 1841.

Too weak are words thy worth to tell,
    Thy wondrous arts to please.
Oh! nothing e'er can break the spell
    Or cause these throbs to cease.

Lovely Euterpe, with thy lyre
    Thou'st kindled into flame
What was till then a smouldering fire,
    A sense without a name.

'Twas rapture sweet—a fond desire,
    To linger about thee;
Oh, with the art, my soul inspire,
    Can make you think of me.

TO ——

Why wilt thou be more cruel than the moon,
    So long thy charms concealing from my view,
'Tis but one night since she on earth did shine,
    While weeks have flown since I gazed on you.

Is it that brighter after storms, the scene
    That thus from view, thy beauties thou dost veil?
Oh, pity thy poor slave, angelic queen,
    Lest his weak sight before thy brightness fail.

Like wearied mariner on storm-tossed sea,
    I've stretched in vain my longing gaze,
I know no star in all the world but thee
    Can guide me safely on life-chequer'd ways.

'Tis said, with love thou dost regard mankind,
  I ask not that on me thou thus wilt look;
All that I beg is, I a smile may find
  To soothe a heart, long absence cannot brook.

TO MISS I. L.
October, 1840.

Ah! should we meet, ten cycles hence,
  How many the tale we'll have to tell,
Of parted joys, of blasted hopes,
  Methinks such meeting were not well.

Yes, yes, we'll meet, and gazing here
  Upon the unchanged scene,
Learn what old Time has done for us
  While we have wanderers been.

If parted we are doomed to rove,
  The flowers of life be thine;
If thorns shall strew my path, may Heaven
  On your blest spirit shine.

THE BROOK.

'Tis the laugh of the mountain,
  The song of the vale,
The life of the fountain,
  It sweetens the gale.

It cheers the bold brigand
  To high, daring deeds;

It alone cools his thirst
    When wounded, he bleeds.

'Tis the harp for love's story
    When told to the maid,
His life and his glory
    In the valley's green shade.

'Tis the wood's infant murmur,
    When the warring storm's gone,
E'er to sweet shades of summer
    Feathered warblers have flown.

'Tis the type of man's life,
    In purity born,
Hastening on in wild strife
    Its bosom is torn.

Till the valley is reached,
    Where with breath of rose
'Mid the music of heaven
    To ocean it flows.

That ocean where mingle
    The sad and the gay;
The sluggish, the sparkling,
    All take the same way;

To where the bright sunbeam
    Shines out upon all,
And they dance in His sight,
    Or shrink from His call.

ON THE CONSECRATION OF "ST. ANN'S" CHURCH, MORRISIANA.

ERECTED BY GOUVERNEUR MORRIS, 1840.

'Twas rightly done, dear friend,
   Thy work proclaims thy praise,
Louder than loudest terms could speak,
   Men are judged by their ways.

Here, 'neath this simple dome,
   Lies she who best loved thee;
It is the holiest, meetest tomb
   O'er a mother reared could be.

While by her side, he lies,
   Thy Father, son of Fame,
Who in his country's heart will dwell
   While Freedom has a name.

Long may you live to hear
   The heavenly anthems rise,
And when in green old age you part,
   Soar on them to the skies.

THE HUDSON RIVER.
1838.

The sea hath had man's worship, and the sun,
The moon which doth 'mid myriad beauties run
Her even course, and the bright beaming stars
Unchanged amid Nature's raging wars,

Have each in due turn, and most justly won
Praise from admiring poets, old and young,
In lute-like madrigals.
                    But who hath sung
Thy beauties, noble stream? These woods have rung
With thy just praises, only nature wild
Could sound them meetly—thou the rarest child
Of this famed wilderness. Naught but the mind
Thy loveliness can scan. Language would bind
Into too narrow span all that it sees,
Thy myriad tongues thy praise—no words could please.

SONNET.

FAITH.   OCTOBER, 1839.

LIKE to the loveliest hour of the day,
The early dawn, which chaseth night away,
With all its darkling beauties, "Faith," art thou.
The wounded spirit unto thee doth bow,
As doth the fevered brain to sweet dawn's glow,
After deep anguish; though we feel it flows,
Like the pure spring, to which the galled hart flees,
Bearing death's arrows, or sane as bracing breeze.
Thou art the North Star of the world's wanderers,
The sweet moon worshipped by the longing lover
Who thinketh on her not as of earth's dreams,
But as the mirror where loved image beams.
Blest are all those who when Life's labor's o'er,
In faith have known what Heaven hath in store.

SONNET.

To the Oak. October, 1839.

The year is in the seer and yellow leaf,
Now winter's whistlers coursing through the air,
The spring's sweet warblers wont the heart to cheer
From verdant boughs of joyous homes bereave.
Thus spring on spring, winter's chill footsteps chase,
Thus leaf on leaf, the fall demands of thee
Oh, dauntless oak.
     Give me thy heart, oh tree!
That I may be the marvel of my race,
Never borne down by blasts or mighty gales,
But nourished by adversity and strife
In mighty deeds, that other mortals pale,
Each season of my days may be more rife.
Thus do I worship thee, thou brave old oak,
That I may learn, like thee, to bear Time's yoke.

TO ———.
1840.

As on a star, the gentle boy
 In mute astonishment doth gaze,
Unequal in that hour of joy,
 The beauties of the sky to praise;
So, lady, on thy lovely face
 In silent wonder gaze I, e'er
Too weak to read the matchless grace,
 Soul of such lineaments doth wear.

TO ELIZABETH.
October, 1842.

They say like life is young Love's dream,
    Now sunshine and now storm,
That shades will flit o'er brightest scene,
    That man's to sadness born.

Oh, dearest, let us prove through life
    That sorrow brings a balm,
That fiercest gale which bears us on
    Is herald of the calm.

In love as life, God sends the test,
    Shall try, if true we are
Proved faithful, we shall sure be blest,
    Let this trust be our star.

TO ELIZABETH.
April, 1843.

Oh, tell me, love, I pray thee,
    What care afflicts you now?
My once loved voice shall cheer thee,
    And chase it from thy brow.

Upon the fragrant myrtle
    The owlets never rest,
But 'mid its boughs the turtle
    E'er builds her downy nest.

The golden cloud o'erhangs thee,
    Drops not a single tear,

Thy beauty doth upbraid thee
  That you this frown wilt wear.

But where's the bird whose wing's unwet,
  O'er whom no cloud hath flown?
One smile, dear love, and I'll forget
  Thy brow this shade hath known.

TO ELIZABETH.

FAIREST and best of the daughters of earth,
Whose smile has for me than Peri more worth—
Thou who dost shine as the stars do in Heaven,
Gilding the shades that steal o'er her at even.

TRUE LOVE.

HE long had loved her dearly,
  Yet never dared to woo;
Her smile he thought betoken'd
  "This lip is not for you."

He loved her as the infant loves
  The starry hosts on high;
But in his wonder never dared
  To breathe for her a sigh.

Their voices mingled oft in song—
  Their hands had often met;
Yet still he never dared to speak,
  Lest she'd say, "Go, forget!"

A rose she wore upon her breast,
    She placed on his, one eve—
He told his love, her hand she gave;
    That gift did never grieve.

TO A VERY DEAR FRIEND.

As the pure moon on misty eve doth shine
    With veiled loveliness, so glows the light
Of a chaste soul, through that dark eye of thine.
    Though I love day, I better love such night.
As on thy face, a heaven of beauty,
    Through which the graces of thy spirit shine,
I gaze in wonderment, I kneel in duty
    Bound, and worship at the glorious outer shrine—
Too deep, too pure—the inner such as I
    Should bow to; for, oh! too much light
Would blind my grovelling sight, and with a sigh
    I'd turn, by self rebuked, to endless night.
Oh! may I kneeling, at the outer shrine,
    Hope that the inner's office may be mine.

TO ———.

Nay, why so downcast? Must thy radiant eye
And laughing lip of rose's tint be fixed
As thus you listless gaze on vacancy?
Oh! for one smile, away the shade to chase
Traced on thy face of beauty. Friends must part,
E'en death may mark the bounds—then wherefore weep—
The barb, we know, sank deep in thy fond heart,
But 'tis Love's part to hold in its own depths

The swelling waters. Then let smiles once more
Light on those left—the true, the tried, the fond—
Who rise bright beacons on Life's rugged shore,
Shall in all trials prove the stoutest bonds,
In hours of joy, thy joys the brighter make,
In hours of grief, from grief its sting shall take.

TO CARE OPPRESSING A DEAR FRIEND.

Away, oh, care! why wilt thou haunt him thus?
He has not wronged thee, or in thought or deed.
Thou canst not say he warred against Man's peace;
This fierce assault 'gainst his, I pray thee cease—
Has he been cruel or unkind to thine?
Has he not raised the fallen from the earth?
Has he not shared his trifle with the poor,
Or 'gainst the hungry has he closed his door?
Has he not borne the taunts and scoffs of men?
Has he not suffered from sharp tooth of want?
Has he been loved by her who was his pride?
That thus thou'st sworn, for aye, to be his bride;
Or is it, that thou fondly lovest him so,
With his life's course thou ceaselessly wilt flow?

TO E. S. N.
1842.

I know not whereto I should liken thee,
For thou, of all things, fairest art to me.
Thy beauties, as the moon's creation fills,
My world of thought with fairer yet instils;

The stars are fleeting, ever changing hosts.
No fleeting charms, my dearest, dost thou boast;
Earth's flowers, sweet with perfume fill the air;
Yet is thy breath a myriad times more rare.
The air with countless melodies abounds,
And yet with naught like thy sweet voice resounds.
The sparkling waves the brightest gems do wear,
And yet are dim to the bright orbs you bear.
Oh! thou art to me, as to earth, the sun,
Causing all griefs my joyous heart to shun.

TO THE ATHEIST.

We are born; we laugh, we weep,
   We live, love, hate, then die;
'Tis the song of all! Wherefore so?
   Who can tell? Alas, not I!

ANSWER.

Turn, erring mortal, to thy Lord,
   Thy Maker, and thy Master's will;
Study and ponder well His Word,
   Thou'lt find the place thou hast to fill.

THE OLD MAN TO HIS WIFE.
At the Village Church, 1840.

Here saw I thee in bloom of youth,
   In flush of beauty and of pride;
Here heard I first the Word of Truth;
   Here gazed I on my bride.

Here have we e'er from year to year
    Our Sabbaths passed together;
Nor have we ever wanted cheer,
    Though stormy was life's weather.

When sad, I've seen thy cheerful smile,
    Thy merry voice e'er heard,
And they my gloomiest hours beguiled,
    As his mate's song, the bird.

Yes, ever when I've bowed beneath
    The heavy blows of care,
You taught me that our God bequeathes
    The lot 'tis best to bear.

TO E. S. N.

Lady, take thou this token,
    From one who fain would tell,
Ere his poor heart be broken,
    The pains it knows too well.

Thy smile could chase this gloom
    O'ershadows now my brow,
And with the flow'rets' bloom,
    Cause this pale cheek to glow.

TO E. S. N.

As I dreamt in my boyhood of beauty,
    To my fancy so bright shone each charm,
That I believed it to be my first duty
    Ne'er to love, lest the trait'ress might harm.

But alas, though with sentinel care
    I watched my poor heart, it would love.
I can guard it no longer—oh, share
    In my joy, and my own "true love" prove.

TO A CLOUD.

Why mov'st thou so majestically proud,
Robed in the panoply of night, oh cloud?
Like a fam'd monarch to earth's gifts most bright,
Thy beauties owing, lovely in thy might.

A royal diadem of myriad stars
Rests on thy beaming brow in nature's wars,
Most stern, yet still most beautiful art thou;
Though evanescent as yon glorious bow.

Art thou thus e'er in purple deck'd, laced
With golden light, never with dark robes graced?
Dost thou demand the heart shall but adore;
Comest thou ne'er to fill the mind with awe?

Shall not the deep-drawn tears with which thou greetest
The parched earth, nursing its flowery sweets,
Soften man's heart, while thro' life's varied vale,
Down time's swift troubled stream he onward sails?

'Tis not unmoved. Thy voice is thunder,
Opposed with lightning-flash, asunder
All is rent, when on thy beauteous course,
Thou'rt borne, on winds resistless horsed.

While on thy beauties lingering I look,
Thought will take wings, and jealous cannot brook
That fleeting vapors should obey His will,
While I, His image, am rebellious still.

TO E.

Love thee? Do I love the stars,
   Those winged handmaids of the moon,
Whose sweeping train they bear afar
   Their seeming labor, dearest boon.

Love thee? Do I love the sky
   Robed in cerulean blue,
Upon whose bosom gleams on high
   The sun with golden hue.

Love thee? Do I love the world?
   No; therefore, dearest, I love thee;
As Heaven makes this fair earth dull,
   So others all thou mak'st to me.

Then ask me not if thou art dear,
   How else couldst thou e'er be?
All things of earth, the good, the fair,
   Bid me, love, think of thee.

The roseate dawn, the noontide gale,
   The silver lakes, the sparkling stream,
The lofty mount, the verdant vale
   With but thy beauties ever gleam.

Oh, say, must I count all as vain?
  Those hopes prove fleeting dreams?
No, thou art true as yonder fane,
  The court where life's ray beams.

"ST. PAUL'S."
October, 18—.

Methought I stood within that ancient fane,
Where in my infancy I had learn'd to name
The name of God: where a sweet babe I saw,
Timing his steps, with his, who totter'd on
In second childishness, companion dearest
Of that gray-haired man, once sage-like
In his intellect. 'Tw s beautiful, to see
How they did tend each other, the dying oak
Sheltering the delicate flower, which with fragrance sweet
In turn nursed it. The time-wearied lion,
Making his lair couch for the innocent lamb.
He was a reverend, just, and upright man,
And when "Old Age" did bear him to his grave,
"Goodness and he filled up one monument."
Those days were numbered by the spring flowers' bloom.
Memory still wandering back, I hear the voice
Of her, who in her spring sank into lifeless earth,
A flow'ret nipped, when in full fragrance,
By thy ruthless blast, consumption. She was the partner
Of a good man's age, the jewel of his soul, the sun
That kept the currents warm which flowed
Time-chilled athrough his veins.
                      Here had I heard
The funeral dirge, swelling with solemn cadence
On the car; here had I seen dust unto dust

Returned, and wept aloud over loved parent's bier;
What wonder, if sad thoughts should then arise,
Though on me they were smiling from the skies.
Soon like the brooklet which from mount doth run,
My memory's melancholy strain was changed
To song harmonious, for I saw the sun
Struggling to free him from the misty bonds
Which the chill morn had round him hung,
And through the vaulted dome the dawn's soft light
Murkily steal, and round the chancel kneeling,
Fair woman and strong man, young babes,
And infants innocent, one nestled close,
Even at the altar's base, and smiling in its mother's face,
Seemèd to say: This is my proper resting-place.
'Twas a sweet thing to see, how fearless 'mid the crowd
That babe could be, smiling with cherub's glee.
A bride and bridegroom at the altar knelt,
And to the bishop's solemn utterance gave
Heartfelt response: then all united in an earnest prayer
That they might fitly wear their promises.
They both were young, each after their nature beautiful;
The rosy morn, ushering in young day,
A gentle dovelet, taking the same way.

TO MRS. GEORGE L. SCHUYLER.
October, 1841.

Poets have sung the praises of sweet streams,
  Their lucid waters and o'ershadowing groves;
  Rich flowery banks where the fond lover roves,
When on their bosoms slumber Luna's beams,

Lisping dear names, harmonious with their song,
Ceaseless, yet varying with fair nature's call;
Yet none have given to the ear the fall
Of waters, singing on their way, the throng
Of changeful beauties, the rapt sense arrest;
The heavenly harmonies, the pure mind fills,
When with your touch, you sound the tinkling rill—
The sweetest music ever heard confest,
Slow stealing o'er smooth rocks, lading the air
With soul-subduing strains, alas! too rare.

TO ———.

So young! so fair! so sweetly sad!
   Thy way of life 'twere strange to tell.
These of thy days should be most glad,
   And yet this sorrow may be well.
Tell me thy tale, I ween of love,
   Of earliest hopes crushed in their bloom,
Of shadows cast o'er thy bright dreams,
   'Tis thus, fair daughter, to the tomb!

TO AN EVER GAY FRIEND.

What sound is that I hear on high,
Speeding its way athrough the sky?
'Tis the thunder's bolt, roaring aloud,
Bounding on in the fiery cloud.
Who hath made that bolt so strong,
With the lightning fierce which urges it on?
He, who made thee, poor mortal man,
He hath made this, and a louder can.

Beware in what course you hurry on,
Soon will your earthly days be gone;
He who hath made the thunder loud,
He also made the lowering cloud;
He, who hath made the form of life,
Stirreth up the elements' strife;
He who hath made all nature fair,
He alone need not death—beware.

TO E. S. N.

Lady, let not fancy roam,
　In those dark and gloomy lands,
Where like vapors from the tomb,
　Sorrow round thee wreathes her bands.

Once thy brow was cloudless, lady,
　And thy smile was sweet and gay,
Brightly beamed thy eye like fairies,
　Joyous as a spring-time's day.

Cheer, sweet mourner, let not grief,
　Like the canker in the bud,
Make thy spring of life so brief,
　Drown thy young heart in its flood.

FAIR WOMAN'S SMILES.

How blest is he for whom the sigh
　Of gentle woman oft is breathed;
Around whose image every thought
　Forever is most fondly wreathed.

For whom affection's tear doth flow,
   Or brightest smile doth sweetly beam,
And in the hour of joy or woe
   To her the spirit of her dream.

And yet how sad it is that she
   So fondly prizes, oft's deceived,
That from the hand should bid it flee,
   The blow most wounds is oft received.

TO A BROOK.

WHY should I not be as the graceful deer,
Heedless of time, exempt from every care?
Light as the air, which bears aloft the cloud,
Pure as the stream, of its reflection proud;
My song as free as is the morning airs,
Singing 'mid tree-tops, where the bird but dares
To soar? As clear, as steady, and as bright,
My way through life as gorgeous stars of night,
Chasing away, with beaming smiles, the gloom
Which haunts each child of sin unto the tomb.
Untrammell'd as the winds, my way shall be
Not man dependent. Such are never free.
No, let me live in nature like to thee,
Thou pearly element—no fear to flee.

THE MINSTREL.
1842.

A LADY fair from her lattice light,
   Gazed on the silver sea
Where the moonbeams played when earth was dight
   In its midnight panoply.

While thus she stood, the sound was heard,
    Of a minstrel sweetly playing
His harp seem'd striving to clothe in words
    What her spirit to heaven was saying.

To sadness soon he changed his strain,
    One sigh by her was given,
He never touched that chord again,
    Their spirits met in heaven.

WRITTEN IN A VOLUME

(Poems of Rogers, Campbell, Montgomery, Lamb, and Kirk White) presented to a friend.

Flowers sweet and fair will early fade and fall;
Fondest pleasures on the light heart pall;
From these pure pages then to thee shall spring
Enduring comforts. Each doth in turn bring
Chaplets meet for the gallant warrior's brow.
Each teaches whence ne'er-fading glories flow.
Of "Memory," one the fond remembrance tells;
On sweets of "Hope," the other sweetly dwells.
In heaven-born anthems "He of Zion" sings.
And to the scene, Lamb fairest flow'rets brings;
While thus the glittering galaxy doth close,
With verse, we feel from gentlest nature flows.
Here ever may the craving spirit find
The purest truths have flow'd from mortal mind.

ON WEIR'S PAINTING, WEST POINT,
In Chapel, 1840.

Happy is he whose faultless hand can trace
The graceful form, the much-endeared face;
Thrice happy he, and oh, how honored too,
Whose works so nobly teach as thine here do,
The soldier's road to proudest glory lies
In warring ever to his Maker's praise;
That bloodless may religion's fight be fought,
Though fierce the strife, they'll win the prize that's sought.
"War's" banner, furlèd, lies beneath his feet;
No clang of arms, no peal the ear doth greet,
But hopeful, smiling "peace," with laurel wreath,
Points to the realm whose warriors know not death;
Much to thy honor, Weir, this gift redounds :
Rich in itself, richer for truths here found.

ON THE PAINTING IN CHANCEL OF WEST POINT CHAPEL.
By Weir, 1840.

Ye youthful sons of war, whose steadfast gaze
Is fixed on glory's star—here learn the way
To highest honors ye can ever wear;
Fadeless as eternity, ye will rear
Proud monuments, if so ye shall but live
True warriors. Your highest ambition give,
Not to the conflict on the battle-field.
"Peace" calls on ye a bloodless sword to wield
In her high cause; a host Religion leads;
Join ye her ranks—true glory's in her deeds;

Promotion's sure beneath her banner,
Preferment to the highest posts of honor,
Where peace and love, contentment e'er shall be,
Are her rewards.   This Weir is taught by thee.

TO ELIZABETH.
1841.

Oh, tell me, must this hour of joy
   Be linked with hours of gloom;
One gold, the rest all steelen rings;
   The chain shall be my doom?

From on thy breast a jewel rare
   Gleams on my wondering sight;
Oh, might I wear that jewel rich,
   Life's links would all be bright.

Oh, shine thou like that diamond pure,
   Hanging on my life's chain,
And thou wilt gild its steelen links,
   And I not love in vain.

TO ELIZABETH.

Oh, what's the art you use to make
   The hours so swiftly fly,
And as they pass their hue to take
   From yonder happy sky?

Oh, whence the smile that lights thy face;
　　Those brightly beaming eyes,
Whose glances every care efface,
　　And bid " away " to sighs?

Is it that time and thou art one,
　　Knowing nor change nor age,
How swift soe'er ye onward run,
　　Owning but one bright stage?

As " he," you know doth never change,
　　So finds he fair in thee,
A gleeful spirit lights the range
　　He takes o'er land and sea.

Oh, if with him I long should sail,
　　Over life's varied sea,
I never would its storms bewail,
　　Heard I your joyous glee.

TO COUSIN ELIZA SCHUYLER.

You should love flowers, for flowers love you,
They bloom in thy hand as fair as they grew.
Thy lily-white hand, so like gem of the vale,
It wooeth my heart to tell its love-tale.

The myrtle that blooms with perfume so sweet,
Wherever thou movest my rapt senses greet,

The orange-bud too, so sweet and so fair,
Recalls unto me thy virtues most rare.

The rose from thy cheek has borrowed its hue,
Its fragrance, the breath it has stolen from you.
Oh, say, may I hope they shine thus for me;
Or would I be a blight to the sweets' bloom for thee?

TO ELIZABETH.

Sin's clouds were lowering all around,
No peace, no comfort e'er was found,
Until, sweet dove, thou camest to me,
And taught me my neglects to see.
Oh, hover ever round me now;
Lead to the streams whence life doth flow;
Grant that, there laving I may glow
With light serene and others show
The gorgeous way which leads to life,
The way with peace forever rife;
Oh, finish this good work so well begun,
And leave me not, back to sin's way to run,
Then shall our spirits meet in regions blest,
By my prov'd worth, my debt to thee confest.

TO ELIZABETH.

Bright star of my soul, to thee I sing,
Trophies, rare trophies, my queen, I bring;
Honors and glory and love are thine,
Oh! on my wondering spirit shine.

Sorrow and sin, henceforth shall flee,
No more my heart shall weary be,
With song and with mirth I'll fill the air,
If thou my home wilt but deign to cheer.

Purity veils from all gaze profane
The "Spirit of Truth" which peerless reigns;
Flowers I'll bring to deck the brow
A chaplet of glory enriches now.

Grace in thy form, life in thy laugh,
Oh, let me ever this goblet quaff;
Earth with its beauties made heaven by thee,
Before thy rare smiles all shadows shall flee.

TO E.

If I, at distance, must gaze on the star,
Gleams as of old, to Chaldean afar,
Silent in worship, on low-bended knee,
Soothed in thy service my spirit will be.

Then on my worship pray do not frown,
If other shall wear the proud victor's crown;
I will fealty swear to him in thy train,
May thee I but serve, glad e'en in my chains.

Glory and honor and praises I've known,
Trophies for good done, proudly have worn;
Dangers have dared by fell and by field,
Yet never quailed, but now humbly yield.

The glance which has conquered,
Leading on battle's hosts, has lowered
'Neath thine, while my face paled and blushed,
In fear lest by thee my heart's prayer should be
   hushed.

For daring to worship, thou star of my soul,
Sweet saint, then in charity, since all control
To him *thou* hast conquered o'er his spirit is lost;
Forgive if he yields to thy charms countless hosts

CHRISTMAS.
1841.

REJOICE, the day hath come,
   To man, a Saviour's given,
Let your glad voices anthems raise;
   Be joy in earth as heaven.

Now want doth lose its sting,
   Care's wrinkled brow is smoothed,
The poor, the rich, the grave, the gay,
   Are all alike beloved.

All are the heirs of life,
   Let all then sing His praise;
The sweetest comes from hearts are true,
   And steadfast in His ways.

Sorrows shall vanish at the thought
   That joy eternal's given;
The universe one choir shall praise
   The Lord of earth and heaven.

LOVE.

Love is a tyrant, whose despotic sway
    None e'er may share;
Reason to fancy must its rule resign,
    Many its care.

Imagination is its direst foe,
    Yet firmest friend;
From it the greatest beauties ever flow,
    Like breath to end.

Jealous by nature, ever on the watch,
    With childish freaks;
Itself in eager haste, it oft doth catch,
    Till reason speaks.

Then creaks the bark of glowing fancy,
    The dream is o'er;
Reason once more hath seized the nervous helm,
    Love's bark's ashore.

SONNET.

When we look back and think of all the days
That we have passed in vain and useless ways,
We ask ourselves if we have pleased God,
If we have obey'd His ever righteous word.
Conscience doth loudly tell us we have erred,
That we from the true path of life have swerved,
That we, most guilty creatures, live to roam
Through the wide world, without or friend or home.

For though 'gainst storms our roofs may shelter be,
Yet are they ill-secured, when we of Thee
So little think, and much less, Lord, obey,
When we in darkness live, altho' the ray
Of Life eternal shines upon the way,
That we should walk, as bright as sun-lit day.

TO MY ELDEST SON.
September 9, 1847.

Welcome to earth, sweet infant, may thy way
Be so far golden that thou may'st not stray
From the straight road leads to eternal life.
May every day, aye, every hour be most rife
In fadeless joys, such as to thee shall last,
When the short summer of thy life is past,
And cheer thy age's winter with bright flame
Of generous deeds, fond friends delight to name;
So that when time and tide shall be no more,
Thou'lt rest secure upon that peaceful shore,
Fertile in richest harvests to all those
Whose bosoms with celestial spirit glow,
Chosen attendants on His high commands,
Who calls to honors in His happy lands.

ANTIETAM.
July, 1862.

Hark to the clarion's blast!
Hark to the fife and drum!
Hark to the cannon's boom!
As fierce and fast they come!

Lie low, till the roar is o'er,
   Ere smoke is curled away;
Fill the field with a sea of gore,
   Check the foe with death's array.

Level your muskets in serried row,
   A solid, fearless front now form;
Rider and horse 'neath your fierce fire's glow
   Shall quickly meet the traitor's doom.

Hark, cannons roar, shells fierce shriek!
   Our bullets sharp, shrill whistle,
Their dying groans, our death-work speak
   While Porter's rifles glisten.

Mansfield has fallen—Hooker too,
   But he shall lead in martial array,
In many a fight, with victor's blow.
   McClellan has saved this bloodiest day.

Wherefore is this? We brothers all—
   Fighting for what? A phantom dream,
A fancied wrong? Is this honor's call?
   No, no, 'tis life to the slave now gleams

Freedom for all, no matter their hue,
   Our God in Heaven has willed to all.
Sons of the South, yield to the Blue,
   Which never before the gray shall fall.

Cheer for the Stars, cheer for the Stripes,
   Cheer for the gallant boys in Blue,
Antietam's blow slavery dooms.
   God stands firm, by the just, the true.

CHANCELLORSVILLE,
May, 1863.

Silent and sullen the scene,
    Silent and sullen the air;
Sudden we start from our dream,
    Awakened by enemy's cheer.

Unheeded, the warning was sent
    To him who commanded the corps,
Wrapt in his confidence, rent
    Was his fame, the foe at his door.

Our picket-guard hurried the word
    That Jackson was massing in wood:
Would strike ere our lines could be formed,
    Not heeding, unmoved, Howard stood.

Loud was the shout, fierce was the charge
    On our men by their camp-fire sitting,
Our evening rations yet warm,
    Not warned of the enemy's greeting.

"Rally, boys—rally, boys; form
    A hollow-square," our hope—
Jackson's horse, in fierce charge come,
    And they make a fearful swoop.

Again, again did we rally,
    Fierce as ocean the sea-shore laves,
His cavalry from the woods sally,
    And our boys are swept to their graves.

Those gallant sons of the North
    Who, following our "fighting Joe,"

Drove from Antietam the South
  All gilded with victory's glow.

The wearied and worn, all through the night
  Our wounded we succor—our dead we bury,
Jackson has fallen, after winning the fight,
  Slain by his own in the turmoil's flurry.

The Sabbath's dawn has broken,
  The battle is fiercely raging,
Hooker has been wounded, fallen,
  Sickles the foe engaging,

Calls for succor in vain,
  None then to take command
And secure our Sickles' gain,
  Line after line disbands.

Kilpatrick is doing his work,
  And Pleasanton charging on;
But Stoneman and Averill lack,
  And our claimed victory's gone.

Fast falls the rain, as fast the foes
  Each claiming the field as theirs,
Till wearied and worn, each one goes
  To their lines 'mid groans, 'mid cheers.

The dead and the dying, there lie close,
  Fire in the forest raging—
Better that all had their lives then lost,
  Than wounded, die in the blazing.

Neither a victor, both fall back
  To meet soon in battle array,

Jackson no more, we now on the rack,
   Shall glory in Gettysburg day.

GETTYSBURG.

The Northern heart was heavy,
   Yet firm in its trust that God,
In His good time, after chastening,
   Would keep His promised word.

The glorious Fourth at hand,
   Day by all nations hailed;
Whose hordes fly to our land,
   As before their tyrants they quailed.

After Chancellorsville's losses,
   Our ranks are filled once more,
Lee with his host is hastening North,
   To flood loyal fields with gore.

July's glorious golden days
   Are gilding the fields with grain,
Orchards with fruits are laden,
   All growing, alas in vain;

For Freedom's calls are heard
   By every loyal son,
And North and West are hurrying on,
   For Freedom must be won.

The first day Reynolds drove
   Back the outnumbering foe,
On the second morn the fight raged fierce,
   The scene was all aglow.

The loyal North victorious,
    Driven the foe from the field,
Again and again repulsed,
    For Ewell would not yield.

Our Sickles, armed with faith,
    Charges this lion's den,
Sweeps through, with vengeful wrath,
    Falls 'mid the myriads slain.

From dawn of the third our Slocum
    Fearless stood—a wall of fire.
While Jackson's old corps, their masses hurled
    In fierce and quenchless ire.

Our foe retired at noon,
    But ere two hours were spent,
Longstreet, sublime in solid mass,
    Against us his corps sent.

Till even raged the deadly strife,
    The foe from the field were driven.
Victory crowned the Union cause
    Under the hand of Heaven.

Oh, glorious Fourth! hailed be this day
    While Gettysburg fight lights our land,
Vicksburg's host, so long stood at bay,
    Falls beneath Grant's heavy hand.

TO E——.
November 15, 1842.

Joy, joy be unto thee, my lovely bride,
   My life's best gift, a rosy dawn salutes thee,
Earth, ocean, sky, glisten in glad delight—
   Henceforth life's ills before thy smile shall flee.

When thus I call thee mine, all thine grow dear,
   Thy mother is a mother, too, to me;
Thy sisters fair a circlet round us form,
   Unto my bosom closer binding thee.

There shalt thou find whatever may betide
   A resting-place secure as dovelets' nest,
'Mid fiercest storms rock'd in the old oak's arms,
   An infant slumbering on a monarch's breast.

Thanks from a heart o'erflowing rise to Him
   Who gives thee me—a holy trust—dear love,
Oh! may I e'er be found true to this trust,
   As worthy it, so worthy thee I'll prove.

A LEGEND OF THE RHINE.

Whose home is yonder castle
   With its turrets high and proud?
There dwell no sons of battle,
   But the warriors of the cloud.

'Tis a castle high and strong
   Of a race famed in story,
Whose glory lasted long,
   But whose end was sad and gory.

Erd was a stern old chieftain,
    Long known far and near;
His call none ever heard in vain,
    Its sound to all was fear.

He had an only daughter,
    Ethelda, fair and proud;
To foe he gave no quarter,
    No ear she to the crowd.

Who woo'd her night and morning,
    Who woo'd her many a year;
She bade them go—all scorning
    Who fear'd "Cleft Rock" to dare.

At last there came a chieftain
    From a far distant land;
He brav'd the rock—its terrors vain—
    Ethelda gave her hand.

High in the air he rais'd it,
    With fire flashed his eye—
"For whom is murderess meet
    Her race shall surely die."

Unto that chief she knelt,
    Ethelda proud and vain;
Rather than lose this lord she felt
    She'd stoop to life of shame.

Her father soon lay dead;
    Her acts had slaughtered him.
She laid in earth—that head
    To man had a terror been.

Ethelda liv'd alone,
    Save when Carodin came;
A lurid light e'er shone
    Around that house of shame.

Till as her spirit pass'd away
    Far brighter burnt that flame;
Then all was quenched at close of day,
    Tho' not quench'd that maiden name.

TO E. S. N.

Dear Bessie, we have known each other
    Scarce more than half a season,
Yet in it I have lived an age,
    Oh, tell me, what's the reason?

The days have flown on eagle's wings
    As blithe as linnet's song,
And yet so full of joy was each
    It seemed a season long.

The moon when passing o'er us, love,
    Alike gilds every scene;
So 'neath thy smiles shines every hour,
    And life's but one sweet dream.

Oh, may we never live to find
    A shadow cross this view;
How loud soe'er Life's storms may rage,
    That moon I'll see in you.

TO A CLOUD.

Beautiful cloud, whither away—
Stay with me, I pray thee, stay;
Thy fleecy train of snowy white,
With its dazzling stars adorn the night,
Like thee our joys, in a gorgeous train,
Deck the dark robes of grief and pain.

TO E. S. H.

Fairest and best of the daughters of earth,
Whose smile has for me than Peri more worth;
Thou who dost shine as the bright stars of heaven,
Gild thou my days till a golden even.

TO ———.

Though fairy is thy form, ladie,
   Adorned by every grace,
'Tis not for this that I love thee,
   The fairest of thy race.

'Tis true thy lip is sweet, ladie,
   Thy smiling rosy lip
As sweet as floweret where the bee
   In summer-time doth sip.

'Tis not thy blooming cheek, ladie,
   Whose hue outvies the flower,
Which now I feel inspires me
   In verse to own thy power.

Nor golden curls, waving, ladie,
    O'er orbs now dazzling bright,
As moonlight clouds o'er stars, ladie,
    When peering forth at night.

'Tis not thy silver voice, ladie,
    Like waters o'er rocks stealing,
Gives to my flinty heart, ladie,
    This true and changeless feeling.

But 'tis thy wit and worth, ladie,
    Flowerets of gentle birth,
Which blooming round the heart, ladie,
    Now win it back to earth.

SONNET.

Oh, Father, grant me, e'er my days are past,
    That I may learn the ways of truth, of life,
Not using years, as I have used my last,
    But that they may with most just deeds be rife;
If I have erred, my heart, I hope, was right.
    None have I willingly abused—no trust
Confided, have I wronged—with all my might
    Hereafter will I labor, Lord, for Thee, but grant
Earth offers not to me too strong allurements.
    Whatever is, is best, that let me learn,
That here all things are vain—preferments
    Follow fast and sure, those who ne'er turn
From virtue; for useless fame
    All else forget, never Thy holy name.

TO EMMA.

Auburn tresses! sparkling eye!
Laughing lips, with their coral dye;
Snowy bosom and faultless form,
Sylph-like step, as she floats along.

"Who is this?" did the Beauty cry,
 Glancing in mirror, passing it by.
"Oh, foolish girl, beware the thought;
 What? Has he lisped? Is thy heart caught?"

Her wooer came—she sang her song—
Did that voice to siren belong?
Perfume of heaven filled the air—
Seraph notes—so rich, so rare!

Gladsome and gleesome. Oh, that smile!
'Twould a saint from his beads beguile.
Yes—he's vanquished, that golden hair,
That laughing voice! that face so fair!

The sceptre of genius is crested there,
Her brow of beauty truth's impress bears,
Yet pales before the rare wit that flows
In her sparkling words, where wisdom glows.

Was it, then, strange she woke from the lair
That lion heart, which all danger dares?
One has come, whom he trembles before—
Cupid has conquered, opened the door.

The troop of beauties he marshalled in dreams,
Have flooded his soul, when he strongest seems;

He has met his fate—wilt thou hear his prayer?
Is thy heart whole?   Sweet maiden, ne'er fear.

No snowflake falls from our dear Father's sky,
But its pillow is spread, where 'twill safely lie;
The hand that mars the pure work of God
Will never escape His avenging rod.

ZENOBIA.

She stands alone in queenly pride,
   Her bearing high as ever;
Fate, thou couldst raise her rock-bound throne,
   But her proud spirit, never.

Around the fierce exulting crowd,
   Revelling in her great fall,
Demand her life—a woman's life—
   Hers, who had lost her all.

Her all—not so, in her proud heart
   That spirit burn'd as pure,
As when she sat Palmyra's queen,
   Far from the Roman's shore.

She was the consort of a king,
   Partner of the Roman's throne,
Despising servitude—he slain,
   She reigned, proud queen, alone.

Rome's Emperor* in mercy bids
   His arm'd attendants cease;

---

* Emperor Aurelian married Zenobia's daughter.

Pardons her errors and her guilt,
   Points out the paths of peace.

On Tiber's shore, her stately step
   And queenly voice is heard:
A mimic court attends her will,
   Obeys each wish, each word.

Oh, was it mercy thus to spare
   To mockery's cruel gibes,
A heart which God had made to rule
   A thousand savage tribes?

Aye, more than mercy; for in Rome
   That heart was tamed, was calm:
She closed her days in virtuous deeds,
   Robed in religion's charms.

TO E.

When he who adores thee
   Shall roam far away,
Will he be to thee, Lissy,
   As dear as to-day?

May the smile of another
   In the hour of mirth,
Not banish the lover
   Like shadow from earth?

Or will thy heart beat,
   Thy rosy cheek burn,
Thy lips fail to meet,
   As you wait his return?

Or open the seal
    Where his love story's writ,
"Thine thro' woe or weal,
    Whate'er life has in it?"

Aye—we'll quaff of its cup
    While its waters shall last;
And when they're drank up,
    We'll sigh that they're past.

For whate'er they may be,
    Or of pleasure or pain,
If they're shared but with thee,
    To me, 'tis the same.

THE TROUBLED SPIRIT'S SONG.

My home, it is by the churchyard side,
    The sharp ring of the spade I hear
As it sounds o'er all from babe to bride,
    When they're borne from the mournful bier.

Oft on my ear, at the midnight hour,
    The whisperings of spirits steal,
Or like the balmy breath of flowers,
    Or the culprits at the wheel.

First come the young babes, their lispings weak,
    Then deep sound the mournful mothers,
Then on the ear strike the young bride's shrieks
    As she weeps the death of lover.

And then, anon, there comes a low sound,
    Like the heaving of the billows,

As tho' many the heads beneath that ground,
  Laid not on easy pillows.

As tho' spirits dread did haunt the tomb
  Of some who there they have laid,
I strive to rest, I see but that gloom,
  Hear naught but that ringing spade.

And then I think how blest are the young,
  Who have sank to peaceful slumbers;
For whate'er our lot, our hearts are wrung,
  If many a year we number.

TO ELIZABETH.

Star of this darksome hour,
  Light of life's gloomy day,
I own thy mighty power,
  Bow to that light's glad ray.

Speak not of sorrow's reign,
  Smile tho' its shafts are sent.
I truly know the pain,
  Sweet maid, thy heart hath rent.

Oh, ye! who kneel to "love,"
  Beware its galling chain,
Tho' it your souls may move,
  'Tis but a golden pain.

ON LAURENS HAMILTON.
July, 1858.

Weep not—he needs no tears—
  They are for those of earth;
But sympathize with him
  Who mourns a brother's worth.

His was a spirit bright—
  Wander'd from yon high sphere
To this vast world of night,
  Where none his joys might share.

ON MY BROTHER LAURENS,

Who lost his life at Richmond, Va., July, 1858, when a member of the Seventh Regiment, escorting President Monroe's remains to their last home.

Weep not for Laurens! he is dead—
  Dead to the world and all its bitter cares,
Where he by Heaven's loving hand was led,
  Though weighty trials did assail him here.

He lived above them, ever in their midst,
  As sea-bird, soaring o'er the raging waves
In wildest storm, his wing unwet, most blest,
  For in God's care he found the love He gave;

Teaching that griefs were but as vestal flames,
  Chastened the spirit, making more meet
When he was called to serve in Heaven's high fane,
  To wear the glory, there God's own shall greet.

He was so loving—gentle, firm, yet kind—
    All hearts unconsciously he ruled ;
Now he is gone—in this our loss we find
    How blest were we by his pure teachings schooled.

Then render adoration unto Him,
    Whose love a season short our darling lent
To teach how golden are the griefs earth dims
    To those receive them in our Lord's intent.

TO-NIGHT.

Oh, lovely night, shinest thou for me alone,
Or to some kindred spirit art thou known?
Some spirit bright, a beacon from afar,
As to the wave-tossed seaman, Polar star.

So fix thy image on my wav'ring mind,
That I in future festive hours may find
All thy rich beauties—rich as now they gleam,
That they may not be fleeting as a dream.

High o'er my head, sweet Luna brightly glows,
Serenely walking thro' yon realm which shows,
Like azure train, on queenly shoulders borne,
With golden stars bespangled, tho' they're shorn,

Of half their lustre, as by thee, my Star,
All other beauties of this wide world are—
So, fond one, live, that here thy course fulfill'd,
There you may shine, as at thy birth was will'd.

TO E.

You say, dear love, your nature's cold,
    When carelessly you greet me,
Oh, rather would I you should scold,
    Than that you thus should meet me.

Beware, beware, take early heed,
    For we but own this minute;
Life, you know, has a headlong speed,
    So drink the joy that's in it.

Flowers which bloom when summer smiles,
    'Neath winter's breath will fall,
So while my heart thy wit beguiles,
    Beneath thy frown it may pall.

Oh, wear no more that careless look;
    Give me no icy hand;
Thy frown, dear love, I cannot brook,
    Thy smile's a fairy's wand.

Awakes to light, to love, to joy—
    A heaven makes of earth;
The weightiest chain becomes a **toy**—
    Oh, has thy smile no worth?

DISAPPOINTMENT.

Who bends beneath thy blow?
    Who bows the head to thee?
His should lie low, so low
    There could no refuge be.

Within the Holy Tome
    The words of truth are writ,
That this is not man's home,
    Earth's fairest joys must flit.

Flit as the taper's light,
    The perfume of the rose,
The songster of the night,
    The cheek with beauty glows.

TO A STORM.

O storm! how fearful, yet how beautiful—
The air all still—swift came a darksome cloud,
And all was gloom. The silence of the tomb
By its shrill voice was broken. Thunder dread
Startling awoke the sleeping—lightning fierce,
With its livid glare, rous'd dreaming nature.
O storm! thou wert a welcome visitant,
Kindred unto me—my thoughts a portion
And a part of thee. Thy fearfulness I love,
For thou wert fashion'd by the hand of God—
Now, through yon cloud gleams the moon's silver light.
The storm is hush'd—the tempest's wrath appeas'd—
And where it raged, beauty and peace now reign;
Thy glorious voice, O storm! came not in vain.

THE WALNUT-TREE.

There's a charm in thee, thou dear old tree,
    With thy branches hoar and broad,
Scene of my play for many a day
    Did thy cooling shades afford.

Now autumn's winds, thy leaves unbind
    And sing amid thy boughs,
While sweet birds' throats, with warbling notes,
    Utter their heavenly vows.

Though winter chill, with voice so shrill
    Shall bow thy graceful form,
We'll love thee still, and the sparkling rill
    Shall nurse thee 'mid the storm.

And if " old time " shall bear away
    Our childhood's dearest friend,
We all will weep, when in dust you sleep,
    And sadly mourn thine end.

DYING CHILD TO HER MOTHER.

MOTHER, why must I die—
    Earth's life but just begun?
Oh, could I live but one short year
    How chang'd the course I'd run.

Cool, cool my fever'd brow!
    A fire is at my heart!
Oh, Father! Mercy, mercy now!
    Let me in peace depart!

I have forgotten Thee, my God,
    But Thou wilt sure forgive.
Grant that I may to learn Thy Word
    Only one season live.

Ha! they attack my brain!
    Those searing flames burn still—

Cool, cool my tongue— 'Tis vain—
But, oh! it is God's will.

Peace, peace, my child, be calm,
  Thy pains will soon be o'er,
Oh, Father, send to her the balm,
  A peaceful mind restores.

A shriek! a sigh! a moan!
  A gasp, all, all is o'er—
She's dead, nor dies she thus alone,
  That mother is no more.

Is this thy way, O life?
  The echo of thy song!
The end of beauty, pride, and pomp,
  Oh! who could love thee long?

TO MRS. SUSAN A. GIBBES.

Whence is the charm, with which thou win'st man's heart?
  To beauty he true knight doth ever bow,
  But with thy converse hours and days do flow
Fast as they even with his true love part.
  Is it His spirit, whom on earth you mourn
Such sweet communion with his reft bride holds
That like the babe, fond mother, thou enfold'st
  In thy chaste bosom his dear image borne?
Ever about thee, Heaven's rich charms instill,
  Celestial born, thy wondrous wit doth fall
  In numbers sweet, making all others pall,
Sweet, aye, more sweet than notes the green woods fill
  May the bright spirit doth attend thee here,
  So live, that she her parents' crown may wear.

TO ———.

Nay, why so downcast? Awake, put on your arms,
   Go forth and war with foes oppose you now.
   You ne'er have bent to care, why will you bow,
So long triumphant over all earth's harms?
   Her gentle spirit calls to thee in love,
She, the companion ever of the good;
List, 'tis her hand offers celestial food:
   Take it and feast, thus feast those dwell above.
Remember thou His cross hast taken up,
   The cross of Him who did but suffering breathe.
   So bear all cares, that thou may'st win the wreath
Those wear who follow Him—
                   Here may'st thou sup
Of pleasures purer than are born of earth—
Those pleasures, only of man's thoughts, are worth.

TO ———.

He weds her, though he loves her not—
   A perjured man he stands,
How could he ever have forgot
   Heaven claims hearts, not hands?

Years number'd by that wronged bride
   Have passed—long, weary years—
As gazing on her babes, her pride,
   In silence flow'd her tears.

Another's heart to win her strove,
   But she's as chaste as fair—
Like vulture over her has flown,
   He left not a shadow there.

His much wrong'd bride has pass'd from earth,
    His wealth has vanished too,
His babes they died—at a lonely hearth
    His deeds shall this murd'rer rue.

TO ———.

IF I have been unkind to thee,
    You felt no pain so great as mine.
He prizes most, whose toil 't must be
    To make the valued diamond shine.

Oft aches my heart, my cheek grows wet
    With tears in sorrow suffering born,
Yet like this grief, who'd e'er forget
    The freshening cloud o'er sun hath flown.

The gentlest bird e'er cheer'd thy heart,
    The softest breeze e'er kiss'd thy brow,
Told thee that joys of earth would part
    Such ever smiling lover's vow.

The constant song would cease to charm,
    The balmy breeze its fragrance lose;
The changeless tone no more would warm,
    He coldly loves, in smiles e'er wooes.

TO E——.

SHE says she loves thee—so do I,—
    "Thou, to each and all art given,"
(Gayly sing earth, ocean, sky)
    "Dearest boon e'er came from Heaven;

"Peace and plenty—joy—be hers,
    Placid as a summer's sea,
When the breeze of even stirs,
    Naught from its sweet harmony;

"Be her days, her hours, minutes—
    Slumbers soft her eyelids close,
Till at dawn the songs of linnets
    Wake her from her sweet repose.

"Spirit from the courts of Heaven,
    Mirror of a spotless life,
Essence to the dew-drop given,
    Free from sorrow, sin, or strife."

Such art thou, fond, dearest Lissy,
    Polar star to me away,
Ever shall this heart reflect thee,
    As the sea that guardian ray.

Oh, be thou about me ever,
    Hover o'er me in my sleep,
From thy "Own Home" wander never,
    O'er my acts strict vigils keep.

TO ———.

Oh, can it be, that I who've wept thee ill,
    Mourn'd o'er thee as forever lost to me,
Should e'en one moment of thy dear hours fill
    With saddest, weightiest melancholy.
Forgive me, oh, forgive me—do I ask,
    Yet ask but to implore the boon once more.

Oh, it is but a thankless, endless task
    To pardon oft—as I do oft implore.
With sad and heavy heart I think o'er days
    Given to us to be but scenes of mirth,
Made by my wanton, wilful, heartless ways,
    Of melancholy thoughts the seeds, the birth.
Awak'd as from a long and mournful dream
    That past, I see, cloth'd in a sombre hue—
While far before thee, brightly shines a beam
    Fill'd with the promise of rich joys to you.
That dark and gloomy past 's a golden land,
    Rich in its fruitful harvests unto both,
Where we, dear love, are walking hand in hand
    In virtue's ways and lovely works of truth.
I oft in sadness think, and thinking, weep
    So much of evil in my nature is,
That I in grief may all thy dear hours steep,
    Those hours which should be but glad hours of bliss.
I know not why, that in my latter days
    The moaning night-bird haunts me with his song.
Once ever glad and joyous were my ways,
    Once sang for me the lark the whole day long.
Oh, intercede for me at that High seat—
    Where all we ask as surely we shall find,
That you hereafter may with sweet smiles greet
    Him who to this world you alone did bind.

TO ———.

Where art thou, my beloved one?
    Gone, gone for aye, from me?
May I no longer hear thy voice,
    Or matchless beauty see?

No longer shall the clear blue sky
    Be dear and lov'd by me;
The day is dark and gloomy now,
    For all is night I see.

But highly do I prize the stars,
    Which loving look on thee ;
And her whose image wears thy smile—
    Yon crescent shines on me.

"THE DEATH BLAST."

It comes from the north,
    In its raiment of ice;
It comes from the south,
    In its garb beyond price.

It comes from the east,
    And it comes from the west,
It comes e'er the same;
    For 'tis "death's" at the best.

Lo! that charger of blood,
    'Tis death's warrior flies,
To the slaughter of thousands;
    Hark, hark ye, the cries

Of the mothers, the babes,
    The sires, the sons,
As they fall 'neath his blow
    Where his blood course he runs.

Lo, the shriek on the gale,
    The moan on the breeze,

The curse on the tempest—
  Naught, naught can appease.

For revengeful he rides,
  Like the storm o'er the billow,
Spares nor maiden nor bride,
  Hark his hillo, his hillo!

Now, a whispering comes,
  'Tis a guilty heart's sorrow,
He heeds not its call,
  It must wait till the morrow.

Like the cry of the hounds
  When they rush on in madness,
Death's yell deepest wounds
  Those who'd fly from their sadness.

Then to shouts of glad tidings
  For victories o'er,
Are chang'd the soul's wailing,
  Leaving earth's darksome shore.

TO JULIA S.

There's a spell in thy dark eye, fair one,
  A light in thy beaming smile;
Flashes like wave where the golden sun
  In sport its last hours beguiles.

There's a grace in every motion,
  A charm in every thought;

But ah! who knows this heart's emotion,
   So dearly, so sadly bought?

Thou art flown with the storied past,
   Whose visions around me rise,
Oh, give me one look, one look ere my last
   From those too well remember'd eyes.

ON OUR MARY.
Feb. 6, 1887.

Hush, hush, tread softly here,
   It is my babe here sleeps;
Dry, dry that foolish tear,
   Who e'er for angel weeps?

Strew, strew those fragrant flowers
   O'er the snow-white garb earth wears,
The handiwork of the virgin showers
   Which could not restrain their tears.

Raise high your voice in praise,
   Till it ascends to Heaven;
Unite with her in joyful lays,
   In those high courts are given.

TO ———.

I lov'd thee once, I lov'd thee well,
Ah dearly bought, ah fatal spell,
Courted you were, all gay and bright,
But won, where is that lov'd eye's light?

Whither has flown the joy joyful smile,
The laugh so many hours beguil'd;
The winsome ways that won my heart,
Those foes of man, fair maiden's arts?

All, all are gone, no light is there,
Those orbs are dark, that raven hair,
That smiling lip, that roseate cheek,
That brow that seem'd almost to speak.

Flown with the knell of all earth's joys,
Time, cruel time, e'en love destroys,
I thought thee one beyond his touch,
But none escape, no, not e'en such.

ON LEAVING MY COUNTRY HOME FOR CITY LABOR.
1850.

One long last kiss, my darling boys,
    For I must hasten far away
And seek to win those gilded toys,
    The light and glory of this day.

Yes, I must leave my darling babes
    And bravely breasting every storm,
Toil with earth's ever restless slaves,
    And worship lucre's filthy form.

Ah! why is nature by our God enrobed
    In beauties brighter than in diamond gleams,
Too weak to bind me, where each hour unfolds
    Glories far mightier than the miser dreams.

Need bids me leave my native hills,
  My darling babes, a fond farewell.
I seek your good. Heaven guard from ills;
  How fond my love, these tears best tell.

Cling ye to her, your mother dear,
  Who bids me go with swelling heart,
Tho' bright her eye, her brow so clear,
  While choosing thus the wiser part.

"THE FROLICSOME PARSON."
By "Delilah's Avenger."

I am a jolly Britisher. I came from Fatherland,
To make a mighty fortune, I thought I'd turn my hand;
I tried a little farming, but found it would not do,
So I turned all may attention to "Cock-a-doodle-do."
I set just twenty eggs, under a great big hen
That I had shut up nicely, in a little lattice pen,
But out of the whole twenty, I got but half all told,
For the lazy, stupid hen left half out in the cold. . . . .
I tried a little painting, but the likeness was so true,
You could not tell, to save you, if it was I or you.
I tried a little carving, and there I hit the nail:
Says I, "Now, Brother Bluster, you surely cannot fail."
I made a set of chairs, such chairs you never see,
They were made after a pattern my daddy left to me;
It was a very ancient chair—Grandsire Adam used
For all his little babies, and it was much abused.
I took it all to pieces, and put it up anew
With twine, and pins, and thread, and a little bit of glue.
And when I had them finished, I tell you I was proud,
I called my neighbors in, and showed them to the crowd.

I thought I had a fortune, that I would reach renown,
Says I: I'll make my pile in this here little town.
But down sat old friend Jones, of just three hundred pound,
Oh! my, in what a hurry he laid upon the ground,
'Twas in my chair he sat—just inside the front-door,
And all the village laughed, to see him sprawling on the floor.
Says I, "By Jolly"—up I jumped just like a flying kite.
I didn't know if I should laugh—I thought I'd like to fight.
But you see my daddy was a parson, and he was used to say
'Twas safest ne'er to fight, but always run away;
For it might be I'd get licked, as I saw my "Sky-and-Tan,"
When he ran out into the street and chased a little man.
So I thought I'd keep my temper, and only "bark it out,"
Or else I might get whipped and then "go up the spout."
So what to do I did not know to make the kettle boil,
For to keep my darling "Duckie"—I then resolved to toil. . . . .
One day as Duck and I were on our way to church,
I thought the "boys a laying round," would be left in the lurch
If something to amuse them on the Sabbath was not done,
Either in the way of "biz"—or in the way of fun.
So early the next morning I hastened into "town,"
To see a mighty bishop, of credit and renown—
"Good-morning, 'Mr. Bishop'—I am a nice young man,
I've come clean from the country, to see you if I can.
There are a lot of fellows, a hanging all about,
Upon the Sabbath morning—they'll all hang, I've no doubt,
If something is not done to make them mend their ways;
So I want you just to show me how a good man prays—

And then if you'll just give me an order to go preach,
I'll call them in and try, how these loafers I can teach."
He gave it and I went, and there I took my stand,
A valley in the mountains, and I looked o'er all the land;
I bade them all come to me, from hours of twelve to four,
For my church was just the next unto the Methodist's door.
I calculated as the crowd all came out of that,
I'd have the whole concern just so nice and pat.
They came, I preached of Heaven, with a little bit of Hell,
Maybe they didn't like it—I bet you it did tell.
I soon was then invited to come to Brother Full,
The Presbyterians were weak—and just give him a pull.
This card it proved a trump—the blue-lights liked me much,
And said *they* only wished *their* church had a such.
The Methodists grew jealous—so I resolved to show
I didn't believe that *one* church would ever make it go,
So I went to a "quarterly meeting"—maybe I didn't talk,
I made their hairs stand on end, when they saw the Devil walk.
They invited me to serve again, and come to a Love Feast—
Oh, didn't Duckie storm at this—"Jist the way with all you priests,
The gals is all you're arter—I seen you peeking at their feets—
Then looking right straight in their eyes, as they walked down the streets."
Oh! law! what could I do—but to the feast I went,
Oh! there, there, there was love unto my heart's content. . . . .
The priest, old Father Riley—he heard of my great fame,
He said "he didn't know—but his flock grew very tame."
I told him *I* would help him—just a little piece.
I went down and talked, but he took all the grease. . . . .

As I and Duck must live, and Dobbin must have his hay,
I found the Romish Church was not the place to stay. . . . .
So I resolved to keep the 'Piscopalian walk—
But now you better believe, I heard the strangest talk.
My people—how I loved the dear, kind, good, sweet souls!—
Said, " they thought the Parson should attend to his own folds."
I asked them for some stamps—they laughed right in my face—
They answered—" that the swift, they heard, always won the race ;
That as I had been riding all around the course,
They thought that I must surely be the real winning horse."
I told them it was true, that I ahead came in,
But for all that, it did not bring Duck and I "*the tin.*"
I prayed, I preached—I sang and preached again,
I found—oh, the hard-hearted curs—that it was all in vain.
So with a heavy heart, I sent my resignation.
I didn't believe they'd take it, but oh, my consternation!
I got a little note, all writ on scented paper,
That the next Sabbath-day they'd just put out "my taper."
I told them, "Very well, I'd give them my last sermon."
I bet you Duck and I sat down, and if we didn't write one—
The church was full of Dutch, of Romans, Blue-lights, all
Of every name, with Methodists—but 'Piscopals was small—
I told *them, they* were safe, that they should have salvation.
Riches and joys forevermore, but 'Piscopals—damnation;
That this was a big country, that I was a Johnny Bull—
That I'd be hanged but I would preach, if the church was empty or full—

That I had thought the Old Boy had lived under the ground,
But now I knew 'mong 'Piscopals was the place where he was found.

ZION MEETIN'–'OUSE.
Sarmont by Ole Brudder Abram, Charleston, S. C., March, 1879.

Darkies all, young and old,
Now har de lesson I bill unfold.
Old Pompey's dead—all must die,
Stop wringing yere hands—dun't yere cry.
Old Pompey, I say, died to-day,
He's gone, I s'pose, de same ole way.
Now, darkies, hear, ob all degree,
And what he's been done and I'll do, you see.
Dar was a garden in olden times,
Whar Adam and Ebe had to walk der lines,
Maybe you've hern how de Moccasin, he
Stole behin' an old apple-tree ;
Adam, he'd gwine to catch some eels,
So he's out ob de way, an' ole Moccasin feels
Roun' Mrs. Adam, and wants her to gwine
Up into dat tree, and shake de limbs,
For he can't climb, with his old stump tail,
And he wun't try—for maybe he'd fail.
A thing what's forbid—be sure we does,
So quick as a wink, up high she goes.
" Shake away "—" shake away "—down they fall
  Apples and branches, Mrs. Adam and all.
" Hullo," said a voice—" whar are you, Ebe ? "
" Here, Adam," said she, " wid ole Moccasin's lebe,

I jist flew'd up to de top ob dis tree,
Now here's de apples, what beauties you see."
" You naughty gal—ye sha'n't eat dat fruit,
If yer do, I'll gie yer my fut"—
'Twas a great big heel, and a great big toe,
Whareber it hit, it was bound to go.
But eat she did, as gals will do,
Took a great big bite, and Adam too;
For she tole him it was the nicest thing
That eber was set before a king. . . .
Out ob de garden dey was hustled straight
Into de wilderness—locked de gate—
Den dey was cold, wide de wind an' de shame,
Dey made leaf-clothes, eat fish, flesh, and game.
Soon little Cain come trottin' along,
An' Abel soon arter—de same ole song;
And as years cum and ages flew,
De more der was—de more dey grew;
But de boys hab a fight, how de wool flew;
But dun't yer know, 'twould never do.
Well, Abel died, just as Pompey too.
Adam was leader ob all you crew.
Pompey was like him, jest his tee;
In tellin' ob Adam, I'se tellin' ob he.
A rare old fellow—fourscore and ten,
I know'd it, breddren, by our ole hen,
For she hatched out, when Pomp cum to town,
I 'members it well, for ob great renown
Was ole Aunt Dinah—a darter true
Ob Adam and Ebe, and all dere crew.
I tell you what ole Pompey was like,
Like all his kind, be dey black o' white,
Mens o' womens—chillen o' babes,
All ob "ole Mock" dey be de slabes;

Dey may sing, and may dance, may talk, may preach,
But dey neber will take what's out ob dere reach.

TO GENERAL GRANT.

Mt. McGregor, July 2, 1885.

The Sumter shot was heard, the Northern heart on fire
From every valley, hill, and mount, rushed forth our sons,
    our sires.
Mothers and maidens urged them on, with smiles they
    forward cheered.
Alone, in silence flowed their tears, heart-riven, while thus
    they dared.
Long weary days, weeks, months, aye, darksome years
Came fast and fleeting, robed in grief and tears.
Defeat and death, and all their bloody train:
Chief after chief was tried, but still in vain;
Till He who ever pities the shorn lamb,
Raised one, our Grant, steadfast, brave, and calm;
Patient in all things, ever firm and true,
A wondrous change was wrought, our country born anew.
Then none but he could hold the helm of State,
In each new duty Grant was proved more great.
The wide world hailed him; prostrate at his feet
All nations fell, eager they sought to greet
The master spirit of the age who bore
The bark of Freedom to oppressed's shore.
On Mount McGregor's heights, now famous for all time,
Soothed by tender care of those most dear, a scene sub-
    lime;
He so generous, meek, so gentle, kind, yet firm,
The wide world's conqueror bows to the great "I am";

Succumbs to ills no human tongue can tell
The bitterest trials ever man befel;
Yet e'en in this he hears his Master's voice
Of love, which leads him to rejoice.
Crowned by his griefs more royally than by gems,
Decked his victorious brow; the wide world's realms
Are but as baubles, as he waits the call,
Will yet declare him "Victor over all."

SARATOGA.
July 15, 1885.

Threescore years past, a boy, I coursed your fields
Chasing butterflies and bees, culling flowers, their yield;
In fancy painting what you yet might be,
But never dreaming such rare sights to see.
Where now your palaces crown your verdant hills,
Or homes of splendor line your pearly rills,
A simple cottage greeted my fond eye;
Home of those loved best, your summer sky,
With its soft air brought roses to the cheek
Of her so fondly prized; in soul so strong, in health so
 weak;
Strength and good cheer to him, honored only the pure,
 the good;
His God revered, and next his sire so loved.
Sisters sweet and gentle, ambrosial made the scene;
Brothers proud, gallant, in devotion crowned " our queen."
So named by sire, as his loved deference shown,
Taught all to bow to her, decked with affection's crown.
From her we learned to rule by works of love,
From him, worthy by virtues of our Master prove,

By all was true and noble and sincere;
None great, but good; all not, "beware."
By Randolph of Roanoke, here was I caressed;
Here Lafayette, blessing with kind hand, pressed
The head of scion of him, his pride.
In camp and council—Yorktown, side by side,
Here have I heard the charming voice of Clay;
While Webster, gilded with prophetic lay,
The future of our land, so great this day
That all the world their tributes to her lay
In honor, not in trembling at her feet,
Memories of those we love in reverence greet.
Here Lincoln with Moses' prophetic lore,
Pictured in eloquence all yet in store,
For such their country's faithful champions prove;
From him I lived to earn confiding love.
Honored and trusted by Seward, Stanton, Chase;
Favored by Grant, the first of that great race,
Called into service in our Master's cause,
Who now in heaviest hours with illumined face,
Gilds with its brightest hues this favored place.
With all my faults, my failings, and my flaws,
Called into service in our Master's cause.
Teaching in forests, preaching in His courts;
Telling how dearly all our gifts were bought.
I trust in duty to those dear ones gone
And now are serving round our Father's throne,
That teachings pure were never lost, but bore
Me fruits I feast on—richer, I trust, in store.

PRESS NOTICES.

From the Boston Traveller.

"CROMWELL: A Tragedy in Five Acts. By the author of 'Thomas A'Becket,' etc. Pamph. 12mo, pp. 124. New York: Dick & Fitzgerald. A noble work, and nobly planned and written. It proceeds on a just conception of Cromwell's character and actions, which alone ought to secure for it a favorable reception from intelligent readers, who must be tired of having the foremost man of all the English world drawn as a compound of ruffian and hypocrite, when there was neither hypocrisy nor ruffianism in his nature. Many passages in the drama show good powers of versification, and a high poetic spirit; and the dramatic faculty of the author is apparent throughout his work. But why does he not devote himself to historical composition? In that he would excel, and in a time, too, as remarkable for its historical productions, their weightiness and variety, as any that has been known since the Augustan age.

"Our author has done in the dramatic form what Mr. Herbert did in the romantic form, but he is hampered by the very form he has adopted to present his hero's career and character in accordance with the well-established facts of historical criticism, which give to Cromwell one of the very highest places in the roll of great men. Even those who agree with Mr. Bissett, who has written the history of the English Commonwealth so well, must admit, that, after all proper deductions have been made, there was much that was grand and majestic in the nature of Cromwell, that he was worthy of a crown, and that, as matters stood in 1654, it would have been wise in the English people had they placed an imperial crown on his head, so that a Cromwellian dynasty might have been established, and which would have ruled till this day, and far into the future. Taking the higher, and therefore the sounder, view of the Lord Protector's character, our dramatist follows him throughout his public life, from 1642, after he began to distinguish himself in

Parliament, to the day when his great soul left the earth, a tempest of wind and rain that occurred at the time being connected in the public mind with his death."

From the N. Y. Herald.

"Thomas A'Becket, a tragedy in five acts, is just published in New York City by Dick & Fitzgerald. It is founded on the ecclesiastical assumptions and violent death of the man whose name it bears. In the main true to history, with touching allusions to Fair Rosamond, it introduces scenes of romance, love, and adventure. The style of the play is sprightly and often elegant. The nature of the subject, and the chaste and beautiful manner in which it is presented, will commend it to favor with all who appreciate artistic literature of this description, and will make it popular in exhibition on the stage. It will soon be produced at one of the leading theatres in that city."

From the Evening Post.

"It is founded on the ecclesiastical assumptions and violent death of the man whose name it bears. The author has availed himself of this remarkable chapter of English history to make his play the vehicle of a rapid series of events, and to give it the interest which arises from crowded action."

From the New-Yorker.

"One of the best recent dramatic productions of American origin. The historical period has been evidently studied with care, the characters are clearly marked and well distributed, the action is decided and the language emphatic and not rarely high-toned and elegant. The author may therefore justly take an honorable place in the roll of American tragic writers."

From the N. Y. Times.

"Some of the scenes are exceedingly powerful."

www.ingramcontent.com/pod-product-compliance
Lightning Source LLC
Chambersburg PA
CBHW020309240426
43673CB00039B/748